TREACHEROUS BEAUTY

Peggy Shippen, the Woman behind
Benedict Arnold's Plot to Betray America

MARK JACOB AND STEPHEN H. CASE

LYONS PRESS
Guilford, Connecticut
An imprint of Globe Pequot Press

Lyons Press is an imprint of Globe Pequot Press.

Layout: Joanna Beyer
Project editor: Ellen Urban

Library of Congress Cataloging-in-Publication Data

Jacob, Mark.
  Treacherous beauty : Peggy Shippen, the woman behind Benedict Arnold's
plot to betray America / Mark Jacob and Stephen H. Case.
    p. cm.
  Includes bibliographical references and index.
  ISBN 978-0-7627-7388-6
  1. Arnold, Margaret Shippen, 1760-1804. 2. Arnold, Benedict,
1741-1801. 3. American loyalists—Biography. 4. United
States—History—Revolution, 1775-1783. I. Case, Stephen H. II. Title.
  E278.A72J34 2012
  973.3'85092—dc23
  [B]

                                                              2012012815

Printed in the United States of America
10 9 8 7 6 5 4 3 2 1

*Dedicated to Stephen's grandchildren—Paul Anguel Case,
Charles Edmonds, Samuel Case, Kathryn Edmonds, Theron Case,
Archer Case, and Benjamin Ayres—and Mark's grandparents, Marian and
Gerald Witham and Helen and C. L. Jacob.*

Contents

Preface

WHEN HISTORIES OF THE AMERICAN REVOLUTION were first written, Peggy Shippen was a mere footnote, if she was mentioned at all. The lovely young lady from Philadelphia had married a man twice her age, General Benedict Arnold, before he conspired to deliver the strategically vital forts at West Point, New York, to the British and perhaps arrange the capture of his supreme commander, George Washington. Peggy Shippen was pitied as the unfortunate, innocent wife of a traitor.

More than a century later, her story took a dramatic turn. The papers of British general Henry Clinton, acquired in the 1920s and donated to the William L. Clements Library at the University of Michigan, implicated Peggy as a key player in the turncoat negotiations between her husband and the British.

By that time, however, there was a lot of history to undo, and Peggy never got the attention she deserved.

This is the first nonfiction book to focus on Peggy's life, rather than depict her as a supporting character in her husband's story or as a subject of historical fiction. It is intended as a popular biography that brings a fascinating yet little known American story to a wider audience. While our narrative and interpretation are original, they rely on the work of renowned historians, among them Carl Van Doren, James Thomas Flexner, Clare Brandt, Robert McConnell Hatch, and Willard Sterne Randall. We also refer to rarely studied letters from Peggy to her son Edward that were provided to us by her descendant Hugh Arnold.

In writing for a general audience, we have edited some quotations to eliminate distracting quirks of punctuation, old-fashioned spellings, and the jarring capitalization style of the era. While presenting Peggy's lushly romantic tale, we have taken great pains to rely on solid information and to exclude accounts that appear unreliable. We have been helped immensely in our quest by academic researchers Andrea Meyer, Stephanie Schmeling, Julianna Monjeau, and Marie Elizabeth Stango.

The Clinton papers document Peggy's involvement, but many details remain unknown, and Peggy was never confronted with the facts and compelled to explain her actions. Even today, some people question her complicity despite the evidence. We hope that the reader will not consider it a repudiation of the Bill of Rights and the concept of "innocent until proven guilty" if we issue our own extralegal verdict: Peggy Shippen was guilty . . . and she was fascinating, too.

CHAPTER I

Princess of Philadelphia

ON AN EARLY AUTUMN MORNING IN 1780, a lovely young woman named Peggy Shippen seemed to go stark raving mad.

Her husband, a hero of the American Revolution named Benedict Arnold, had just fled to the enemy, abandoning her in a tidy country estate in New York's Hudson Highlands. Left alone to answer for the treason, she screamed and wailed and shrieked, her cries of anguish reverberating throughout the house. Half dressed in the presence of proper men, she clutched her infant son to her breast and gave voice to fevered hallucinations. She declared that her husband had risen through the ceiling, and that hot irons had been put into his head. The hot irons were torturing her, too, and only the commander in chief, George Washington, had the power to take them away.

But when Washington arrived in her bedroom to comfort her, she declared him an impostor who was planning to murder her child. And she wept, and she wept some more.

Washington and other men of honor vouched for her innocence and virtually worshiped at her bedside. And so a woman whose espionage and treachery brought the new nation to the brink of disaster was allowed to go free, vilified by a few but pitied and admired by many more.

She was only twenty years old, and she had fooled the Founding Fathers. This is the story of how Peggy Shippen arrived at this mad scene, and how she found a way to overcome it.

On June 11, 1760, a prominent Philadelphia lawyer named Edward Shippen wrote a letter to his father, leading with the news that a debtor was willing to pay up—if only his father would send the vouchers before the man left for England. The second most important item of business was personal: Shippen had received "a present of a fine baby, which though of the worst sex, is yet entirely welcome."[1]

The "worst sex" was female, and the baby was given her mother's name, Margaret, along with her nickname, Peggy.

She was born with brilliant prospects. In a new country, she was from old money. She was the descendant of not one but two mayors of Philadelphia, and was the granddaughter of one of Princeton University's founding trustees.[2] She joined a family that was filled with affluent skeptics, well-educated, modern, and somewhat quirky people who were part of Philadelphia's power structure but didn't always run with the pack.

The Shippens had three daughters, then a son, then Peggy. Two more sons followed Peggy, but neither lived beyond age three, leaving Peggy as the baby of the family. Because the single surviving son was a disappointment to his parents, Peggy was treated as the star, the offspring with the greatest potential, despite the perceived handicap of being female. Though not deemed worthy of the first paragraph in her father's letter, Peggy would become his favorite child.

She had blond hair, delicate features, and an endearing manner. Her eyes were variously described as blue, hazel, and gray, but in any case they were bright and flashing, an advertisement for the intelligence that lay behind them.[3]

People often remarked on her charisma and physical allure. As she grew to adulthood, women would admire her and want to be her friends. Men would describe her as the most beautiful woman in the room, or the most beautiful in the city, or the most beautiful in North America or in all of England. But Peggy was no bauble. She would also impress men on two continents with her sharp-eyed view of the world, her command of social situations, and her savvy in negotiating financial matters.

Peggy was raised like many wealthy children of her time, constantly attended by servants. She had a sense of entitlement but also a sense of obligation, with a mission of education, self-improvement, and family achievement. She had little interest in politics, but it was her misfortune to live at a time when politics was unavoidable. She came of age with the country—turning sixteen less than a month before the Declaration of Independence was approved in Independence Hall a few blocks from her home.

She grew up on Society Hill, the best neighborhood in a bustling, brash city. Over the three decades that preceded the Revolutionary War, Philadelphia's population more than tripled, from thirteen thousand to forty thousand, making it the most populous city in North America and one of the most populous in the English-speaking world.[4]

The Shippen mansion on Fourth Street near Prune (now Locust) sat amid tall pines. It was four stories high, forty-two feet wide, and about the same depth. The facade was made of red and black bricks, with the long and short sides of the bricks alternated in the style known as Flemish bond, which was favored by the affluent.[5] A formal garden and orchard graced the property. The interior featured fine furniture, an excellent library, and another common property of the wealthy: African slaves.

There was no indication that the Shippens struggled with their consciences over slavery, as some colonists were beginning to do. Indeed, a 1790 letter by Peggy's father offered to sell his slave Will for half of the one hundred pounds he had paid for him. Peggy's father described Will as "tolerably honest" but complained that he was "rather an eye servant," meaning that he worked only under the watchful eye of his master.[6]

The Shippen family was Quaker when it settled in Philadelphia four generations earlier, but had embraced the Church of England by the time Peggy was born. She was baptized at Christ Church, a center of worship that was founded in 1695 and is spreading the Episcopal message even today.[7]

A high point for the church came six years before Peggy's birth with the construction of a steeple and installation of eight bells weighing a total of eight thousand pounds. The initial bell-ringing marked the funeral of Pennsylvania governor Anthony Palmer's wife, who was said to have been the mother of twenty-one children and to have lost all twenty-one to tuberculosis, then known as consumption.[8]

While the first ringing of Christ Church's bells marked one death, it caused another. An early history reported that a bell ringer was fatally crushed because of his "ignorance and ill-judged management of the bell rope."[9]

Colonial Philadelphia was full of risks and rewards. Indeed the city's growth was built on gambling—Christ Church's steeple was financed by lotteries, as was the paving of roads.

In an era when ship travel was supreme, the city's location upriver from Delaware Bay made it a great center of commerce. By the time of the American Revolution, more than five hundred hatters were counted in Philadelphia alone.[10] Wealthy families like the Shippens sipped imported Madeira and French wines and dined on turtles shipped live from Jamaica.[11]

The markets were meccas for both the rich and the working class. All ears could hear the peal of Christ Church's bells on Tuesday and Friday nights, announcing that markets would be open the next morning. Farmers brought the predictable staples, of course, but also sold frogs that they caught in their ponds. At market, a lady's social standing might be signaled by whether a maid trailed behind her with basket in hand or she carried the basket herself. When buying butter, it was customary to take a taste first, and the sellers set up small pyramids of butter for that purpose, providing a spoon or a fork. Prominent men of Philadelphia eschewed the common utensils, using their own coins to scoop tastes of butter.[12]

Peggy's Philadelphia was as cosmopolitan as the colonies could be, with strong religious foundations but a measure of tolerance and acceptance of diversity that was far from universal in America. Pennsylvanians were "a people free from the extremes both of vice and virtue," as Thomas Jefferson put it.[13]

Even before Peggy began to make history, she was surrounded by it.

Philadelphia's role as both a destination and a crossroads allowed her father to play host to the most accomplished and influential visitors of his day. During Peggy's childhood, houseguests included George Washington, the wealthy Virginian who would later become the Father of His Country, and Benedict Arnold, the audacious military officer who would later become Peggy's husband—and his nation's most famous traitor.[14]

Another transformative figure in American history, Benjamin Franklin, was a friend of both of Peggy's grandfathers. By the time Peggy was born, Franklin's famous electricity experiment with a kite and a key was eight years old, and Franklin was often gone from Philadelphia on long diplomatic trips to London.[15]

Among the visitors to Philadelphia when Peggy was three years old were a pair of English surveyors named Charles Mason and Jeremiah Dixon, who were hired to establish the Maryland-Pennsylvania border, later known as the Mason-Dixon Line, one of the most famous borders in American history.[16]

Indeed, Peggy was in the company of greatness from the very start.

A Philadelphian born the same year as Peggy—but of far lower caste—was Richard Allen, a slave who gained his freedom and became the leading founder of the African Methodist Episcopal Church. Allen's owner was Benjamin Chew, the chief justice of Pennsylvania, whose daughter was one of Peggy's childhood friends.[17]

When Peggy was a child, her father's cousin Dr. William Shippen caused an uproar in Philadelphia by using cadavers in medical education and advocating the involvement of men in midwifery. Rocks were thrown through his windows, and charges abounded that he was a grave robber.[18] But his efforts advanced medicine, especially in the battle against infant mortality, which was ten to twenty times higher in the American colonies than it is in the United States today.[19] (Dr. Shippen's father, William, also a physician, famously assessed his profession by saying, "Nature does a great deal, and the grave covers up our mistakes.")[20]

There was yet another noteworthy person in Peggy's vicinity—Elizabeth Griscom, who was eight years old and lived about three blocks away when Peggy was born. Griscom, whose married name was Betsy Ross, served the needs of American mythmaking and is remembered, accurately or not, as the woman who made the first American flag.[21] Today Betsy Ross is far more famous than Peggy Shippen, though far less significant in the events of her time. But she fit the stereotype better: Women were meant to sew flags, not to sow conspiracies.

The Reverend Andrew Burnaby, a British travel writer who visited Philadelphia around the time of Peggy's birth, said, "The women are exceedingly handsome and polite. They are naturally sprightly and fond of pleasure, and, upon the whole, are much more accomplished and agreeable than the men."[22]

But the men were in charge, and always had been.

Two of the most accomplished patriarchs among Peggy's Shippen ancestors—her grandfather and great-great-grandfather—showed a special ambition and intelligence, like hers. And also like Peggy, they were tortured by the harsh judgments of society.

Peggy's great-great-grandfather, the first Shippen to cross the Atlantic from England to America, was Edward Shippen, son of an overseer of highways in Yorkshire. By 1668, when Edward was about thirty years old, he had arrived in Massachusetts and set up as a merchant, leasing dock space in Boston and developing trade with the Caribbean, then typically called the West Indies.

Edward soon married a Quaker woman and shed his Anglican roots to join her faith. It was not a popular move; it separated him from the majority of Bostonians and invited persecution.[23] The Quakers—formally the Society of Friends—were known for their pacifism, their rejection of social distinctions, and their refusal to swear allegiance to government.[24] In 1677 Edward Shippen was arrested twice and subjected to public whippings for the crime of attending Quaker meetings.

Edward nonetheless found business success in Boston. His family thrived, too, with his wife bearing eight children in seventeen years before her death in 1688. Shippen remarried and, in 1694 at the age of fifty-five, resettled in Philadelphia. The reasons for the move are in dispute. According to some historians, a meteor over Boston prompted superstitious Puritans to launch a new wave of persecution against Baptists and Quakers. But others insist that no such pogrom occurred.[25]

In any case, Edward's Quaker beliefs were far more welcome in Pennsylvania, a province founded by a Quaker, William Penn. Also very welcome was Edward's wealth. When he arrived, he may have been the wealthiest man in the Philadelphia area.

Edward was immediately invited into the government and served as the city's first mayor. He acquired hundreds of acres of property, rode in a fine carriage, had his portrait painted, and lived in a mansion overlooking the city and the Delaware River. His Second Street estate, later known as Governor's House, featured orchards, gardens, and herds of deer.[26] When William Penn visited Pennsylvania, Shippen turned over his mansion as temporary home for the province's "absolute proprietor."[27]

Despite trappings of elegance, the Shippens were considered to be an acceptably circumspect Quaker family. Edward's wife and daughter signed the Quaker women's annual declaration against fancy language, striped and gaudy clothing, overlong scarves, and hair piled high upon their heads.

Four generations later, when Peggy Shippen was dressing for dances, such a pledge against extravagance would have been unthinkable. But perhaps Peggy could relate to another aspect of her ancestor's life—how her great-great-grandfather experienced the family's first major scandal in North America.

A year after Edward's second wife died, he married a third woman in a hurried fashion. Something had caused the woman's "apron to rise too fast," as one Quaker put it. She was pregnant. The sixty-seven-year-old newlywed was labeled an "old lecher" by that same Quaker, and an excruciating two-year period of reproach and humiliation ensued. Finally the Quakers accepted Edward's testimony of sinfulness, and the text of his confession was distributed to other Quaker groups in New England, New Jersey, and Maryland, as well as overseas to Barbados, Antigua, and even London. That admission restored Edward to social acceptability. Before he died at age seventy-four, he was offered another term as Philadelphia mayor, but declined.

Next came Peggy's great-grandfather, Joseph, a country gentleman who fell away from the Quakers and left little of note to history except his money and his eldest son Edward, Peggy's grandfather.

This Edward, like the first Edward, had a talent for business. He married the daughter of his father's second wife—more proof that the family by this time had rejected Quaker values. Under Quaker law, marrying a stepsister was the same as marrying a sister—the sin of incest. But that was no matter to Edward; he was a Presbyterian.[28]

The young Edward was apprenticed to a wealthy Philadelphian who slipped on the ice and shattered his hip. Bedridden for three months and relying on crutches thereafter, the businessman gave Edward his power of attorney and made him a partner.

Their business involved trading with Native Americans for furs and skins, including deer, raccoon, bear, mink, and otter. Those furs were shipped to England, and in return came knives, axes, gunpowder, blankets, and other goods in demand in North America. The enterprise involved a great deal of credit, forcing Edward to track down debtors, a job that increased his visibility if not his popularity.

Edward plowed much of his money into real estate in the city and well beyond, acquiring land that later became the town of Shippensburg in south-central Pennsylvania. In 1744 he became mayor of Philadelphia. In 1758 he became a founding trustee of the College of New Jersey, now known as Princeton University.

Edward's business and political interests thrived, but the pursuit of love proved disastrous for him, as it had for his grandfather and would for his granddaughter. His stepsister-wife died at age twenty-nine, leaving him with three small children. He waited eight years to remarry and then chose a woman whose husband had departed for the Caribbean island of Barbados several years earlier and had not been heard from since. The man was presumed dead, and Edward obtained the opinion of the Reverend Aaron Burr, president of the College of New Jersey, that the woman was free to marry him.[29]

Weeks after the wedding, an unconfirmed report from Barbados indicated that the bride's first husband was indeed alive. Edward's business partner urged the newlyweds to split up, but instead they "agreed to separate beds," in Edward's words.

For several years their anguish remained private and there was no sign of the missing first husband. But around 1750, authorities learned of the possibility that he remained alive, and a grand jury indicted Edward for adultery and his wife for bigamy. The crime of bigamy was punishable by thirty-nine lashes and life imprisonment, though it is doubtful that the wife of such a prominent person would have suffered that fate. In any case, executive clemency resolved the legal issues: The governor pardoned them both.

But another form of punishment was administered through public humiliation—through the whispers of "so many spiteful enemies who are always wrongfully condemning us," as Edward's son Joseph described them. Edward's wife departed to live with her parents while he and his friends collected witness statements to try to establish that the missing man's funeral had taken place in Barbados. Eventually they claimed they had enough proof, and the unfortunate couple were reunited.

Edward and his wife left the judgments of Philadelphia for a peaceful life in the frontier town of Lancaster, Pennsylvania, where they enjoyed many happy and vigorous years. Edward grew asparagus and peaches and danced a jig at a wedding at age sixty-nine. He was a great lover of learning and of life. A family history recalled that Edward believed that "a little wine upon the strawberries improves them very much."[30] An in-law and law clerk wrote: "In a minute, he relates to me ten different stories, interlarding each narrative with choice scraps of Latin, Greek, and French."[31]

Edward's retreat to Lancaster provided a vital resource for historians, since his absence from the city compelled him to exchange frequent letters with his son, letters that tell the family's story in depth and intimacy.

Edward's son—Peggy's father—signed his letters to his father as "Edw. Shippen Jr." Though generally assessed as being less colorful and original than his father, this Edward was a deep thinker and scholar in his own right.[32] Given every chance at success, he took full advantage. He first became an apprentice to a respected lawyer, Tench Francis, who served for a time as attorney general of Pennsylvania. Then, at age nineteen, Edward received an expensive and invaluable gift from his father—a legal education in England.

Getting there was an adventure. In a letter to his brother Joseph, Edward described a winter ocean voyage in which a storm nearly overturned the ship. "The sailors were so disheartened that they would not work a stroke, but quitted the deck, every man but one, and retired to their cabins to pray."[33] Eventually Edward and his fellow passengers arrived in London, "where we have had the pleasure of congratulating one another upon our deliverance."

Edward attended the Middle Temple, so named because it was home to the Knights Templar, the Roman Catholic military order that was disbanded in the 1300s but has survived as the subject of numerous documentaries and contemporary thriller novels.[34] Edward enjoyed his own set of thrills in London, achieving an education unattainable in North America and having an enjoyable time while doing it.

His father's generous nature toward him is evident in a letter that urged him not to let his studies get in the way of having a good time: "I much approve of your conduct, for you will have an opportunity of reading books on your return, but not so good a one to read men; you may remember my advice to you upon parting (among other things) was to rise early and to study hard till dinner time that you might have the afternoons to look about you; and notwithstanding that you will cost me a great deal, yet if I had money to spare I would send you as much more."[35]

Peggy's father toured Paris and Versailles and wrote that he enjoyed speaking French in "the metropolis of the polite worlds." Then he returned to Philadelphia to make a career. It would have been difficult for him to fail, with so many blood relatives and in-laws in so many positions of power. The Shippens were virtual royalty, despite the occasional scandals. Happy to use his family connections to his advantage, Edward Jr. became a judge of the Admiralty Court, which enforced law from London in the colonies. He also served on the Philadelphia Common Council and was chief clerk of the Pennsylvania Supreme Court.

But like the Shippens before him, he was not cynical or calculating about love.

He considered Margaret Francis, the eldest daughter of his mentor Tench Francis, to be "the most amiable of her sex." While many men of the era would have appraised a prominent lawyer's daughter as an excellent catch, Edward thought his prospects were so high that he could have found an even wealthier family to join. He virtually apologized to his father for his choice of a wife.

"If I had obtained a girl with a considerable fortune, no doubt the world would have pronounced me happier," but he preferred "internal satisfaction and contentment of the mind," he wrote.[36]

Margaret Francis came with a dowry of five hundred pounds, and Edward spent much of it on his library. As a gift, Edward's father gave the young couple the fine house on Fourth Street.[37] The newlywed Shippens promptly began their family. First came Elizabeth, the sister to whom Peggy was closest. Then Sarah and Mary, and yet another Edward. And then Peggy.

The childhood of Peggy Shippen is not well documented. We know she received the common lessons for upper-class girls—in sewing, dancing, drawing, and music. It is unlikely that Peggy ever attended school, which would have been a rare privilege for a young woman in that era, though Peggy would send her own daughter to school decades later. Well-off children were more likely to be tutored. In any case, Peggy was well armed intellectually, and the quality of her later writings demonstrates her command of the English language.[38] As an adult, she told her father that she had enjoyed "the most useful and best education that America at that time afforded."[39]

Sadly for historians, any letters written by Peggy in the first eighteen years of her life were lost or destroyed in the panic after Benedict Arnold's treason was discovered. It is unknown whether her family and friends got rid of her correspondence because it contained incriminating evidence or because they feared that any innocent sentence could be twisted and wielded as a weapon against her.

Peggy's family and friends may have destroyed a part of her story, but enough remains from the surviving letters of her later years to indicate that she possessed a razor-sharp intelligence and a practical nature, the kind of pragmatism that would have sent her earlier letters to the fire. The destruction of her letters protected the myth of Peggy's innocence—a most fortunate occurrence for her.

Edward Shippen, Peggy's father, steered a middle course through a bloody revolution and ultimately won the job of Pennsylvania chief justice—but lost his daughter to exile. PHOTO BY HULTON ARCHIVE/GETTY IMAGES

Peggy was indeed lucky in life, except in the timing of her birth, which came only a few years before a wrenching war would ruin her chances at happiness. And she was lucky, except that her beauty brought her into the highest circles of fame, and intrigue, and danger. And she was lucky, except that when she found love, it was with a man incapable of returning the fidelity she showed him.

Which means that Peggy Shippen, a princess of Philadelphia, wasn't lucky in the least.

Chapter 2

No Safe Haven

Peggy was not raised to be famous. She was raised to be a cultured woman, a credit to her family, a supportive wife to a worthy husband, and a vessel for the greatness of her children.

"Needlework, the care of domestic affairs, and a serious and retired life, is the proper function of women, and for this they were designed by Providence," declared Caleb Bingham's *American Preceptor,* a textbook of the era that denounced modern female tendencies such as "a soft indolence, a stupid idleness, frivolous conversation, vain amusements, and a strong passion for public shows."[40]

Far from rebelling against the roles that society assigned to her, Peggy embraced them. She even adopted the self-deprecating writing style common to females of that period, with phrases such as "weak woman as I am."[41] But before she was ready for the "retired life" of a married woman, she was eager to sample the amusements of youth and the pursuits by handsome suitors.

She seemed to grasp the importance of her good looks and her family's affluence in the quest for the best match. Decades later she wrote bluntly that her daughter Sophia was well-read and cultured but there was "little chance of her marrying, having but a moderate share of beauty and no money."[42]

The young Peggy had neither of those problems. Instead, she was perfectly qualified to attract male attention in an era of great public fascination with the flowering of young women, as reflected in a 1754 almanac poem:

At fourteen years young females are
contriving tricks to tempt ye
At sixteen years come on and woo,
and take of kisses plenty,
At eighteen years full grown and ripe,
they're ready to content ye,
At nineteen sly and mischievous,
but the Devil at one and twenty.[43]

For Peggy and other young women gaining sexual power, there was peril in socializing. Any indiscretion might ruin a young woman's prospects for a good marriage. And a pregnancy out of wedlock would likely make a hasty marriage decision for them. In some New England towns in the late eighteenth century, up to a third of the brides were pregnant at the altar, according to one study.[44]

Women were likely to take the brunt of the blame for any sexual misconduct. According to the prevailing attitudes, females were less ruled by reason than males were, and thus were more prone to lustful temptation.

Group activities were encouraged, such as polite conversation in the parlor, where young people of the opposite sex could be watched. For upper-class young ladies, sewing circles were a popular and safe way to pass the time, with one girl reading aloud while the others cut and stitched cloth. Peggy was known to gossip on occasion, but was discreet enough to maintain close and loyal friendships.

Though Peggy would later be viewed as a scandalous party girl who dallied with men on both sides of the revolutionary struggle, a far more sympathetic portrait of her also survives. By these accounts, she was a homebody who doted on her family.

A relative praised her as "so gentle and timorous a girl."[45] The daughter of a Shippen family friend recalled how her mother was impressed by Peggy's "affectionate and exemplary conduct" and "great purity of mind and principles." The friend's daughter also noted: "Miss Peggy Shippen was particularly devoted to her father, making his comfort her leading thought, often preferring to remain with him when evening parties and amusements would attract her sisters from home. She was the darling of the family circle, and never fond of gadding. There was nothing of frivolity either in her dress, demeanor, or conduct, and though deservedly admired, she had too much good sense to be vain."[46]

In addition to her high regard for her father, Peggy adored her "Grandpapa" and looked forward to his visits to the city.[47] Peggy's grandfather likewise treasured the occasions when Peggy and her family made the two-day journey to Lancaster. When Peggy was fourteen, her grandfather wrote that he would duck out of his work as a court official when she visited next: "I will ride out more than once to meet her, though it is even on a court day."[48]

Undoubtedly, the two men who dominated Peggy's childhood tried to shield her from the harsh uncertainties that steadily enveloped her family, her city, and all of North America.

Peggy was two years old when a treaty ended the French and Indian War, part of a transatlantic struggle between Britain and France known in Britain as the Seven Years' War. The British won the war and collected Canada as a prize, but they amassed debts that they tried to pay by imposing taxes on the American colonists. In the treaty that ended the fighting, the British also agreed to protect Indian lands by limiting westward expansion—another point of irritation with the colonists.[49]

The Stamp Act, which imposed a tax on paper products, was passed by the British Parliament in early 1765, when Peggy was four years of age.[50] Opposition to it was vocal in Philadelphia but achieved its full volume in Boston—a dynamic that would continue as New England's radicals led the other colonists away from moderation and ultimately to revolution.

"You observe by the public papers that great riots and disturbances are going forward in New England in opposition to the Stamp Act and stamp officers," Peggy's father wrote to his own father. "I think the act is an oppressive one, and I wish any scheme for a repeal could be fallen on; but I am afraid these violent methods will only tend to fix chains upon us sooner than they would otherwise come.... Poor America! It has seen its best days."[51]

As the Stamp Act was about to take effect, he wrote his father again, noting that his newborn son "had just time enough to breathe about three weeks the air of freedom; for after the first of November we may call ourselves the slaves of England."[52]

Disapproving of the Stamp Act but also disapproving of its opponents, Peggy's father simply avoided doing any business that would force him to take a stand. When the Stamp Act was rescinded the next year, Edward exulted to Peggy's grandfather: "I am stopped with the joyful news of the Stamp Act being repealed. I wish you and all America joy."[53]

This easing of tensions was short-lived, and merely preceded such incidents as the Boston Massacre and the Boston Tea Party and such measures as the "Intolerable Acts." Even so, the idea of independence from Britain seemed a remote possibility, and was opposed by the Shippens and many if not most of their fellow colonists.

The growing grievances led to a gathering of politicians—the First Continental Congress in 1774. Philadelphia was picked as the meeting site for many reasons. It had the lodging and amenities, and it was a good place to balance the conservatives of the South against the fire-breathers of New England.

On September 28, 1774, Peggy's father brought one of the delegates home for dinner. The guest was a tall, wealthy forty-two-year-old Virginia landowner who had become a land surveyor, then had gone into the military and barely survived the French and Indian War, with two horses shot from under him and four bullets whizzing through his coat.[54] The man was George Washington, and his life was soon to become perilous again, with war less than a year away.

Washington may have been an impressive guest at the Shippen home that day, though dinnertime was never his finest hour. One biographer described meals with him as "excruciating" and noted his habit of using his knife and fork as drumsticks, tapping on the table to cope with his unease at small talk.[55]

Fourteen-year-old Peggy dined with Washington that day, and a family relationship was established that would later prove crucial to her freedom. She would admire him her entire life, writing after his death a quarter century later: "Nobody in America could revere his character more than I did."[56]

Certainly Washington didn't consider Peggy's family to be a collection of toadies subservient to the whims of King George III across the sea. But as the political atmosphere became increasingly polarized, the Shippens were often mislabeled as Loyalists. Of course, public opinion in general was ill-defined and volatile, allowing for radical activists like the Sons of Liberty to deliver inspiration through persuasive essays and impose fear through cruel mob tactics such as tar-and-feathering.

In 1777, with the Revolutionary War under way, a writer identified only as "S." in the *Pennsylvania Packet* newspaper divided the citizenry into five political categories:

- The "Rank Tories" were defined as Loyalists who favored "unconditional submission to Great Britain."
- The "Moderate Men" preferred a continued place in the British Empire and took a stand "to hate the people of New England and to love all Rank Tories."
- The "Timid Whigs" were open to independence but pessimistic about the colonists' ability to resist British power.
- The "Furious Whigs" hurt the cause of liberty by their indiscriminate violence.
- And the "Staunch Whigs" were depicted as heroes, resolute and resilient, who "would rather renounce their existence than their beloved independence."[57]

Peggy's family fit into none of these categories neatly. Her father and grandfather might have been considered "moderate men" who opposed independence, but they had sympathy toward New England, not antipathy. When the Intolerable Acts were imposed to try to bring the colonists to heel, "Grandpapa" Shippen contributed ten pounds to ease the suffering of Bostonians. He also was active in Lancaster's citizen committees, which aimed to build strength and solidarity as resistance to British rule grew.

Peggy's father would not go that far. Educated in England and seen as a symbol of the old guard, he was under the Patriots' constant suspicion. But he was not a Loyalist; he was merely a Shippenist, seeking to preserve his family's long-held privileges against any challenges from either liberty-minded firebrands or authority-imposing British officials.

While the Shippens experienced life under severe political pressure, they did so with rich food in their stomachs and fine carpets underfoot. Peggy's father wrote Edward Sr. that the boycott of British tea was inconvenient, forcing the family to adopt coffee drinking. His wife "has searched every shop in town for a blue and white china coffee pot, but no such thing is to be had, nor indeed any other sort that can be called handsome. Since the disuse of tea, great numbers of people have been endeavoring to supply themselves with coffee pots. My brother, having no silver one, has taken pains to get a china one, but without success."[58]

Soon the quest for a handsome coffee pot would be far from Edward's mind. Events had started spinning out of control.

In March 1775 Patrick Henry raised patriotic fervor by telling the Virginia Convention, "Give me liberty or give me death!" The next month in Massachusetts, the Revolutionary War erupted, with violent clashes of British forces and armed colonists at Lexington and Concord.

Uncertainty reigned, but some members of the Shippen family finally took a stand. Peggy's cousin Neddy Burd, who served as a law clerk to her father in Philadelphia, volunteered as a lieutenant in a Pennsylvania rifle battalion and set off for Boston to oppose the British, inspiring Peggy's father to write a letter rebuking him. "I wrote him my sentiments about this step the other day," Edward told his father, "and represented to him that not having been used to the woods; nor to hunting, nor to use of rifles, he would be deemed a very unfit person for that service, and that it would appear to all the world a ridiculous thing for a young man bred in an office to attempt to command riflemen, who are expected to be men bred in the woods and enured to hardships."[59]

Peggy's grandfather also disapproved, but Neddy would not relent.[60] The news was especially painful to the Shippens because he not only was a beloved cousin but also was romantically involved with Elizabeth "Betsy" Shippen, Peggy's oldest sister.

Another Shippen—Dr. William Shippen, the alleged "graverobber" who was Peggy's father's cousin—also cast his lot with the revolution, becoming director of hospitals for the Continental Army. And one of Peggy's cousins on her mother's side, Tench Tilghman, became a trusted aide to General Washington.[61]

The Revolutionary War was a civil war, with many families deeply divided. But Peggy's father tried to defy that painful reality by clinging desperately to neutrality. It was as if Edward had lashed his arms to two different ships that were leaving port in opposite directions.

In early 1776, Thomas Paine's pamphlet *Common Sense* pushed the colonies well past the point of no return. Its sales in that year alone were estimated at a staggering half million—in other words, one copy for every five colonists.[62]

Edward wrote to an in-law: "A book called *Common Sense*, wrote in favor of a total separation from England, seems to gain ground with the common people; it is artfully wrote, yet might be easily refuted. This idea of an independence, though some time ago abhorred, may possibly by degrees become so familiar as to be cherished. It is in everybody's mouth as a thing absolutely necessary in case foreign troops should be landed, as if this step alone would enable us to oppose them with success."[63]

Indeed, the British were taking steps to remind the colonists of their military might. Two warships, the *Roebuck* and the *Liverpool*, came up the Delaware River in early May of 1776 to test Philadelphia's defenses. A hurriedly assembled flotilla chased them away, with minimal casualties on both sides but enough booming of cannon to alarm the citizenry, including the Shippens.[64]

Edward decided to lead his family's retreat from Philadelphia.

He picked an improbable new career—rural shopkeeper—and set up near Flemington, New Jersey, about fifty miles northeast of Philadelphia, on 260 acres of land featuring a home recently built by John Reading, former governor of the colony of New Jersey.[65] Putting a happy face on a less than ideal situation, he described their new residence as a "fine house" on "a clever tract of land with a good deal of meadows." Granted, the house would have to be shared with another family come winter, but there was no reason to complain.[66]

It's safe to say that Peggy loathed her rural exile. In a letter later in life, she made clear that she considered herself a city sophisticate, describing the prospect of associating with regular country people as "extremely painful" and the atmosphere in a country town as even worse, "chiefly composed of card-playing, tattling old maids, and people wholly unaccustomed to genteel life."[67]

But at least rural New Jersey seemed safe. Writing to an in-law, Edward declared: "Every moderate-thinking man must remain silent and inactive."[68] It was quite a contrast to Patrick Henry's cry of "Give me liberty or give me death," but it perfectly reflected Edward's formula for survival.

The shopkeeping was a failure, and the Shippens never felt at home. It is not difficult to imagine Edward and his wife enduring the grumbling of four daughters and a son who were accustomed to city comforts.

Meanwhile, within two blocks of their home in Philadelphia, a crowd gathered on July 8 and heard the reading of a new document completed a few days earlier, a document that would transform the colonies and rewrite the Shippens' lives. The Declaration of Independence announced that the crown's control was over. A new Pennsylvania constitution soon followed, abolishing the government that had brought the Shippens their wealth.

There was, of course, the likelihood that the British would quash this uprising, as they had done with so many others as they extended their global empire. Many observers, especially in England, viewed the developments as little more than a fit thrown by a bunch of toddlers. "I look upon America to be our spoilt child," said British general John Burgoyne.[69] Even a delegate to the Continental Congress, John Dickinson, had embraced the metaphor nearly a decade earlier, urging colonists to "behave like dutiful children who have received unmerited blows from a beloved parent."[70]

Yet the American independence movement had grown up enough to be dangerous in all the colonies. For the first year of the war, combat was largely confined to the Boston area. But cannon, cleverly captured at Fort Ticonderoga on Lake Champlain in upstate New York by Colonel Benedict Arnold, were even more cleverly emplaced on Dorchester Heights overlooking Boston Harbor, frightening the British into sailing away.

The king's army went briefly to Halifax, Nova Scotia, then south to New York City, where heavy fighting resumed in August 1776. There were three major engagements: at Brooklyn, White Plains, and Fort Washington, near the east end of the present-day George Washington Bridge. Each battle was a disaster for George Washington and the Continental Army.

One of the New York casualties was Neddy Burd, who by this time was the fiancé of Peggy's sister Betsy. Word came back that Neddy had been killed in action. The news plunged the Shippens into grief, but then a more reliable report indicated that Neddy had been captured rather than killed.[71] He was being held on one of the notorious prison ships off Long Island, where thousands died from malnutrition, scurvy, typhus, dysentery, and bayonetings by guards. Few prisoners lasted six months, and far fewer made it a year. Neddy was fortunate enough to be freed after three months.[72]

The remnants of Washington's army retreated across New Jersey and into Pennsylvania. Peggy's family also decided to leave New Jersey, but for a different reason. New Jersey's legislature passed a measure in October "to punish traitors and other disaffected persons." Edward was given two choices: renounce all allegiance to the king, or be tried for treason.

The Shippens initially returned to their home on Fourth Street, but fears grew that Philadelphia might come under siege or fall to the enemy. There were even rumors that the city would be put to the torch rather than surrendered. The city's Council of Safety advised that women and children flee the city to avoid "the insults and oppressions of a licentious soldiery" if the British should take Philadelphia.[73]

Peggy's father moved his family out of the city to a farm near the Schuylkill River four miles upstream from the Delaware. "I live near the Falls of Schuylkill, a very clever retired place," he wrote his father.[74] But both father and son were watching their wealth drain away, as he noted in the same letter: "I think another summer must necessarily show us our fate. If the war should continue longer than that, we are all ruined as to our estates, whatever may be the state of our liberties."

While Peggy and her family lived quietly near the Falls, her father feared seizure of their Fourth Street mansion as a barracks for colonial troops. He went into the city nearly every day "that I may be seen in and about my house, which is constantly opened every day, and has all the appearance of being inhabited, and is really lodged in by two or three women every night," most likely his servants.[75] "By this means I hope to escape the mischief," he wrote.

A most surprising development relieved British pressure on Philadelphia. On Christmas night, Washington and his troops crossed the Delaware and attacked Trenton, New Jersey, where the British had stationed a force of Hessian soldiers. The Hessians were expecting festivities, not hostilities, and about a thousand were captured along with a young Philadelphian named Edward Shippen, Peggy's brother.

The eighteen-year-old Edward had been on a business errand in New Jersey when he ran across three Loyalist cousins who persuaded him to join the British army with them. The cousins moved on to New York, leaving Edward with the Hessians in Trenton, where Christmas frivolity ensued until Washington spoiled the party.

The young man's capture, coming at a time when his father was desperately trying to avoid any appearance of Loyalist sympathies, might have proved disastrous to the entire family. But luckily for the Shippens, Washington determined that young Edward had taken no action against the colonial forces and that he was, in essence, a dolt. The gracious general released the young man, dispatching him to his family near the Falls.

In explaining the incident, Peggy's father showed himself to be a bit of a dupe, writing: "Though I highly disapproved of what he had done, yet I could not condemn him as much as I should have done, if he had not been enticed to it by those who were much older, and ought to have judged better than himself."[76]

Even so, Peggy's father, who had briefly tried to turn over some business affairs to his son so that the family could make money, gave up the idea. He vowed never "to put it again in his power to trade or make any improper use of money."[77] From then on, it was clear to Peggy's father that if he wanted to discuss business with one of his offspring, he would choose his youngest daughter.

A higher priority than his wallet was his freedom, and that was under great threat as Pennsylvania's revolutionary government rounded up suspected Loyalists. A group of militiamen showed up with a warrant for his arrest and were persuaded to relent only upon his pledge not to leave the farm or speak of politics. Later the State Council loosened the reins, allowing Edward to travel anywhere in Pennsylvania.[78]

Though Peggy's father must have felt vulnerable to arrest or banishment at any time, he was saved from such a fate by his many friends and admirers, such as Thomas McKean, a signer of the Declaration of Independence, who declared his "special trust and confidence" in Edward's patriotism.[79]

By March 1777 it was obvious to Edward that the British forces of General William Howe would soon be in Philadelphia, with "General Washington's army in no condition to prevent him." Then, he predicted, the American army would lay siege "and the country will be laid waste by the two contending parties."[80] Peggy's father, though not always astute about politics and war, was an accurate prognosticator this time. But he didn't see a clear path to safety.

"In this dreadful situation of affairs I am at a loss to know how to dispose of my family," he wrote his father. "Advantages and disadvantages present themselves by turns, whether I determine to remain in Philadelphia or remove to a distance."

At some point, either before the British captured Philadelphia or immediately afterward, the Shippens moved out of the increasingly dangerous countryside and back into the city, which posed its own dangers.

Improbably, the next nine months would be one of the most wonderful periods of Peggy's life.

CHAPTER 3

Enter André

THE BELLS OF THE SHIPPENS' CHRIST CHURCH—the bells that had killed that very first ringer back in 1754—were taken out of the city to prevent the advancing British from melting them down for ammunition.[81]

But the belles of Philadelphia remained.

Dressed in their fine gowns and high hair, Peggy Shippen and other young aristocratic women were ready to be courted by the sharply uniformed officers who conquered their city in the first weeks of autumn 1777.

To most Americans, the times were grim and desperate. At least a dozen Tory spies and recruiters were executed that year, so many that 1777 was known as "the year of the hangman" because the sevens in 1777 looked like gallows.[82] But to Peggy and her lavishly attired friends, the sevens might just as easily have represented bowing gentlemen asking them to dance.

The British occupation, rather than spoiling the ladies' party, simply brought a new set of admirers and a new style and abundance of dances and dinners. A series of galas known as the Dancing Assembly had been a tradition in Philadelphia for three decades, serving the dual function of fun and social stratification. The families of import-export merchants were welcome; shopkeepers' kin were not. Lawyers and doctors could join; artisans could not. The Assembly was tightly run. Dancers formed themselves into sets of exactly ten couples, first come, first served. Minuets were performed first, then country dances. If a gentleman or lady arrived alone, a partner would be assigned by lot, with no protest allowed. And the gentleman would be considered rude if he did not have tea with the lady the next day, to see if their relationship might go further. For those who preferred not to dance, card tables were provided. Wine, rum, and coffee were served, along with a modest supper consisting of tea, chocolate, and a hard cake called rusk.[83]

But the Dancing Assembly system was far too tidy and controlled for a year like 1777. As the war brought social chaos to Philadelphia, the Assembly met irregularly, and enterprising British officers filled every vacuum with their own dizzying series of social events, creating an atmosphere of festivity that the city had never before seen. The British also brought new rules. While the provincial custom called for the ladies to keep the same dancing partner all night, the opposite was true with the British.[84]

At the center of the celebration—and the new level of romantic competition—were four young ladies: two Peggys and two Beckys.

There was Peggy Shippen, of course, and her friend Peggy Chew, whose father had served as attorney general and chief justice of Pennsylvania.[85] Then there was Becky Redman, daughter of a former high sheriff of Philadelphia, and Becky Franks, daughter of a prominent importer who had brought the Liberty Bell to town.[86]

Peggy Shippen was the youngest of the group, only seventeen when the British seized her city. Peggy Chew was about a year older, Becky Franks a year older still, and Becky Redman quite a bit beyond them, in her mid-twenties.

Peggy Shippen seems to have been the prettiest, though the dark-haired Peggy Chew was also described as quite beautiful. Chew, who was more the philosopher than her friend, once wrote: "What is life, in short, but one continued scene of pain and pleasure varied and chequered with black spots like the chessboard, only to set the fairer ones in a purer light?"[87]

Becky Redman was known as a lover of German music. Becky Franks, perhaps Peggy Shippen's closest friend, was the mischievous and funny one, and an unabashed Loyalist. According to a story told early in the British occupation, a Continental Army officer once asked Franks

John André, poet, thespian, artist, soldier, and spymaster. THE ART ARCHIVE, REF: AA532551

whether she thought "their arms had not been crowned with great success" in the war, and she replied that she didn't know about their arms, but she thought their legs had succeeded in running away.[88]

All four of the young women became enamored of an enthralling British officer who had recently been promoted to captain. His name was John André.

André was five-foot-nine, with dark hair and eyes, and olive skin inherited from his ancestors in the South of France. Just as people tended

Miss Margaret Shippen.
daughter of Chief Justice Shippen

Peggy Shippen as drawn by her friend John André. Hers was a life of high hair, high drama, and high treason. PORTRAIT OF MARGARET SHIPPEN (MRS. BENEDICT ARNOLD), YALE UNIVERSITY ART GALLERY

to dwell on Peggy Shippen's physical attractiveness, men and women remarked on André's fine features. A Connecticut militiaman once described André as "the handsomest man I ever laid eyes on."[89]

But, like Peggy, John André was gifted on the inside as well. He spoke a cultured English, plus French, Italian, and German. He played the flute and sang. He danced superbly. He wrote and recited poetry. And he showed exceptional talent as an artist, drawing sketches of street scenes and portraits of his friends.[90]

He was twenty-seven, a decade older than Peggy, and his life experience was even further beyond hers. But his playfulness and youthful sense of wonder drew them close. He made regular pilgrimages to Peggy's home on Fourth Street to discuss the arts and to flirt. He sketched a drawing of the young Peggy that is one of the few remaining images of her, with high hair, a headdress, wise eyes, and a Mona Lisa smile.

John André lavished attention on the other young women as well.

For Becky Franks, he painted a miniature portrait and wrote a few lines of poetry.[91]

At Becky Redman's request, he cut silhouette portraits. He also wrote verses to her, set to her favorite German music, such as:

> Return, enraptured hours,
> When Delia's heart was mine
> When she with wreaths of flowers
> My temples would entwine.[92]

He paid special attention to Peggy Chew, and if he loved any of them, she was probably the one. But he seemed to be fond of them all. And they of him.

―――

Nothing about André was typical, including his path to the British army, and to America. Both his parents' families were Huguenots, a sect of French Protestants who had suffered persecution. His paternal ancestors fled the South of France for safety in Genoa and Geneva. Eventually his father immigrated to London, where he became wealthy in the import business. He married a Parisian Huguenot, and they settled in a London suburb, raising their children—first John, then three daughters and another son.

André was instructed by a private tutor in his youth, then went to the Academy in Geneva where he mastered music, illustration, and other liberal arts that charmed so many of those he later encountered. He majored in mathematics and military drawing, and met other intellectuals such as Pierre-Eugene Du Simitiere, who would later befriend André in America and create the first design for the Great Seal of the United States, including the phrase "E Pluribus unum" (Out of many, one).[93]

André found that his father's ambitions for him were not artistic in the least. Summoned home at age seventeen, André was put to work in his father's counting house in London's Warnford Court. About two years later his father died, leaving a will in which each of his five children inherited five thousand pounds (roughly nine hundred thousand dollars in today's currency).[94] However, the children would not get their money until age twenty-one, and as the oldest son, André was under pressure to support the family business.[95]

The summer after André's father died, the family vacationed in Buxton Spa in Derbyshire. The spa, known as a sort of poor man's Bath, offered springs that were said to heal, and sometimes to induce an "inebriating giddiness." There André met a woman who would raise his intellectual game—Anna Seward, daughter of a clergyman then serving as canon of Lichfield Cathedral.[96]

Seward, a few years older than André, was a poetess known as the Swan of Lichfield. She and André became fast friends, and she brought him into her literary circle. She also guided his romantic interest toward her friend Honora Sneyd, a pretty seventeen-year-old girl who lived with the Sewards. Honora suffered from tuberculosis and also was afflicted with a shyness that made her more of a pet than a full partner in Seward's group. Nonetheless, André was enraptured with Honora, and they became engaged. They were not allowed by their families to marry, however, unless André returned to London and established his business career first. André and Anna exchanged long letters, but

Honora was not much of a correspondent, complaining that her illness made it difficult to write. She did, however, deign to add postscripts to Anna's letters.

André resolved to endure the long-distance relationship and succeed at the family business. "When an impertinent conscience whispers in my ear that I am not of the right stuff for a merchant," he wrote, "I draw my Honora's picture from my bosom, and that sight of that dear talisman so inspirits my industry that no toil seems oppressive."[97]

After a year living in London away from her, André returned to Lichfield for Christmas 1770 to find that Honora had developed a curious interest in an inventor and educational theorist named Richard Lovell Edgeworth, who was a married father of three. Rejected, André fled Lichfield. Edgeworth later wrote that "Miss Honora Sneyd was never much disappointed by the conclusion of this attachment." But Edgeworth was hardly objective. After Edgeworth's wife died in childbirth, he married Honora.[98]

And so the lover became a soldier. André, shattered by his disastrous romance, abandoned his father's business and joined the Royal Welch Fusiliers as a second lieutenant. But it would be years before he saw any fighting. Partly because of his fluency in German, he was sent to a military training program associated with the University of Göttingen. As always, he made many friends, including poets in the Göttinger Hain literary movement, which promoted sentimental themes of nature, friendship, and love.[99] And he kept up his art, painting portraits of the Duke and Duchess of Gotha.[100]

Finally, in 1774, he was ordered to America to catch up with his regiment, which had already been sent to Quebec. He took an indirect route, arriving by ship in Philadelphia at the same time that colonial politicians gathered for the First Continental Congress, the event that occasioned George Washington's dinner with the Shippens.

André found Philadelphia restive, and when a false rumor spread through the city that British warships had shelled Boston, André witnessed the potential for trouble in America—the gathering of angry, armed men in Philadelphia's streets. Another inaccurate report indicated that André's regiment had been sent to Boston, so André sailed there. He

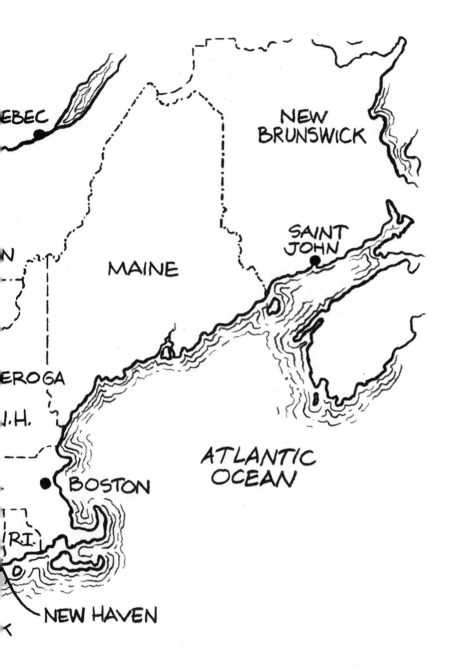

EBEC

NEW BRUNSWICK

MAINE

SAINT JOHN

N

EROGA

I.H.

ATLANTIC OCEAN

BOSTON

R.I.

NEW HAVEN

The vast stage for the drama of Peggy, Arnold, and André. At the time of the American Revolution, Vermont wasn't a separate colony, nor was Maine. They're included here for purposes of orientation. ILLUSTRATION BY RICK TUMA learned that his unit was still in Quebec, and it appears likely that he was happy to depart Boston, where the port was closed to merchant traffic, the citizens were agitated, and the British troops seemed either apathetic or oblivious to the gathering storm.[101]

André could have taken a ship straight to Quebec, but he chose an overland route. Some have speculated that André wanted to see the countryside because he was gathering intelligence for the British high command, but others say he was simply collecting intelligence for himself, filling notebooks with sketches and words about colorfully painted Indians, lush valleys, and rushing rivers, with the goal of someday writing a book. In any case, André sailed first to New York City and then up the Hudson River past Haverstraw, West Point, and other picturesque places that would figure prominently in his and Peggy Shippen's story a few years later.

After disembarking at Albany, he walked to Lake George, hunting for small game along the way. Then on Lake Champlain he boarded a flat-bottomed boat called a bateau and traveled farther north, past Fort Ticonderoga in New York and Fort St. Jean in southwestern Quebec, two British outposts in rundown condition. From Montreal he traveled by schooner east on the St. Lawrence River to Quebec, wearing a bearskin robe to fight off the Canadian chill.[102] "We had scarce any provision on board," he wrote his sister Louisa, "and were clustered up, by way of keeping out of the cold, with a black woman, an Indian squaw in a blanket, an Indian boy, and the sailors round a stove in a dungeon-like part of the vessel."[103]

Civilization awaited him in Quebec. He was invited to a fine ball thrown by the British commander in Canada, General Guy Carleton, and also enjoyed sleigh rides in the countryside with groups of friends, including ladies. "We dine, dance rondes, toss pancakes, make a noise and return, sometimes overturn, and sometimes are frostbit," André wrote.[104]

He expected his regiment to be transferred to Boston or Montreal, but instead the Continental Army's activity in northern New York kept him in place. In May 1775 colonial forces led by Ethan Allen and Benedict Arnold captured Fort Ticonderoga in a surprise attack. Arnold then raided Fort St. Jean, seizing a sloop with military supplies before being driven back.[105] André's regiment was sent to St. Jean and set to work improving the defenses. For a time, the most serious threat faced by André came from swarms of mosquitoes.

Suddenly the military life became more than fancy balls and sleigh rides for André. Two formidable colonial armies under Generals Arnold and Richard Montgomery headed north. Montgomery's force laid siege to St. Jean, greatly outnumbering the British regulars and French Canadian volunteers. As the siege stretched from days into weeks, food ran short, volunteers deserted, soldiers lost limbs and lives, and no help arrived from Montreal. Montgomery's cannon grew closer and more lethal.

André, keeping the official journal for the outpost, wrote that its buildings were steadily being reduced to rubble. The soldiers crowded into the basements to sleep, except for those "unable either to get a place or bear the heat and disagreeable smell arising from such members being crowded together." The rest slept above ground, coping with the shelling, the chill, and the rain. Some simply wandered around the camp at night, unable to get any rest.

Finally Montgomery sent a blindfolded messenger, a Montreal hairdresser named Lacoste, to the British with the news that a force sent by Carleton to rescue Fort St. Jean had been beaten back. Further resistance was futile. The hairdresser had been part of the British relief force and spoke the truth, but the British doubted him, writing back to the colonials that Lacoste was "frequently subject to fits of insanity." Montgomery offered to have a British officer talk with a more prominent Canadian who had witnessed the relief force's defeat.

The British agreed, sending a blindfolded John André into the enemy's lines. André was taken to the same sloop that Arnold had captured in his earlier raid, and after a short talk with the witness, he was convinced.

André and the rest of the British force surrendered.

Many years later, Anna Seward quoted André as writing at the time: "I have been taken prisoner by the Americans and stripped of every thing except the picture of Honora, which I concealed in my mouth. Preserving that, I yet think myself fortunate."[106] But that was a hackneyed bit of mythmaking by either André or, more likely, Seward. André kept his possessions, as demonstrated later when he showed his friend Du Simitiere the drawings he had made during his trek across New York.[107]

In fact, the captured Britons were treated exceptionally well, under rules for prisoners of war that appear absurdly genteel when compared to modern standards. Montgomery let the British officers keep their swords. And André and a few others were "paroled" so that they could go to Montreal and fetch the personal belongings of those captured. André and his fellow quartermasters returned to captivity with about twenty-two bateaux filled with possessions, thereby infuriating their colonial captors, who were much less well provisioned.

According to the terms of the surrender, the British troops would not be held at any prison camp. Rather, they would be assigned to rural colonial areas, to wait out the war, and would be banned from traveling outside their assigned districts. The officers were supposed to be held in Connecticut, with the enlisted men sent to Pennsylvania,[108] but André never made it to Connecticut. He dawdled for nearly a month in Albany, making friends and providing dinner entertainment for an unlikely host: General Philip Schuyler, the Patriot general in overall command of northern New York. As André was preparing to leave Albany, the orders changed. The British officers would spend their captivity in Pennsylvania with their men. André was sent seventy-five miles west of Philadelphia to Lancaster, Pennsylvania, coincidentally the home of Peggy Shippen's grandfather. The charming lieutenant headed down the Hudson in January 1776, enjoying a dinner in Haverstraw with a group that included attorney Joshua Hett Smith, who would later play a crucial role in the lives of both André and Peggy.

Most prisoners crossed the Delaware north of Philadelphia, some of them accompanied by their wives and children. André, drawn to places where people could appreciate his charm, went farther south to Philadelphia. His official reason was to talk with David Franks—Becky's father—who had been hired by the British to supply André and the other prisoners with food and other necessities. Under the protocol of the time, the British government was responsible for supplying its soldiers who had been taken prisoner by the enemy, and vice versa.

In Philadelphia, while making arrangements with David Franks, André is believed to have first met Becky Franks. As he earned her admiration by giving her a miniature portrait and writing her some poetry, he also made the brief acquaintance of her friend Peggy Shippen.[109]

Then it was on to Lancaster, where he reported to authorities and promised not to stray more than six miles from the town or conduct any correspondence related to the war. Most Lancaster residents refused to lodge the British soldiers. Pennsylvanians who were British sympathizers did not want to appear to be so, while those who hated the British could not abide having them in their houses. Both Loyalists and Patriots could agree on one thing: Soldiers could be loutish, drunken guests who might pose a threat to the womenfolk. Some enlisted men were consigned to shabby old barracks, while officers such as André were billeted in local taverns, where they got into bitter disputes with the tavern owners over their rent.

André was more at ease interacting with the settlers, especially the Germans, who appreciated his fluency in their language. He and the other captured officers were eventually transferred even farther away from Philadelphia, to Carlisle, where André found the residents to be "a stubborn, illiberal crew called the Scotch-Irish." Soldiers from Carlisle had suffered casualties in recent fighting in Quebec, and the locals took out their hostility on André and his fellow prisoners. For example, when André and a comrade were spotted talking to two suspected Tories, local authorities seized letters signed by André that seemed to be written in code. But the "code" was simply French, which no one in town could read. Even so, André was then restricted to the streets of town, rather than allowed his initial six-mile radius.

In late November 1776 the Patriots, in need of manpower while retreating across New Jersey, engineered a prisoner exchange. André and other British captives were marched eastward, past retreating, disorganized elements of Washington's army. All the while, André drew maps and carefully observed the enemy. In New Brunswick, New Jersey, he and his comrades were turned over to the main British army.[110] Once in New York City, he wrote his mother: "You may conclude my carcass to be very safe for this winter, and, as I have some regard for myself, you may depend upon it."[111]

Within the eighteenth-century British military structure, officers could purchase higher ranks, subject to approval, and upon his return André did so, rising from first lieutenant to captain. Again making use of his German language skills, André offered himself as a liaison to the growing number of Hessian troops arriving in America to augment His Majesty's army.

André was appointed aide-de-camp to General Charles Grey, and in June 1777 he joined his new unit aboard a huge flotilla whose destination was top secret. Before leaving, André executed a will giving seven hundred pounds apiece to his brother and three sisters, plus smaller bequests to friends.

Many people on both sides of the conflict expected the British force, led by General William Howe, to sail up the Hudson and support General John Burgoyne's army, which was invading southward from Canada. Instead, André and the rest of Howe's force went south to Norfolk, Virginia, then up Chesapeake Bay, landing at its most northerly point and heading for the city where independence was born—Philadelphia. Washington's effort to stop them south of Philadelphia led to the Battle of Brandywine, a British victory.[112]

As Howe's army approached Philadelphia, André was involved in one of the most shocking episodes of the war, dubbed the Paoli Massacre by Patriots. At about one in the morning on September 21, 1777, Grey's force surprised enemy troops near Paoli Tavern, west of Philadelphia. To avoid detection, General Grey ordered his soldiers to unload their firearms or remove the flints so they would not fire accidentally. Instead, their weapons of choice were swords and bayonets. In an exceptionally bloody attack, they killed scores of surprised troops—including some who tried to surrender, according to rebel accounts.

André seemed to be cheered up by the gruesome victory, noting that he and other officers drank "good gin" seized from the American camp. Grey earned the nickname "No Flint" Grey, as well as burnishing his already formidable reputation as a butcher on the battlefield.[113] (Today the Grey family name has a more cultured connotation—Earl Grey tea was named for the general's son.)[114]

Less than a week after Paoli, Washington's army set up camp at Valley Forge, northwest of Philadelphia, and the British marched into a city that the fleeing future president John Adams labeled a "mass of cowardice and Toryism."[115]

André was quartered in what he called a "most sumptuous house" on Philadelphia's outskirts in Germantown, where the Chew family owned an estate called Cliveden. Benjamin Chew had been arrested and banished from Pennsylvania by Patriot authorities, but his daughter Peggy and other family members were staying at Cliveden, and they welcomed visits by André.

The estate suddenly became a key battleground in early October, when Washington's forces attacked Germantown. British troops barricaded themselves behind the estate's thick brick walls and held up Washington's troops for hours, depriving the Patriots of a decisive victory. Bodies littered the beautiful garden and grounds of the estate. The Chew family safely avoided the fighting, and André also was uninvolved, having already been transferred into the city proper.[116]

Serious fighting was over for the year, and the British prepared for a long winter in Philadelphia.

For André, the chilly city would be a warm oasis from the war, a chance for an absurd and idyllic frolic with the two Peggys and two Beckys who reigned over what he called "the little society of Third and Fourth Streets."[117]

CHAPTER 4

The Meschianza

HEAVY SNOW, SLEET, AND HAIL PUNISHED British-occupied Philadelphia during the winter of 1777–78. Food was scarce, high-priced, and often spoiled. The Continental Army tried to seal off the city from the countryside, thereby keeping fresh food from reaching the city. Even the conquering warriors were put on reduced rations as some of the provisions stored on British ships were ridden with maggots.

American prisoners in British custody especially suffered and were routinely denied any food at all for their first few days in jail. Some reportedly ate clay. One jailer purposely spilled broth and other food on the ground to watch the desperate prisoners lap it up.[118]

The demand for firewood compelled soldiers to pull apart fences and even houses. Even the Shippens were not immune: British soldiers invaded their stable, removing the wooden ties that held the rafters together.[119] Public outrage at firewood raiding by the invaders prompted a barrage of complaints to the British commander, General Howe. Military justice for all manner of crimes was swift, but sometimes excessive. A civilian accused of stealing a piece of linen was sentenced to five hundred lashes in public.

For many, the winter was excruciating. But for Peggy Shippen, it was wonderful. She and her friends felt neither chill nor hunger nor want. They were warmed by male attention and fed by a constant supply of compliments. Becky Franks summed up their gaiety in a letter:

You can have no idea of the life of continued amusement I live in. I can scarce have a moment to myself. . . . I am dressed for a ball this evening at Smith's [City Tavern] where we have one every Thursday. You would not know the room 'tis so much improved.... The dress is more ridiculous and pretty than anything I ever saw—great quantities of different colored feathers on the head at a time besides a thousand other things. The hair dressed very high.... I spent Tuesday evening at Sir William Howe's, where we had a concert and dance.... No loss for partners, even I am engaged to seven different gentlemen, for you must know 'tis a fixed rule never to dance but two dances at a time with the same person.... I've been but three evenings alone since we moved to town.[120]

Meanwhile, Captain John André had found impressive living quarters in Benjamin Franklin's three-story brick mansion, where the diplomat-inventor-publisher's wife had died three years earlier. Franklin was promoting American independence to the French court, but had left behind his books, scientific equipment, and even a portrait of himself painted by Benjamin Wilson.[121]

While other British officers formed eating clubs, played cricket, and bet on cockfights, André and his friends put together their own theater troupe. They called themselves Howe's Thespians. In the years before the British occupation, theater had been strongly discouraged in Philadelphia. The First Continental Congress passed a resolution against "every species of extravagance and dissipation, especially all horseracing, and all kinds of gaming, cock-fighting, exhibition of shows, plays, and other expensive diversions and entertainments."[122]

Not bound by this legislation, André and a friend, Captain Oliver DeLancey, took over a cobweb-ridden theater called the Southwark and dressed it up. André painted a backdrop that a theater historian described as "a landscape presenting a distant champagne country and a winding rivulet, extending from the front of the picture to the extreme distance. In the foreground and center, a gentle cascade—the water exquisitely executed—was overshadowed by a group of majestic forest trees." The much-admired backdrop was used at the theater until its destruction in an 1821 fire.[123]

Howe's Thespians sold all the tickets in advance, with theatergoers warned not to attempt to bribe the doorkeeper for admittance. Thirteen different plays were performed, with André taking minor roles and sometimes writing a prologue to kick off the night's events.[124] Among the plays was William Shakespeare's *Henry IV, Part 1,* an appropriate choice both for its story line about putting down a revolt and its most amusing character, the drunken, dissolute Falstaff.[125] The famous Falstaff quotation "The better part of valour is discretion" [126] could have been the motto for British occupiers who preferred to enjoy the city's comforts rather than venture into the countryside to confront the enemy.

During the British occupation, Peggy Shippen spent many a delightful hour with André. She visited Southwark to see him onstage and also joined him on sleigh rides around town. When the captain wasn't working on his latest stage production, he could be found enjoying refreshments or playing the flute at the Shippen house on Fourth Street.

He sometimes brought along friends such as Lord Rawdon and Captain Andrew Snape Hamond, both of whom offered effusive praise of Peggy, adding to her reputation as an object of tremendous desire. Rawdon, a hero at the Battle of Bunker Hill who would soon become adjutant general of British forces in America and much later would serve as governor-general of India,[127] declared that Peggy was the most beautiful woman he had seen in England or America. Hamond, captain of the British warship *Roebuck,* one of the ships that had tested Philadelphia's defenses early in the war, said of Peggy, "We were all in love with her."

André and Peggy were undoubtedly fond of each other, and writers of historical fiction have succumbed to the temptation to depict them as lovers. But that is far too tidy and fanciful. Most evidence suggests that André's primary romantic interest was Peggy Chew, not Peggy Shippen. If any British officer in particular won the attention of Peggy Shippen, it may have been Hamond, who was nearly forty years old at the time, more than two decades her senior. One of the most memorable social events of the occupation was a dinner dance aboard the *Roebuck,* which was bedecked with lanterns and two hundred guests. Peggy Shippen sat at Hamond's right at the dinner table.[128]

Hamond's floating fete featured dancing till dawn. At that event and others, the British officers were having so much fun with the local ladies that there never seemed to be enough hours in the night. André and the others treated the Peggys and Beckys with gentlemanly respect, as far as we know, but they showed a baser and more ravenous interest in other representatives of Philadelphia womanhood. Indeed, it was a period of great licentiousness, from the highest office to the lowest alley. General Howe carried on publicly with a married woman, a fetching blonde named Elizabeth Loring, while he distracted her husband, Joshua, by appointing him as commissioner of prisoners. The husband seemed fully aware of the affair and tolerant of it while using his position to collect bribes from vendors.[129] Howe's heavy drinking and gambling, as well as his affair with Mrs. Loring, were well known on both sides of the Atlantic. After Patriots floated kegs filled with gunpowder down the Delaware River in a futile attempt to damage the British fleet in January 1778, Howe earned special mention in a poem called "The Battle of the Kegs" by Francis Hopkinson, a signer of the Declaration of Independence:

> Sir William, he, snug as a flea
> Lay all this time a-snoring
> Nor dreamed of harm, as he lay warm,
> In bed with Mrs. Loring.[130]

Many British officers—though not André, as far as is known—followed the womanizing example of their top commander.

Becky Franks wrote to Peggy Shippen's cousin Nancy about an encounter with three officers on the street. "After talking a few minutes with me they walked off," Becky recalled. "There's a house next door . . . that a Mrs. McKoy lives in, a lady well known to the gentlemen." In other words, a prostitute.[131] Becky said two of the officers "had the impudence to go in while I was looking right at them." The third officer explained to Becky that he was a married man and would abstain. He told her that his comrades had visited Mrs. McKoy's home "to look at a tube rose." This infuriated Becky. "I was never half so angry in my life," she wrote. "I never think of it but I feel my face glow with rage."

Lord Rawdon, who presumably behaved like a gentleman when visiting Peggy Shippen on Fourth Street, was a cad in his own mind, writing a year earlier in New York that British soldiers were as "riotous as satyrs." He added, "A girl cannot step into the bushes to pluck a rose without running the most imminent risk of being ravished, and they are so little accustomed to these vigorous methods that they don't bear them with the proper resignation."[132]

In the randy atmosphere of British-held Philadelphia, it was little wonder that two anonymous men thought they might get lucky by placing an advertisement in a local newspaper. It read: "Wanted to live with two single gentlemen: a young woman to act in the capacity of housekeeper, and who can occasionally put her hand to anything. Extravagant wages will be given, and no character required."[133]

The British tactics in the streets of Philadelphia were far more successful than their strategy elsewhere in North America. At first blush, the loss of such a major city would be considered a crushing defeat for the Patriots. But Washington's army remained intact, if barely, northwest of Philadelphia at Valley Forge. The British had lengthened their supply lines and raised their exposure without dealing a fatal blow to the enemy. Soon after Howe took Philadelphia, the other major British army in the field met a shocking disaster. At Saratoga, New York, in October 1777, General Burgoyne's entire force surrendered after a decisive attack led by rebel Benedict Arnold. Howe was criticized for settling safely into Philadelphia rather than moving his army north to assist Burgoyne.

Burgoyne's defeat brought the French officially into the war on the rebel side. Before Saratoga, the French had confined their support to running guns through a dummy company operated by Pierre-Augustin Caron de Beaumarchais, playwright of *The Marriage of Figaro*. After Saratoga, Benjamin Franklin persuaded the French to send their navy and ground forces.

As winter turned to spring, it became apparent that the British occupation of Philadelphia would be a short stay. Rather than directly attacking the enemy at Valley Forge, the British nibbled around the edges, setting up a seine in the Schuykill River to try to block shad and other fish from getting to Washington's camp.[134]

Amid backbiting in British military and political circles, Howe was replaced by General Henry Clinton, who was so unenthusiastic about his new job that he wrote to his cousin, the Duke of Newcastle: "I should have wished to avoid the arduous task of attempting to retrieve a game so unfortunately circumstanced."[135] Clinton's first task was to pull the army out of Philadelphia and return to New York City. But there was much to do before they could leave—including a farewell party for Howe, an extravaganza bigger than anyone's imagination, except André's.

They called it the Meschianza. It was the most shameful carousing amid catastrophe since Nero fiddled while Rome burned. But while Nero's fiddling in all likelihood is a myth, the Meschianza on May 18, 1778, was real. The party's name was loosely based on the Italian for medley or mixture, and was chosen because the event would be, as André put it, "a variety of entertainments." The spelling varied, and included Mischianza, Mischeanza, Mesquinza, and Mesquienza. The name on the specially designed ticket was Meschianza.

A group of twenty-one officers were to pay a total of 3,312 pounds—roughly twenty-five thousand dollars apiece in today's currency—to sponsor the celebration, and André would serve as impresario, developing the themes, costumes, decorations, and activities.

The guest list numbered four hundred, and featured a court of fourteen prominent "knights" and their damsels. The ladies—"selected from the foremost in youth, beauty, and fashion," according to André—included Peggy Shippen, of course, along with Peggy Chew and both Beckys. In addition, Peggy Shippen's sisters Sarah and Mary accepted invitations, as did Peggy Chew's half sister Sarah and Becky Redman's sister Nancy.

The ambitions for the event were of such magnitude that André and the young ladies had to scurry to complete their tasks in a month's time. Armor was impractical for these "knights," so they were equipped instead with shields and spears to accompany costumes from the French court of Henry IV.

The ladies' garments were more exotic, described as Turkish and meant to suggest they were beauties from lands conquered in the Crusades. But to some, the ladies seemed to be dressed as slave girls.[136] "They wore turbans spangled and edged with gold or silver, on the right side a veil of the same kind hung as low as the waist, and the left side of the turban was enriched with pearl and tassels of gold or silver and crested with a feather," André wrote. "The dress was of the polonaise kind and of white silk with long sleeves, the sashes which were worn round the waist and were tied with a large bow on the left side hung very low and were trimmed, spangled and fringed according to the colors of the knight."[137]

The cost of the costumes was mind-boggling. A shop set up in Philadelphia by London's Coffin and Anderson sold silks and other finery for the Meschianza at an estimated total price of twelve thousand pounds, roughly equivalent to nearly two million dollars in today's currency.

The clothing expenses for Edward Shippen's three daughters were quickly draining his treasury, which was not being replenished as he lost one government position after another and avoided business dealings that might put him in political danger. Beyond the financial costs, the ladies' participation in the Meschianza posed a serious risk to their fathers' attempts to avoid direct confrontations or alliances with either side in the war. It's not clear that the ladies even considered this. Granted, the pressure to marry well was intense. The ladies knew that a flower is most admired in full bloom, and there was no time to waste in finding the right husband. But as the Peggys and Beckys threw their passion and pocketbooks into the Meschianza, their families suffered from the despotism of the debutantes.

Benjamin Chew, for example, had been arrested as a suspected Loyalist the previous year, and he was on parole in New Jersey when his daughters began preparing for the great event. Just three days before the Meschianza, the former chief justice won a congressional order allowing him to return to Pennsylvania.[138]

Becky Franks's father, David, was in an especially vulnerable position because he was a Jew who had done business with the British, and therefore was subject to a double dose of prejudice from some Patriots. Franks's commerce with the crown before the occupation had been aboveboard. In fact, he had to fight to receive payment for the nearly 1.4 million rations he delivered. Yet some independence-minded Philadelphians considered Franks a Tory and thought he should be forced to leave town after Washington's army returned.[139]

Regardless of the risk to their fathers, the Peggys and the Beckys were not to be dissuaded from the pageant of a lifetime.

André and his theater friend DeLancey were busy turning the confiscated mansion of an exiled Patriot, Joseph Wharton, into the party venue. The mansion, with a gorgeous view of the Delaware River, was decorated with flowers, ribbons, and ornamental candleholders called girandoles. The walls of a large hall were painted "in imitation of Sienna marble," according to André. Upstairs, four rooms were opened up to form a ballroom. André, meticulously describing his own elaborate designs, wrote that the upstairs was "decorated in a light, elegant style of painting. The ground was a pale blue, paneled with a small gold bead, and in the interior filled with drooping festoons of flowers in their natural colors. . . . These decorations were heightened by eighty-five mirrors, decked with rose-pink silk ribbands, and artificial flowers, and in the intermediate spaces were thirty-four branches with wax-lights, ornamented in a similar manner."[140]

Adjoining the house, a separate banquet hall was specially constructed for the Meschianza, with canvas stretched over framework and painted with scenes. Cut-glass lustres hung from the ceiling, with flowers, ribbons, and other ornament on the walls. Outside, two triumphal arches were installed on the lawn, and an area was staked out for a tournament of knights, with pavilions constructed as viewing areas on two sides.

While the guests were given plenty of notice, tickets printed with the official invitation were delivered only a day before the May 18 event. They read: "The favor of your meeting the subscribers to the Meschianza at Knight's Wharf near Poole's Bridge tomorrow at half past three is desired."[141]

André had chosen Peggy Chew as the lady who would accompany him. His shield featured the image of two gamecocks fighting and his motto was "No rival." Peggy Shippen was to be paired with a Lieutenant Winyard; his shield was decorated with a bay leaf and his motto was "Unchangeable."[142] But at the last minute, everything may have changed for Peggy Shippen. Simply put, Peggy either attended the Meschianza or she didn't. On this, the evidence is hazy at best.

André wrote two accounts of the festivities, one in late May to be published in a London periodical, *Gentleman's Magazine,* and the other in June as a private keepsake for Peggy Chew. In the first account, the Shippen sisters indeed attended the splendid party. In the second account, the sisters were off the roster, with no explanation for their absence.

According to a story told by later generations of the Shippen family, a group of disapproving Quakers paid a visit to Peggy's father on Fourth Street just before the Meschianza. They thought it would be scandalous if Edward Shippen's girls participated in such a spectacle. The Quakers reportedly didn't complain about the girls' dalliances with the British invaders, or the ladies' ravenous consumption during a time of great privation. Instead they picked the argument that would work: that the girls' "Turkish" costumes were indecent.

According to this story, related by descendant Lewis Burd Walker more than a century after the events, the father who had been so indulgent with his daughters finally put his foot down. And although Peggy and her sisters were "in a dancing fury" over their father's edict, "they were obliged to stay away."[143]

The Shippen family lore reveals that Peggy was prone to hysterical fits, and it has prompted speculation that her reaction to her father's decision must have been an outburst on a grand scale. In Walker's family history, he described Peggy's tendency toward hysteria in the nicest possible terms, saying she sometimes experienced "nervous attacks of a hysterical nature when under mental excitement" and had "a susceptibility to fainting spells, to which she was subject whenever perturbation of mind reacted upon a delicately organized body."[144]

Despite certain family accounts, some scholars believe the Shippen girls did indeed attend the Meschianza, and this view is supported by another Shippen descendant who wrote in the late nineteenth century, "I am in a position to sweep away all doubt on the subject, since Sarah Shippen was my grandmother, and was never tired of telling me all the delight and glory of that memorable fete. . . . They *were* there."[145]

Neither version can be proven. But the case against the Shippens' attendance seems stronger. Some believe André wrote his first account of the festivities ahead of time—before the Shippens pulled out—and then wrote the second version based on what actually occurred, sans Shippens. More likely than not, Peggy Shippen missed the Meschianza, the grandest party that she would ever have the opportunity to attend.

And what a time it was. First came a flotilla along the Delaware River. Three brightly decorated galleys carried the most honored guests. These were accompanied by twenty-seven barges holding the rest of the four hundred guests along with three bands of musicians. "The gaudy fleet, freighted with all that was distinguished by rank, beauty, and gallantry, was conveyed down the river, along the whole length of the city," André wrote, "whilst every ship at the wharfs or in the stream was decked in all her maritime ornaments and covered with spectators." Crowds lined the shore, "full of curiosity and admiration." As the floating parade passed Captain Hamond's *Roebuck*, his ship provided a nineteen-gun salute.

The party arrived at the Wharton house, and the musical bands combined to lead a procession that "advanced through an avenue formed by two files of grenadiers" to the field where a knightly tournament commenced. There the guests were divided into two groups of spectators, with special viewing spots awarded to the fourteen ladies chosen by the knights. If the Shippen girls were at home pining and weeping, as is likely, no one knows which three lucky ladies replaced them.

Uninvited gawkers gathered on the periphery to witness the show, and "a very strong guard controlled their curiosity."

Three trumpeters and a herald entered the tournament grounds, followed by André and his six comrades, well dressed in pink and white silk, and riding gray horses finely attired in the same colors. The knights were accompanied by squires in similar colors who carried their lances and shields. André's group called itself the Knights of the Blended Rose, with the motto "We droop when separated."

After the knights circled the field and saluted General Howe and the ladies, their herald made an announcement three times to different sections of his audience: "The Knights of the Blended Rose, by me their herald, proclaim and assert that the ladies of the Blended Rose excel in wit, beauty, and every accomplishment, those of the whole world; and should any knight or knights be so hardy as to dispute or deny it, they are ready to enter the list with them, and maintain their assertions by deeds of arms, according to the laws of ancient chivalry."

From the other end of the tournament field came the Rose's rivals: three trumpeters and a herald, followed by the seven Knights of the Burning Mountain, dressed in black and orange, with black horses and squires in similar colors. Their motto was "I burn forever."

The Mountain's herald offered a counter-declaration: "The Knights of the Burning Mountain present themselves here, not to contest by words, but to disprove by deeds, the vainglorious assertion of the knights of the Blended Rose, and enter these lists to maintain that the ladies of the Burning Mountain are not excelled in beauty, virtue, or accomplishments by any in the universe."

The chivalric showmen faced off and commenced a series of charges, waving swords and spears at each other, and even firing pistols as they passed. The battles wounded none and ennobled all, proving "the knights so brave that it would have been impious to decide in favor of either."

The four hundred guests then left the tournament field in fine order, passing through two triumphal arches as the bands played martial music. The knights went through the first arch and lined up with their troops to form an avenue. "The colors of all the army, planted at proper distances, had a beautiful effect in diversifying the scene," André wrote.

The guests promenaded past the troops and knights, through a second arch specifically dedicated to Howe that featured the figure of Fame and the Latin phrase *I, bone, quo virtus, tua te vocet; I pede fausto* (Go, thou good man, where thy excellence may direct thee; go with thy foot of happy omen).[146] Beyond the second arch, guests encountered a garden full of flowers, and then the mansion. They repaired inside for tea, lemonade, and "cooling liquors," followed by dancing, fireworks, and more dancing—"one pleasure ever substituted to another throughout this various evening."

At some point in the night's revelry, the rebels tried to spoil the party. A Patriot captain named Allen McLane arranged for his troops to set fire to camp kettles filled with explosives on the city's outskirts. The series of blasts alarmed the British enough to send cavalry after the fleeing McLane. But guests at the Wharton house were told that it was simply a distant tribute to Howe.

At midnight, supper was set up in the specially built pavilion and served by slaves, "twenty-four negroes in blue and white turbans and sashes with bright bracelets and collars bowing profoundly together." The four hundred guests settled in at tables set with twelve hundred dishes, which were filled with chicken, lamb, buttered ham, Yorkshire pie, veal, puddings, rare fruit from the Caribbean, jellies, cakes, sweetmeats, and syllabub, a then-popular English dessert featuring sugar, lemon juice, wine or brandy, and whipped cream.[147]

The banquet ended with a series of toasts—to the king and queen, to General Howe, to the festivities' sponsors, and to the ladies. All in attendance sang "God Save the King." After the banquet the throng returned to the house, where some played faro,[148] a popular card game for gamblers that later fell out of fashion, partly because it was so vulnerable to cheating. Other guests danced and drank until "daylight overtook them in all the festive mirth with which a youthful band could be animated."[149]

Not surprisingly, the Meschianza inspired a medley of criticism from both sides of the Atlantic.

Diarist Elizabeth Drinker wrote: "This day may be remembered by many for the scenes of folly and vanity—promoted by the officers of the army—under the pretense of showing respect to Gen. Howe. . . . How insensible do these people appear, while our land is so greatly desolated, and death and sore destruction has overtaken, and now depends over so many!"[150]

The London press used words such as "nauseous" to describe the event, believing it was especially inappropriate considering Howe's sorry performance as a military commander.[151] Loyalist historian Thomas Jones wrote after the war, "Had the general been properly rewarded for his conduct while commander-in-chief in America, an execution, and not a Meschianza, would have been the consequence."[152]

There were no turbans or lustres at Valley Forge, where Howe's enemy and the Shippens' friend George Washington was emerging from an excruciating winter. His soldiers had sometimes gone without blankets and shoes while surviving on firecake, a crude paste of flour and water cooked on stones in the campfire's embers.[153] About two thousand soldiers had died, and five hundred horses had starved to death.[154] But the army had survived, and would soon reenter Philadelphia. It is tempting to imagine how history might have been different if the British had used the money, manpower, and creativity of the Meschianza for some other purpose—such as, perhaps, attacking the enemy.

André remained optimistic and ambitious as he prepared to depart for New York with the rest of Howe's army. Packing up at Benjamin Franklin's home, he received a farewell visit from his old friend from Geneva, Pierre-Eugene Du Simitiere, who had settled in Philadelphia. Du Simitiere was shocked to find that André was looting the place, taking away books, musical instruments, and even that prized portrait of Franklin.

André was most likely operating under the orders of his superior, "No Flint" Grey. The portrait of Philadelphia's most famous Patriot hung for more than a century in the Greys' Northumberland estate before the family donated it to the United States government. In modern times it has been displayed prominently in the White House.[155]

André took away pictures of his ladies, too, if only in his highly visual mind. And he left them tender and personal souvenirs. For Becky Redman, he snipped a button from his coat and presented it as a keepsake.[156] For Peggy Chew, he wrote a poem:

If at the close of war and strife
My destiny once more
Should in the various paths of life
Conduct me to this shore
Should British banners guard the land
And faction be restrained
And Cliveden's peaceful mansion stand
No more with blood bestained
Say, wilt though then receive again
And welcome to thy sight
The youth who bids with stifled pain
His sad farewell tonight?[157]

When André bade farewell to Peggy Shippen, he gave her a lock of his hair.[158] Peggy didn't know if she would ever see him again; in fact she probably never did. But in the next few years, the two of them would certainly manage to stay in touch.

CHAPTER 5

Arnold Arrives

THE BRITISH ARMY'S IMMINENT DEPARTURE from Philadelphia was supposed to be a military secret, but the signs were obvious. Captain McLane, who had made the big noise that barely distracted the Meschianza revelers, passed on intelligence to General Washington that cannon had been "broke and thrown off wharf—likewise thousands of broken muskets—a large number of barrels of pork and beef also thrown over—and not less than four thousand blankets burnt that came out of the hospital."[159] Half-built ships were set afire, along with building materials in the shipyard that could not be hauled away. Blazes grew out of control, burning several homes of Philadelphia's poor. Twenty thousand troops and three thousand Loyalists left by sea, but the Peggys and Beckys stayed behind.[160]

Americans who had fled Philadelphia when the British invaded began making their way home on June 18, 1778, exactly a month after the Meschianza. They often found their homes in wreckage. Empty houses had been converted into barracks and badly abused by the inhabitants, with doors and windows missing and furniture long gone. In some cases, holes had been cut into the parlor floors so that excrement and garbage could be tossed into the cellars. Letter writers of the time described the ever-presence of flies.

Congressmen quickly returned, meeting at the College of Philadelphia (now the University of Pennsylvania) because of the poor condition of their former facilities at the State House, now known as Independence Hall.[161] Henry Laurens, a member of Congress, wrote of the "offensiveness of the air in and around the State House, which the enemy had made a hospital and left it in a condition disgraceful to the character of civility. Particularly they had opened a large square pit near the House, a receptacle for filth, into which they had also cast dead horses and bodies of men who by the mercy of death had escaped from their further cruelties."[162]

Radical Patriots demanded retribution against the Loyalists who had lacked the good sense to flee. One rebel proposed to mark the front of every Tory house with black paint. But that idea was cast aside because it would only advertise the strong Loyalist sentiment that remained.[163] Suspected Loyalists who stayed in Philadelphia sometimes were turned out of their houses or arrested. Two met the executioner.[164] Even in minor matters, those who had befriended the British felt the backlash.

A mild form of punishment was issued to the "Meschianza ladies"— which included Peggy whether or not she actually attended the event. The ladies were initially banned from Philadelphia's dances, such as a gala at the City Tavern a few days after liberation that was limited to those ladies "who had manifested their attachment to the cause of virtue and freedom by sacrificing every convenience to the love of their country," as a nineteenth-century historian put it.[165]

In a letter, General "Mad Anthony" Wayne of the Continental Army mocked the Meschianza: "The Knights of the Blended Roses and Burning Mounts [sic] have resigned their laurels to rebel officers, who will lay them at the feet of those virtuous daughters of America who cheerfully gave up ease and affluence in a city for liberty and peace of mind in a cottage." Going even further, Wayne suggested that the ladies who had consorted with British troops had "in a great measure lost that native innocence, which was their former characteristic, and supplied its place with what they call an easy behavior."[166]

Peggy and her friends certainly didn't consider themselves fallen women, and they didn't suffer from ostracism for long. Organizers of dances quickly realized that their events would be far less glamorous if they shunned the city's most cultured, gorgeous, and eligible women.[167]

Mary Morris, a Philadelphian whose husband, Robert, was a signer of the Declaration of Independence, noted how quickly the Meschianza ladies were accepted. "We have a great many balls and entertainments, and soon the [Dancing] Assembly will begin," she wrote. "Even our military gentlemen are too liberal to make any distinction between Whig and Tory ladies. If they make any, it is in favor of the latter."[168]

Peggy and her friends were known for their "high rolls." It seemed that hair height was the easiest way to discern the ladies with British sympathies from those who favored the rebels. A report from a Philadelphia ball describes an unidentified lady whose hair was calculated to be eight feet seven and a half inches above ground level, causing the rest of the ladies to seem like "grasshoppers" compared to her.[169]

Such extreme fashion earned mockery on the streets of liberated Philadelphia. On Independence Day, July 4, 1778, a crowd organized a makeshift parade featuring a person wearing a high roll. Accounts varied widely, with witnesses describing the high-haired marcher as a whore or an "old Negro wench" or even a man. But in all cases the crowd's intention was to ridicule women like Peggy who had consorted with the British.[170]

The attitude in the ballrooms was far different from the sentiment of the streets. Even such a caustic and unabashedly Loyalist lady as Becky Franks was invited to dances, though other guests may have been offended by her presence. The Americans and the French, who wore cockades on their hats, celebrated their alliance by creating a "union cockade" combining the American black ribbon with the French white. At a dance to celebrate the alliance, Franks put the new cockade around the neck of a dog and set it loose in the ballroom.[171] On another occasion, a Continental lieutenant colonel from Maryland greeted Franks wearing a suit of scarlet—a color more commonly associated with the British army. "I have adopted your colors, my princess, the better to secure a courteous reception," he said. "Deign to smile on a true knight." To which Franks told the people around her, "How the ass glories in the lion's skin."[172]

Franks was eventually banished from Philadelphia and moved to New York, then married a British colonel, Sir Henry Johnson, in 1782 and moved to Bath, England's fashionable spa. Her husband distinguished himself in helping suppress the Irish Rebellion of 1798, and was promoted to general. She bore two sons, one of whom was a captain who died during the Napoleonic Wars. Franks died a decade later in 1823, but not before her husband became a baronet, giving her a title of her own: Lady Johnson.[173]

The other Becky, Becky Redman, married even more quickly in December 1779. Her husband, Elisha Lawrence, was a colonel in the New Jersey Loyalist volunteers who had been captured in 1777. The wedding announcement in the *Pennsylvania Gazette* called her "a young lady whose superior beauty, joined with an elegance both of person and manners, rendered her justly admired by all who have the pleasure of her acquaintance."[174]

Peggy Chew waited longer to wed, but when she did, she married well. Her husband was Colonel John Eager Howard, a hero of the Continental Army who had fought in Germantown near her family's Cliveden estate and had won a silver medal from Congress for his heroism at the Battle of Cowpens in South Carolina. They married at Cliveden in 1787, with George Washington attending.[175] Howard served as governor of Maryland and as a United States senator. They had two daughters and six sons, one of whom also became Maryland's governor.[176]

Even in her later years, Peggy Chew thought fondly of John André, much to the annoyance of her husband. According to a story told by her great-granddaughter, the Howards were entertaining foreign visitors at their Baltimore estate Belvedere when the Philadelphia years came up. "Major André was a most witty and cultivated gentleman," Peggy told her guests, and the colonel interrupted, cursing and denouncing André's memory.[177]

Meanwhile, what about Peggy Shippen? Certainly her friends were making interesting matches, but hers was matchless. The youngest of the group, she was the first to wed. Even though she was strongly sympathetic to British ways, she embraced a rebel, who was as brash and self-promoting as she was demure. Shortly after the reentry of the Continental Army into Philadelphia, Peggy met the man whose life would transform hers. And she, his.

***

Benedict Arnold was a fifth-generation New Englander, born in 1741. His great-great-grandfather had emigrated from England and helped Roger

Williams found Rhode Island. His great-grandfather, the first Benedict Arnold, had served as governor of the colony and made himself wealthy. The second Benedict Arnold had spent his father's fortune, forcing the third Benedict Arnold to become an apprentice cooper, or barrel-maker.

But the cooper had greater ambitions. He moved to Norwich, Connecticut, and joined a shipowner in trading voyages to the Caribbean and Europe. When the shipowner died at sea after a trip to Ireland, Arnold delivered the news to his widow, and later married her.

Taking over the shipowner's business and expanding it, Arnold built a fine home and a family in Norwich. His wife gave birth to a son, Benedict, who died in infancy. When they had a second son, he was given the same name, a not uncommon practice at the time.[178]

This Benedict Arnold was a vibrant child, known for his love of skating, sledding, swimming, and fishing. Stories of his daredevil childhood abound, including one in which he grabbed hold of Norwich's giant waterwheel and rode it under the water and back up.[179]

The boy was sent to a classical academy to study under a recent graduate of Yale College. His mother wrote the school: "It is with a great deal of satisfaction that I commit my uncultured child to your care under God. Pray don't spare the rod and spoil the child." Arnold embraced his studies, but was also known for his pranks and adventures. His teacher wrote his mother to report that when a barn in the area had caught fire, Arnold was spotted amid the smoke on the building's roof, walking from one end to the other before escaping the flames. The boy's stay at the elite school lasted only two years, until his family's finances could no longer sustain it. Arnold's father had badly mismanaged his business and had tried to find the answers in alcohol.

Arnold was called home to work as an apprentice to a druggist, fortunate for the chance to learn a valuable trade but forced to endure the humiliation of his father's public descent into alcoholism. While the family held on to its fine house and a pew in the front row of the First Church of Norwich, Arnold's father was arrested for public drunkenness and for failing to pay his debts. The apprentice was eighteen when his mother died, twenty when his father followed.

Bankrolled by his employer, Arnold traveled to London to buy supplies to open his own shop in New Haven, Connecticut. Returning to America, he rented store space and hung out a sign with the Latin phrase *Sibi Totique* (For himself and for everyone). The store featured medicine, books, and cosmetics. Because Arnold was a druggist who had been to England, he encouraged people to refer to him as "Dr. Arnold from London."

Arnold was too restive to remain a mere shopkeeper, however. He began acquiring ships, and for months at a time he sailed to London, Quebec, and the Caribbean in pursuit of trade.

He also was an active overseer to his sister Hannah, who remained in the family home in Norwich. One day he and a friend stopped by the home and spotted the nineteen-year-old Hannah inside, being courted by a Frenchman. Arnold disapproved of this suitor, as he might have of any Frenchman, since the French and Indian War had recently ended. And it is doubtful that any male pursuing Hannah would have been acceptable to Arnold. He arranged for his friend to loudly enter the house, pretending to be Arnold. When the Frenchman climbed out a window, Arnold shot at him with a pistol, but missed. The Frenchman left town, and Arnold moved Hannah to New Haven to help take care of his house. She never married.[180]

Arnold, however, did take a spouse. She was Margaret Mansfield, the daughter of a trader who served as high sheriff of New Haven County. Like other Margarets, she was nicknamed Peggy. Their first child was the latest in the long line of Benedicts, and next came Richard.

Arnold was often at sea, and often on the financial shoals. Part of the fault lay with the times: The British imposed restrictions such as the Sugar Act and the Stamp Act that disrupted trading. Arnold, like most import-export businessmen, was involved in smuggling, and the British crackdown made his business more risky. He became increasingly active in protests against British authority, and led a mob that beat up and whipped a man who had threatened to turn him in as a smuggler. Arnold began to sink into debt, and his London creditors threatened to seize his ships.[181]

Benedict Arnold was loved by Peggy, but was one of the most hated men in American history. NATIONAL ARCHIVES (NWDNS-148-GW-617)

Benedict Arnold had a talent for making enemies. In 1770 a Jamaican trader came to town with a rumor that Arnold had been on a bender while in the Caribbean—an apparently false report, since Arnold avoided strong drink after seeing it ruin his father's life. But the trader brought along another rumor, which Arnold's wife seemed to believe: that Arnold had kept one or more whores during his travels, and had contracted a venereal disease. Arnold went to extraordinary lengths to dispel the rumors, filing a slander suit and recruiting his friends to attest to his good behavior in the Caribbean.

Arnold did not push the case to trial, but he did distribute the depositions in New Haven in an attempt to clean up his image. The campaign worked with his wife at least. Their third son, Henry, was born about a year after the whoring rumors began.[182]

Never one to retrench in difficult times, Arnold started construction of a grand estate along New Haven's waterfront, featuring a house with two chimneys, marble fireplaces, stables for a dozen horses, and an orchard of one hundred fruit trees.

But the house was only half finished when politics began pulling him away from the life he was building in New Haven.[183] Arnold, active in the then-radical Sons of Liberty, accompanied Connecticut's delegates to the First Continental Congress in Philadelphia in 1774. He attended a dinner at Edward Shippen's house and met Shippen's fourteen-year-old daughter Peggy there, but no details have survived. (Coincidentally, John André also was in Philadelphia at that time, but there is no indication that he and Arnold met.)[184]

That first Congress reached quite a conservative compromise, affirming British sovereignty while calling for Britain to end its trade restrictions. But forces were moving in a more extreme direction. Arnold was accused of leading mobs in Connecticut that attacked Loyalists. And mob action was accompanied by military training: Arnold and his friends formed a militia company, with him as captain.

About a month later and 120 miles away from New Haven, the Revolutionary War began. A British expedition to seize Patriot arms caches outside Boston led to bloody gun battles in Lexington and Concord and a humiliating retreat by the redcoats.

When Arnold heard about the clashes, he mobilized his company to head northeast for combat. New Haven authorities chose to remain neutral and locked up the city's supply of gunpowder. Arnold, who had been involved in one scrape or another for his whole life, was ready at age thirty-four to join an organized war. When he and his militiamen threatened to break down the door of the powder house, a local official reluctantly turned over the keys. Arnold's militia loaded up and headed for Boston.

Apprehending that the rebels lacked firepower, Arnold suggested that he lead a force to Fort Ticonderoga in upstate New York to seize the British cannon there. The fort had military significance for another reason: It lay at a critical point on the strategic "line of the Hudson" running from Montreal to New York City, an important lifeline that would be a frequent battleground in the war—and would be in jeopardy during Arnold's treason years later.

Massachusetts politicians liked Arnold's idea of seizing Ticonderoga and commissioned him as a colonel. Complicating things, a group called the Green Mountain Boys, led by Ethan Allen, was already headed to Ticonderoga with the same idea. Arnold rode ahead of his men and caught up with Allen's force, then tried to pull rank. But Allen's motley militia refused to serve under Arnold. The two egotistical leaders reached a compromise and mounted the attack under a joint command.

In a surprise predawn raid, Arnold and Allen captured the fort without a single fatality on either side. Then they immediately fell into dispute. Allen's boys chose the rum supply as their next target, while Arnold tried to order them to improve the fort for the inevitable British counterattack and prepare the cannon for shipment to Boston. The Green Mountain Boys ignored him, and Allen stripped him of his share of the command.

Insulted and impatient, Arnold saw a chance for vindication when a schooner showed up carrying fifty recruits. He persuaded the force to sail north on Lake Champlain and raid the British-held Fort St. Jean in Canada. Approaching undetected, they seized a sloop and destroyed other ships, deftly escaping and leaving the enemy ill equipped to mount an attack on Ticonderoga. The first military mission under Arnold's sole command was a smashing success.

His glory was brief. Massachusetts washed its hands of any jurisdiction in the Ticonderoga area, and Connecticut appointed a new colonel to take Arnold's place. Though Arnold first refused to step down, he ultimately relented.[185]

While he was without command and pondering his future, he received the news that his wife had died of unknown causes.[186] Arnold went home to New Haven, and could have stayed there to raise his three young sons and try to salvage his business, which had been devastated by the British blockade. Instead he left his sister Hannah to assume the roles of surrogate mother and business manager and went to General Washington's headquarters in Cambridge, Massachusetts, to lobby for his plan to launch an invasion of Canada.

Eventually colonial leaders agreed to challenge the British in the North, but political negotiations put off the mission until the summer of 1775 was nearly over—a delay that would prove decisive.

The Americans moved into Canada on two tracks. One force took the conventional route over Lake Champlain and along the Richelieu River to Fort St. Jean, the same path that Arnold had chosen when he captured the sloop during his raid after Ticonderoga. This time the invaders aimed to capture St. Jean—whose defenders now included British lieutenant John André—and then push on to Montreal. Meanwhile, a second force to the east sailed up Maine's Kennebec River and tried to cross a forbidding, little-traveled wilderness to Quebec. If all went well, the first force would tie up the British in Montreal while the second force sprang upon an unaware and undermanned Quebec.

Arnold accepted the more difficult assignment—command of the thousand-plus soldiers who set off over roaring rivers, thickly wooded heights, and mazelike swamps en route to Quebec. The odds, which were against them from the start, grew steadily longer as they struggled with leaky boats, torrential rain, a devastating flood, a blinding snowstorm, and severe shortages of food that compelled them to eat their own moccasins and dogs.

Arnold somehow kept this series of disasters from dooming them all. Nearly a third of his troops turned back, but Arnold's strong will pulled the rest of his bedraggled army over a difficult rise called the Height of Land and down an often wild river named the Chaudière, the French word for cauldron.

When Arnold arrived outside the fortified city of Quebec, he had earned comparisons with Hannibal, famed for crossing the Alps with elephants. But Arnold was facing a more difficult task than the one he had just completed. By the time he reached Quebec, its defenders were reinforced and ready.[187] Arnold's force, on the other hand, was tired, hungry, ill clothed, and undermanned as it assembled on the pastures outside the city walls—the same Plains of Abraham where British forces had defeated the French in 1759. Recognizing that a direct attack would be futile, Arnold marched his army near Quebec's walls in an attempt to lure the British outside and engage them on more even ground. But they didn't emerge. When Arnold realized that his army was perilously short of ammunition—a fact that his officers had hidden from him—he pulled back and awaited support from the other rebel invasion force, which had captured Montreal and was headed his way.

That force was led by Richard Montgomery, the general who had taken André prisoner at Fort St. Jean. A former British officer turned rebel, Montgomery was one of the few military leaders whom Arnold viewed more as a comrade than a rival. Even after Montgomery joined him, the rebel force was outnumbered by Quebec's defenders. But Arnold had come too far to simply withdraw. Many of his soldiers' enlistments were up on December 31, so he had to make his assault before year's end or abandon the plan. At 5 a.m. on that last day of 1775, in the midst of a raging snowstorm, Montgomery and Arnold launched their attack on Quebec.

Some colonial troops wore a piece of white paper on their caps to help distinguish friend from foe. On the paper was written "Liberty or death." Bravery was in abundance, with each of the two commanders at the vanguard of one prong of the attack. For Arnold, the battle was short. As his troops attempted to breach the first barricade, a musket ball struck him in the left calf. At first he refused to withdraw, but loss of blood made him faint, and he was taken to an aid station outside the walls. Montgomery was less fortunate. As he led a charge, a cannon filled with small iron balls known as grapeshot erupted in his direction. He was struck in the head and thighs, dying instantly.

With both leaders fallen, the attack descended into disaster. Hundreds were captured. Arnold lay at the hospital with his sword and two loaded pistols beside him, ready to fight to the death rather than be taken prisoner.[188] But the British simply savored their victory and left the remnants of the Patriot army sitting outside Quebec.

The wounded Colonel Arnold was promoted to brigadier general a week and a half after the battle. But the American version of Hannibal was far from gratified. Congress seemed slow to respond to his calls for reinforcements, but did ask for a full accounting of his expenses. Financial issues would plague Arnold throughout the war as many Continental officials questioned his demands for reimbursement for the personal funds he had used to pay for supplies. If only Arnold had been followed around by a battalion of accountants, the hard feelings and distrust might have been avoided.

Reinforcements came to Arnold in dribs and drabs, and many of them were sick when they showed up. Another newcomer only annoyed Arnold—David Wooster, the man who had hesitated to unlock the New Haven powder house, and who now outranked Arnold. More misfortune befell Arnold when his horse shied and collapsed on his already injured leg.

Securing a reassignment to Montreal, Arnold left Quebec unconquered. With good weather came more British troops, and they drove Arnold and the rest of the rebel army out of Canada.[189] During the retreat, Arnold accused a subordinate of improperly seizing goods, and the subordinate accused him of the same. Arnold went on such a rant during the subordinate's court-martial that officers issued an arrest warrant against him for "profane oaths." Arnold was saved by the intervention of General Horatio Gates, who decided that Arnold's combative nature was more useful on the battlefield than in court.[190]

And indeed it was. As the British sought to move south, control of Lake Champlain became vital. Realizing that Arnold's civilian shipping experience made him "perfectly skilled in maritime affairs," Gates arranged for him to build and command a fleet of small wooden boats to oppose the superior British navy carrying an invasion force south to attack Ticonderoga.[191]

The British fleet boasted about three dozen ships, trailed by canoes carrying hundreds of Indians. Arnold could not risk a fight in the open lake. Instead he hid his sixteen ships behind Valcour Island, which was not even on the British military's map of the lake. Here he was hoping to spring a trap.

On the morning of October 11, 1776, the British fleet was strung out over ten miles of lake when Arnold sent a few of his ships into plain view to lure the enemy piecemeal into the channel behind the island. The British took the bait, and a seven-hour battle ensued in which both sides lost ships but the British could not concentrate their firepower. By nightfall the American fleet had expended three-fourths of its ammunition and appeared trapped, but Arnold quietly sneaked his ships past the inattentive British and made a run for it.

Two days later, the British caught up with Arnold. His command ship, named *Congress* after a group with which he often feuded, was encircled by seven enemy vessels. Nonetheless Arnold found a way to reach a shallow bay, set the ship afire, and escape by land.

Arnold had lost two-thirds of his fleet. But the British had lost even more valuable assets: time and momentum. Embarrassed, bloodied, and stunned into caution, the British abandoned the idea of seizing Ticonderoga that year and turned back to spend the winter at the Canadian end of the lake.[192]

Arnold spent the winter traveling, and he was often greeted as a war hero. Neither Quebec nor Valcour Island had been victories, but in each case he had shown the kind of audacity that was desperately needed—and was so far lacking—in the Continental Army.

During his travels, Arnold brought troops to the beleaguered Washington along the Delaware River, and shared intelligence and stories with the top general, whom he hadn't seen since leaving for Quebec. Then Arnold went to New Haven, where he visited his sister Hannah and his three sons, and paid a thousand pounds of his own money to bankroll a regiment started by some friends. After that, it was on to Rhode Island, where he was ordered to be prepared to confront British forces that had seized Newport. On a side trip, Arnold went to Boston, where he asked shopkeeper Paul Revere to find a sword knot, sash, epaulets and silk hose for his navy-blue uniform.[193]

Arnold was at a high point in his military career, but two significant events would pull him down.

While in Boston—the cradle of colonial radicalism—he met a young beauty from a Loyalist family named Elizabeth DeBlois. Despite her mother's disapproval, the widowed, thirty-six-year-old Arnold tried to woo the fifteen-year-old DeBlois by smuggling her a love letter and a trunk of gowns. It's not clear whether she ever answered the letter, but she did reject the gowns, and soon after accepted a different marriage proposal from an apprentice druggist.[194]

Meanwhile, a career disappointment may have permanently soured Arnold's view toward American independence. When Congress announced the promotion of five men to major general, it passed over Arnold even though he had been a brigadier longer than any of them and had proved himself to be one of America's most brave and resourceful military men.

Arnold immediately wrote to Washington, threatening to resign. Washington asked him to wait while he investigated. "I know some villain has been busy with my fame and easily slandered me," Arnold wrote to Gates, in a sentence remarkable only because he used the singular "villain" rather than the plural.[195] Arnold's brash style had made scores of political foes, for reasons both petty and well founded.

Instead of dwelling on Arnold's polarizing behavior, however, Washington diplomatically blamed the slight on a new congressional policy designed to spread out high-ranking officers among the states. Connecticut already had its share of major generals, Washington explained.[196]

Though Arnold was threatening to quit the war, even he must have known that warmaking was his gift, his calling, his perfect use. While he was brooding over the promotion snub, he was alerted that the British were raiding Danbury, Connecticut, and he immediately gathered militiamen to attack the invaders. During the fighting, Arnold's horse was wounded, and the general fell to the ground, with one foot stuck in the stirrup. An enemy soldier rushed at him, bayonet flashing, and demanded his surrender. Instead Arnold drew his firearm and shot the man dead.[197]

Arnold's apparent willingness to shelve his bitterness and risk his life for his country impressed Congress—or at least enough of its members so that Arnold was belatedly named a major general. That wasn't enough for him, however. He went to Philadelphia and demanded that his seniority be made retroactive to when the other five had been promoted. And when Congress ignored him, he submitted his resignation.[198]

But the call of battle intervened. The British under General John Burgoyne, continuing their effort to control the line of the Hudson, invaded from Canada, seizing Ticonderoga for starters. Arnold asked Congress to put his resignation aside, and he again plunged into a desperate military action at Washington's behest. He joined American defenders near Saratoga, New York, seeking to block the advancing British force. But Arnold found himself embroiled in a feud with Gates, his commanding officer and onetime friend, that nearly sacrificed victory to pettiness.

The Battle of Saratoga was actually two battles eighteen days apart. On September 19, 1777, the aggressive Arnold's division clashed with the British, and Gates refused Arnold's demand for reinforcements that could have defeated Burgoyne then and there. Late in the day, Gates relented, but the troops arrived too late to make a difference. Gates then reported to Congress that Burgoyne had been ably opposed by "a detachment from the army," not mentioning that it was Arnold's division.[199]

As the armies faced each other, Arnold smoldered, and he finally exploded when Gates decreed that one of Arnold's best corps would take orders only from Gates's staff. The bypassed Arnold angrily confronted Gates, who pulled a joker out of his sleeve. Citing the resignation still pending before Congress, Gates declared that Arnold—who had managed one of Gates's divisions for weeks—might not be legitimately in command.

When General Benjamin Lincoln arrived on the scene, Arnold's humiliation was complete: Gates removed Arnold from command in favor of Lincoln, who had been one of the five generals promoted ahead of Arnold half a year earlier. Though Gates wrote a letter giving Arnold permission to leave the battlefront, the disgruntled general stayed in camp, with little to do. It was not in his nature to leave a battlefield with combat still to come.

The second fight came October 7, with Burgoyne's army clashing with the troops formerly led by Arnold. After hearing musket fire at the front, Arnold could stand it no longer. He climbed atop his black stallion and rode toward the sound of the gunfire, waving his sword over his head. Gates sent one of his majors riding after Arnold, to order him back. But Arnold was too swift, too driven. He rallied troops to attack one British strongpoint, then another. Gates's major still had not reached him. With bullets flying all around, Arnold led his soldiers toward a small fort on a rise manned by two hundred Hessians. Arnold's horse was shot, and then Arnold was, too.

Arnold's wound did not stop the Americans from overtaking the Hessians' position, a key advance in the Continental Army's most important victory to that point. Soldiers who came to Arnold's aid found him wounded in the left leg, the one he had injured twice at Quebec. Asked by a comrade where he had been shot, Arnold said, "In the same leg. I wish it had been my heart."[200] When Gates's major finally reached the scene, he absurdly ordered Arnold to withdraw from the front lines.[201]

Arnold endured a painful thirty-mile wagon ride to a military hospital in Albany, where doctors assessed his shattered femur and decided that amputation was necessary. Arnold refused, risking gangrene and death. But again Arnold defied the odds. He was fitted with a wooden fracture box to hold the leg stable, and endured about three months of hospitalization, an excruciating period for a man as active as Arnold.

As his condition improved and regressed and improved again, Arnold was as combative as ever, railing at his doctors. "His peevishness could degrade the most capricious of the fair sex," wrote Dr. James Browne.[202]

All the news was not bad. Burgoyne surrendered soon after Arnold's heroics, and Congress eventually agreed to its own form of surrender, giving Arnold the seniority he had demanded.

After leaving the hospital, Arnold continued his recuperation in Middletown, Connecticut, where he visited his children in school and underwent more surgery to remove bone splinters.[203]

~~

In the spring of 1778, when Peggy Shippen was in Philadelphia preparing for the Meschianza, another young woman in Boston fended off a second round of advances from Arnold.

Betsy DeBlois, now sixteen, who had rejected Arnold the year before and intended marrying an apprentice druggist, was available again. Her mother had stood up in church before the ceremony and forbidden the union. The ever ambitious Arnold saw an opportunity, thinking somehow that a crippled war hero might be more attractive to Betsy than an uninjured general had been the year before. His love letter reveals Arnold at the height of emotionalism: "Twenty times have I taken up my pen to write to you, and as often has my trembling hand refused to obey the dictates of my heart, a heart which has often been calm and serene amidst the clashing of arms."[204]

Betsy—or perhaps her mother—responded by asking Arnold to leave her alone. Such requests were "impossibilities I cannot obey," he wrote, adding that she might as well "wish me to exist without breathing as cease to love you."[205] But eventually he did give up. Betsy, who lived into her eighties, never married.[206]

After a hero's welcome in New Haven, Arnold traveled by coach to Valley Forge to join Washington's army. The commander, noticing that Arnold could not stand on his wounded leg, decided he was not yet fit for the battlefield.[207] Accordingly, Arnold was assigned to be military governor of Philadelphia, that majestic American city vacated by the British, that city of divided loyalties and unending intrigues, that city where a lovely young woman named Peggy Shippen awaited.

CHAPTER 6

Love and Money

To MANY MEN, PEGGY SHIPPEN was the most desirable young woman in Philadelphia, but to Benedict Arnold, she was second choice. As stark evidence of this, Arnold wooed Peggy with a letter that contained many of the same words he had written to Betsy DeBlois only months earlier.

There is no indication that Peggy ever learned that his expressions of love were secondhand. And in any case, Arnold piled on a new layer of heavily perfumed language that is remarkable for its self-deprecating tone:

Dear madam, your charms have lighted a flame in my bosom which can never be extinguished; your heavenly image is too deeply impressed ever to be effaced. My passion is not founded on personal charms only: that sweetness of disposition and goodness of heart, that sentiment and sensibility which so strongly mark the character of the lovely Miss P. Shippen renders her amiable beyond expression, and will ever retain the heart she has once captivated. . . . Shall I expect no return to the most sincere, ardent, and disinterested passion? Do you feel no pity in your gentle bosom for the man who would die to make you happy? May I presume to hope it is not impossible I may make a favorable impression on your heart? Friendship and esteem, you acknowledge. . . . Consider before you doom me to misery, which I have not deserved but by loving you too extravagantly. Consult your own happiness, and if incompatible, forget there is so unhappy a wretch; for may I perish if I would give you one moment's inquietude to purchase the greatest possible felicity to myself. Whatever my fate may be, my most ardent

wish is for your happiness, and my latest breath will be to implore the bless-
ing of heaven on the idol and only wish of my soul.[208]

Arnold and Peggy had met once in 1774 when she was fourteen.
There is no reliable account of their second meeting as the summer of
1778 began, when Arnold returned to Philadelphia as military governor.
But within two weeks of his arrival, the thirty-seven-year-old general was
spending time with the barely eighteen-year-old Peggy.[209]

Though Arnold hobbled and was only five-foot-seven—two inches
shorter than John André—he managed to cut an impressive figure, with
broad shoulders, a muscular physique, and a fearless manner.[210] He was as
aggressive and determined in his assault on Fourth Street as he had been
in Quebec and Saratoga. "I must tell you that Cupid has given our little
general a more mortal wound than all the host of Britons could. . . . Miss
Peggy Shippen is the fair one," gossiped Mary Morris in a letter to her
mother.[211]

Arnold's entry into Philadelphia's social scene was well timed to capture Peggy.

Her father, still on the political sidelines and therefore without significant income, was so worried about his finances that he considered
leaving Philadelphia for Lancaster. "The common articles of life, such
as are absolutely necessary for a family, are not much higher here than
at Lancaster," he wrote his father, "but the style of living my fashionable daughters have introduced into my family and their dress will, I fear,
before long oblige me to change the scene."[212]

Continental paper money was in freefall, dropping from one-third of
its face value to one-tenth in an eight-month period and causing severe
privation for common Philadelphians who had recently survived a difficult
occupation by an invading army.[213] Yet Edward Shippen, who found fault
with his daughters' spendthrift ways, complained about any reduction in
extravagances for himself or his father. "I have sent you . . . half a dozen
pounds of chocolate," he wrote his father in Lancaster, "but I am afraid it
will be very difficult to procure Madeira wine at any price. . . . There is no
such thing as syrup, the sugar bakers having all dropped the business a long

while. It is possible after some time there may be an importation of French molasses; if so, I will try to get you some."[214]

In a time of economic uncertainty, Arnold may have appeared to be a good match for Peggy because of his seemingly bottomless treasury. But in fact, he was badly overextended, having spent his own money to supply the expedition to Canada, for which he was never properly reimbursed. Like other rebel military leaders, he found himself working for free. Congress was three years behind in paying Arnold's salary. But to a man like Arnold, lack of money was no reason to stop spending.

Arnold moved into the Penn Mansion at Sixth and Market Streets, which had been headquarters for his British predecessor as Philadelphia's military ruler, General Howe. The fleeing enemy had stripped the great house of its furnishings, so Arnold restored its grandeur at high cost with the help of a Loyalist-leaning merchant named Joseph Stansbury, who would soon assist Arnold in far more secret arrangements.

The general staffed the mansion lavishly, since he was expected to entertain politicians, merchants, and others with business before him. He rode around town in a carriage, which some critics took as a regal pretension, though in fact Arnold's leg was simply not well enough to allow him to ride a horse.

Arnold's high style of living attracted much attention, coming amid the crisis in Continental paper money. To stay afloat, Arnold arranged secretive and questionable business deals that posed serious conflicts with his official duties. It was routine for an officer to maintain his private livelihood while serving his country. But the manner in which Arnold was compelled to juggle his business affairs and his combat duties proved both absurd and impossible. It was the equivalent of expecting General Dwight Eisenhower to find a few minutes to sell insurance when he wasn't busy planning the invasion of Normandy.

Profiteering like Arnold's was widespread during the Revolutionary War, and not necessarily against the rules. When sailors at sea captured an enemy ship, they were allowed to split the goods they seized. On land, soldiers were generally permitted to profit from their warmaking as long as their business affairs did not get in the way of their public duty.

As the colonial leaders retook Philadelphia, they correctly anticipated a wild scramble to smuggle goods out of the city, and they wanted to make sure that Loyalist-owned property did not escape.

While still at Valley Forge, Arnold wrote a pass for a merchant so he could leave with goods on his ship, the *Charming Nancy*, even as Congress was preparing to impose an embargo on such shipments. Arnold later bought a part interest in the ship's cargo, which included linens, glassware, nails, and tea. Still later, when the ship was stuck in the port of Egg Harbor, New Jersey, and at risk of British seizure, Arnold ordered the use of twelve government wagons to go overland and rescue the cargo. Successful in bringing the goods back to Philadelphia, he and his partners turned a considerable profit. Arnold said later that he intended to repay the government for the use of the wagons.

Before taking control of Philadelphia, Arnold hatched another moneymaking plot. His new aide David Franks, a Canadian cousin of Becky Franks's father, would hurry into the city and buy up as many goods as possible for Arnold on the sly before civil authority was reestablished.[215] But that plan was foiled by the intervention of a powerful Pennsylvania congressman named Joseph Reed, who would soon become Arnold's greatest enemy. Reed strongly urged Arnold to order the closure of the city's shops for a week while authorities assessed what was needed to provision the army. Arnold publicly acquiesced, and privately called off Franks's shopping spree. But the scheming general found a secret way to profit from the week's embargo. Arnold and his partners ignored the trading ban and paid bargain prices for Loyalist-owned luxury goods that would soon be subject to seizure. Because these were luxury items rather than essentials, Arnold could tell himself he was not hurting the war effort, but there was no doubt he was using his authority to gain an unfair competitive advantage.[216]

Arnold's acquiescence to Reed's call for the shop closures did little to satisfy the ambitious and increasingly vengeful politician. While Arnold collected enemies the way some men collected snuffboxes, he would have done well to avoid clashing with Reed. No nemesis in Arnold's life would be more damaging.

Joseph Reed, the Pennsylvania politician whose vendetta against Benedict Arnold pushed the general and Peggy toward treachery.
PHOTO BY HULTON ARCHIVE/GETTY IMAGES

Joseph Reed was the son of a merchant and iron forge owner from Trenton, New Jersey, and received the finest education available in the area, at the Academy of Philadelphia (a forerunner of the University of Pennsylvania) and the College of New Jersey (now Princeton University). Then he crossed the ocean to study law at London's Middle Temple, the same place where Peggy Shippen's father had been called to the bar.

Reed was no colonial radical early on. He was a loyal subject of the king who considered making his living in England, but he came home when his father's drinking and erratic behavior endangered the family business. He built a successful law practice in Philadelphia and eventually brought over an Englishwoman as his wife. While many foreign visitors praised the women of Philadelphia, Esther Reed was unimpressed, finding her new companions "pretty but no beauties; they all stoop, like country girls."[217]

Reed prospered and eventually owned land in New York, New Jersey, and Pennsylvania, plus a home equipped with a wine cellar and two slaves. Though not a delegate to the 1774 Continental Congress, he was an active host, taking prominent American politicians on sightseeing tours of Philadelphia.[218] "This Mr. Reed is a very sensible and accomplished lawyer, of an amiable disposition, soft, tender, friendly, etc.; he is a friend to his country and to liberty," wrote the future president John Adams.[219]

Reed also maintained strong contacts across the ocean, writing a series of letters to Lord Dartmouth, Britain's secretary of state for the colonies. Though Reed was not yet in favor of independence, he warned Dartmouth that "this country will be deluged with blood before it will submit to any other taxation than by their own assemblies."[220]

After blood started to flow at Lexington and Concord in April 1775, Reed joined Washington's army as his secretary, a position that some thought was beneath him because of his legal prominence and that others thought was beyond him because of his lack of military seasoning. Reed admitted that he was no more ready to be a general's secretary than to be an interpreter of Native American languages. But he drafted vital correspondence for Washington, including the letter approving plans for Benedict Arnold's march to Quebec.

In June 1776, Reed received an even more surprising post for a non-military man. He joined Washington in New York as adjutant general, a job that required a deep and nuanced understanding of how an army operates. When the British pushed Washington's forces out of the city, Reed saw battle, but his closest brush with death came from his own side. Reed confronted a Connecticut private who was fleeing the battlefield, and the soldier aimed his musket at Reed and pulled the trigger. The gun misfired, and when Reed grabbed a musket from another soldier and tried to shoot the private, his gun malfunctioned as well. Reed slashed the private with his sword and took him into custody. Court-martialed and sentenced to die, the private was saved only by Reed's intercession.[221]

As Washington's army conducted a desperate and disorganized retreat across New Jersey, Reed made a mistake that left a permanent stain on his reputation. He played politics, and got caught.

General Charles Lee, a former British officer who was second in command to Washington in the Continental Army, wrote a backbiting letter to Reed, complaining about the Patriots' ragged withdrawal from New York. Reed wrote back, lamenting Washington's indecisiveness and telling Lee that it was "entirely owing to you" that complete disaster was averted. In what seemed like a betrayal of Washington, Reed suggested that Lee "and others should go to Congress and form the plan of the new army." Then Reed went on a mission to recruit reinforcements. While he was gone, a second letter from Lee to Reed arrived at headquarters, and Washington opened it. The commander explained later that he was simply eager for news about Lee's forces, but skeptical historians have wondered whether Washington was even more curious about the motives of his rival Lee. In any case, Lee's letter revealed that he was defying Washington's orders on where to move his troops, and it also contained enough references to Reed's letter to let Washington know that his adjutant was badmouthing him. Specifically, Lee agreed that "fatal indecision . . . is a much greater disqualification than stupidity or even want of personal courage." Washington knew they were talking about him.

Reed's relationship with his commander was badly wounded, though he partly repaired it through strong support for Washington's battles at Trenton and Princeton. Lee, on the other hand, went from intrigue to ignominy: Suspected of visiting a woman of loose morals a few miles away from his army, he was captured by British horsemen tipped off to his whereabouts by local Tories.[222] Reed, who slowly evolved into a strident advocate of independence, was offered the post of chief justice in Pennsylvania's new government, but declined. Instead he was elected to Congress in September 1777, just before the British seized Philadelphia. A year later, with the city back in Patriot hands, Reed quit Congress to concentrate on Pennsylvania politics.

He became the area's civilian leader, while Benedict Arnold was the military one. And they quickly found themselves in a war within the war. The two men were so different, and so ambitious, with roles so intertwined, it was like a cold front colliding with a warm front: thunder and lightning were inevitable.

Their disputes involved both style and substance, with one of the most heated battles erupting over a simple desire for hair care. On October 5, 1778, Arnold's aide David Franks ordered a sergeant to fetch a barber for him. The sergeant did so but then began to wonder if it was proper for Franks to treat a volunteer in the great cause of liberty as his personal servant.[223]

The sergeant told his father—who happened to be Timothy Matlack, secretary to the Pennsylvania Council and a confidant of Reed. The elder Matlack, who was a leading promoter of cockfights and specialized in human skirmishing as well, penned a letter lecturing Arnold about how militiamen had more important things to do than arrange for barbers.[224] "Freemen will be hardly brought to submit to such indignities," he wrote.[225]

Never one to tamp down a fire, Arnold responded by explaining that citizens had rights but soldiers had duties, and one duty was to obey orders "without judging of the propriety of them."[226]

Matlack threatened to pull his son out of the militia and go public with the reason. Arnold blasted back: "If the declaration that you will withdraw your son from the service and publish the reasons is intended as a threat, you have mistaken your object. I am not to be intimidated by a newspaper."[227]

The Reed camp had indeed made Arnold an object—of scorn, anger, and suspicion. It didn't help that Arnold was from Connecticut, since Reed seemed to have a special enmity for New Englanders. Colonel Joseph Trumbull, son of Connecticut's governor, once wrote that Reed "has done more to raise and keep up a jealousy between the New England and other troops than all the men in the army beside. Indeed, his stinking pride ... has gone so far that I expect every day to hear he is called to account by some officer or other."[228]

Reed certainly raised a stink about Arnold's social merriment in Philadelphia, especially his willingness to play host to guests with Loyalist leanings. In November 1778, Pennsylvania authorities ordered the execution of two Quaker men for conspiring with the enemy, and hanged them despite appeals by many prominent citizens, including Patriots. Reed was strongly in favor of "a speedy execution for both animals," and was mightily annoyed by a party that Arnold held the night before the hangings, quite likely accompanied by Peggy Shippen.[229] The day after the execution, Reed wrote: "Will you not think it extraordinary that General Arnold made a public entertainment the night before last, of which not only numerous Tory ladies but the wives and daughters of persons proscribed by the state, and now with the enemy in New York, formed a very considerable number?"[230]

Arnold heard the disapproving comments about his interest in Peggy and other politically impure ladies, and dismissed them. "Some gentlemen ... were offended by my paying a polite attention to the ladies of this city without first discovering if they were Whigs at bottom," Arnold wrote to a friend, General Nathanael Greene. "Those gentlemen who avow such illiberal sentiments I shall treat with the contempt which I think they deserve by taking no notice of them."[231] But whether he was indulging in hedonistic pleasures with Tories or with Whigs, he was indulging himself at a time of extreme crisis for the cause of liberty.

General Washington, in Philadelphia that December, saw the Roman fiddling firsthand. While not singling out Arnold, the Continental commander wrote: "Our money is now sinking 50 percent a day in this city, and I shall not be surprised if in the course of a few months a total stop is put to the currency of it; and yet an assembly, a concert, a dinner, or supper will not only take men off from acting in this business, but even from thinking of it."[232]

When Arnold complained about not receiving his military salary yet provided endless food and drink for Philadelphia's social swans, hard-headed men like Reed were certain to wonder about the general's business machinations. Collecting both evidence and rumors, Reed and his allies began building a case against Arnold.

Reed had strong suspicions but no solid proof about Arnold's plot to buy up goods while Philadelphia's stores were closed that first week after liberation. But he soon learned about the questionable use of government wagons in the *Charming Nancy* case. What Reed didn't know was that Arnold had recently signed an agreement with those very same *Charming Nancy* partners to smuggle goods out of British-held New York, an activity that seemed uncomfortably close to trafficking with the enemy.

Reed was well aware of another maritime case involving Arnold. The *Active* was a seized British sloop whose cargo was the subject of intense legal wrangling. Arnold became involved in the case, saying that his only interest was in supporting a party to the case who was a fellow citizen of Connecticut. Reed suspected, but could not prove, that Arnold had a financial stake in the court case. Reed planted rumors to that effect in a newspaper called the *Pennsylvania Packet*. And in fact Reed was right: Arnold had reached a secret agreement with the fellow Connecticuter for half the proceeds if they succeeded in court.

Reed also knew about Arnold's issuance of a pass allowing a woman named Hannah Levy to go to New York City, and he persuaded Congress to order Arnold to get any such passes countersigned by Pennsylvania authorities, which was an insulting public rebuke for Arnold. The general explained that the pass was intended to allow Levy to collect a debt owed to her blind, elderly mother. But Arnold's enemies suspected that she planned to carry a message into the British-held city to further one of the general's business schemes. The truth about Levy's intentions remains a mystery to this day.[233]

Clearly, Reed had reason to question Arnold's actions. But it is fair to ask whether Reed's attacks on Arnold were motivated by patriotism, politics, or personal vendetta. Was he bringing integrity to the independence movement or crippling it by harassing its most gifted battlefield general? Was he helping or hurting the cause?

Reed was a stickler. He granted no genius exemptions. Instead he went for Arnold's throat.

CHAPTER 7

The General's Wife

IT WAS MARRYING TIME IN THE SHIPPEN HOUSEHOLD. In December 1778, Peggy's favorite sister, Betsy, prepared to wed her first cousin Neddy Burd, the former prisoner of war. One of the bridesmaids, cousin Elizabeth Tilghman, recalled that Betsy experienced "quakes, tremblings and a thousand other quirks" as the wedding approached. Her nervousness frightened "poor Peggy and myself into a solemn oath never to change our state"—never to get married.[234]

A family friend, Continental general John Cadwalader, was about to get married, too—to one of the Meschianza ladies, Williamina Bond.[235] Cadwalader bet Peggy a dozen pairs of gloves that a dozen of her acquaintances would be wed by the next Christmas. The winner of the wager is unknown, but as it turned out, Peggy would have been one of the dozen.[236]

Betsy went first, however, committing her future to the extremely popular Neddy in a large and joyous ceremony featuring twenty-five bridesmaids. The socializing lasted for three days and included "a little hop for our unmarried acquaintants," wrote Peggy's new brother-in-law. "This, with punch drinking etc., is all the entertainment that was given, and even this expense must have been considerable."[237]

Peggy's father reported to his own father: "I gave my daughter Betsy to Neddy Burd last Thursday evening, and all is jollity and mirth." Then he went on to another looming issue: "My youngest daughter is much solicited by a certain general on the same subject; whether this will take place or not depends upon circumstances. If it should, I think it will not be till spring."[238]

Arnold had declared his intentions in two September 1778 letters—the love note to Peggy that included recycled phrases from his letter to Betsy DeBlois, and a letter to Peggy's father in which he asked for permission to pursue her, with the goal of marriage. "My public character is well known," Arnold told Peggy's father. "My private one is, I hope, irreproachable." After stating simply that "my fortune is not large, though sufficient," Arnold delivered some undoubtedly welcome news about a dowry: "I neither expect one nor wish one with Miss Shippen." Arnold also addressed politics. "Our difference in political sentiments will, I hope, be no bar to my happiness. I flatter myself the time is at hand when our unhappy contests will be at an end, and peace and domestic happiness be restored to every one."[239]

In fact, Arnold and his future father-in-law were not as divided in their political sentiments as some may have thought. Neither was a strident ideologue, and each was far more concerned with advancing the interests of himself and his family. Edward Shippen was a Shippenist; Benedict Arnold was an Arnoldian.

At first the idea of having Arnold as a son-in-law did not seem to appeal to Edward Shippen. Among the downsides was Arnold's age—thirty-seven, to Peggy's eighteen. And his leg was badly crippled, with the prospects for recovery uncertain. In addition, he already had financial obligations to his three sons and sister Hannah.

Certainly, Arnold was a celebrity, but the Shippens were not easily impressed by that. After all, they had already played host to George Washington for dinner. And fame could be fleeting. Shippens were supposed to marry people from mainline, established families; they weren't supposed to marry mavericks like Arnold.

In the Shippens' world, the matrimony of Peggy's parents was the proper way to stitch together families. It was a marriage of both love and business, quite attractive to the father of the bride. It solidified the alliance of Edward Shippen and Tench Francis in Philadelphia's legal profession, while keeping Tench's daughter Margaret—Peggy's mother—close to home.

A marriage of Peggy and Arnold would be nothing like that. He was from another world altogether, and seemed likely to take her far away from Philadelphia. No wonder Edward Shippen had misgivings.

At some point in the negotiations over Peggy, the Shippens rejected Arnold's proposal. But Arnold, characteristically, would not give up. The chatty Elizabeth Tilghman wrote to Peggy's sister Betsy: "The gentle Arnold, where is he, how does he, and when is he like to convert our dear Peggy? They say she intends to surrender soon. I thought the fort would not hold out long. Well, after all, there is nothing like perseverance, and a regular attack."[240] Despite Tilghman's whimsy, the choice of marriage partners was often a frightening and risky decision—a "dark leap," as a woman of the time put it.[241] Under the common-law doctrine of coverture, a man and woman who married became one legal entity, meaning that the wife could not file a lawsuit, sign a contract, or purchase property. If the couple had children, legal custody went to the husband, automatically. And absolute divorce with a right to remarry was not allowed in Pennsylvania until enactment of a 1786 law.[242]

Because marital mistakes were permanent, decisions were rarely made individually and often required extensive consultation with family members.[243] Some historians have speculated that Peggy fought with her family for permission to marry Arnold, but more likely it was a deliberative process, with Peggy's growing love for the general factored in.

By January 1779, Peggy's new brother-in-law, Neddy Burd, was referring to the Shippen family's "refusal" of Arnold as a thing of the past, and gloating about his earlier prediction that Peggy's engagement would ultimately be approved.[244] Even then, however, there were conditions. The Shippens apparently were waiting to see if Arnold's leg became healthier, a position that was untenable to Peggy, as Burd perceptively noted. "A lame leg is at present the only obstacle," Burd wrote. "But a lady who makes that the only objection, and is firmly persuaded that it will soon be well can never retract, however expressly conditional an engagement may have been made. However, we have every reason to hope it will be well again, though I am not so sanguine as he is with respect to the time; but the leg will be a couple inches shorter than the other and disfigured." Socialites monitoring the courtship of Arnold and Peggy focused on the leg, engaging in extended debates over its prospects for recovery.

Determined to improve his bargaining position, Arnold tossed away his crutches in favor of a cane.[245]

But the leg was not really the only obstacle. The Shippens expected a dramatic financial gesture from Arnold to prove his sincerity. "He has acquired something handsome," Burd wrote, "and a settlement will be previously made." The greatest prospect for Arnold to achieve economic security seemed to come from his friends in upstate New York, where the general had risked his life repeatedly and had ultimately sacrificed his health to protect the colony from British invaders. The New Yorkers were interested in offering Arnold one of two large manors seized from Loyalists, with the idea that he would settle there with some of his soldiers, providing a frontier buffer against future British attacks. As a reward for his heroic sacrifices, New York would sell Arnold the land at a bargain price. The properties were Kingsland, a 130,000-acre estate in the Mohawk Valley, and Skenesboro, a 40,000-acre estate on Lake Champlain.[246]

By the first week of February, when Arnold said goodbye to Peggy and left on a trip to negotiate the New York deal, the two were officially engaged to be married. It was entirely plausible for Peggy to look forward to life in a fine home in the New York countryside as queen of the manor, with dominion over all the land as far as her eyes could see.

Joseph Reed had other plans. The Pennsylvania Council issued eight charges against Arnold:

- That he had written a pass to a "disaffected person"—a Loyalist— to take the *Charming Nancy* out of Philadelphia.
- That he had purchased goods in Philadelphia while ordering the stores closed.
- That he had forced militiamen to perform menial tasks, such as summoning the barber.
- That he had acquired an unethical financial interest in the *Active* shipping case.
- That he had commandeered public wagons to move his private property.

- That he had written an illegal pass for Hannah Levy, the woman planning a mysterious mission to New York City.
- That he had responded in an "indecent and disrespectful" manner to Pennsylvania authorities' inquiries.
- That his support for Tories was "too notorious to need proof or illustration."[247]

Some of the charges were valid, yet Reed was armed with more rumors than evidence. Moreover, his timing was suspect, seemingly designed to catch Arnold out of town and to scuttle his mission to New York.

Arnold had reached the Pennsylvania town of Bristol, on the Delaware River northeast of Philadelphia, when a messenger rode up. Along with an enumeration of charges, the message disclosed that the accusations also had been sent to Congress, to General Washington, and to the leaders of the other twelve states. Reed seemed determined to destroy Arnold.

The besieged general decided then and there to cross the Delaware River into New Jersey and proceed to Washington's headquarters to confer with his commander. This allowed Reed's forces to state accurately but misleadingly that Arnold had left the state after hearing about the charges. Rumors spread that the general had gone over to the enemy. Reed's accusations put Washington in a bind, since the council threatened to refuse to assist in any military actions as long as Arnold was in authority. Washington suggested that Arnold ask Congress for a military court-martial to address the charges. Arnold embraced that strategy rather than submit to Reed's Council, whom he accused of "as gross a prostitution of power as ever disgraced a weak and wicked administration."[248]

Arnold waited at Washington's headquarters for several days, confronted by a dilemma: He could return immediately to Philadelphia and give up his hopes of a New York manor, or he could continue with his planned trip to New York, risking further assaults on his character in Philadelphia.

Perhaps Reed's charges had poisoned the well anyway and no mission to New York could have succeeded. Or perhaps the silence of his fiancée

Peggy compelled him back to Philadelphia. Arnold was hoping for some sign from Peggy, some letter of encouragement, and he did not get it. "Never did I so long to see or hear from you as at this instant," he wrote to Peggy five days after the charges were issued, begging for her to write. "Make me happy by one line."[249]

Was Peggy wavering? Did she feel trapped? She had agreed to marry a man despite his severe physical disability. But now she was being asked to accept another handicap—that he had been declared a public enemy and might be subject to imprisonment and permanent disgrace. She wasn't married yet. There was still time to change her mind. Peggy's thoughts are not on paper—or at least not on any paper that wasn't consumed by fire long ago. But the fact is, she did not promptly write to Arnold at this moment of crisis in his life.

Arnold's letter announced that he was coming home because bad winter roads had prevented his journey to New York. He even dismissed the purpose of the trip as a quest for "a few dirty acres." But those dirty acres had been a great opportunity for the two of them, a great opportunity lost. Arnold wrote to Peggy:

Six days' absence without hearing from my dear Peggy is intolerable. Heavens! What must I have suffered had I continued my journey: the loss of happiness for a few dirty acres. I can almost bless the villainous roads and the most villainous men who oblige me to return. . . . I daily discover so much baseness and ingratitude among mankind that I almost blush at being of the same species, and could quit the stage without regret were it not for some few gentle, generous souls like my dear Peggy who still retain the lively impression of their Maker's image. . . . I am treated with the greatest politeness by General Washington and the officers of the army, who bitterly execrate Mr. Reed and the Council for their villainous attempt to injure me. They have advised me to proceed on my journey. The badness of the roads will not permit.[250]

Arnold's upbeat tone could not have fooled Peggy. The general was coming back to Philadelphia to wage a desperate battle for his reputation, and also to cement her commitment. As she would throughout her life with Arnold, Peggy remained true to her word.

Peggy's cousin Elizabeth Tilghman remained reliably chatty, writing: "I think all the world are running mad, what demon has possessed the people with regard to General Arnold, he is certainly much abused; ungrateful monsters, to attack a character that has been looked up to, in more instances than one, since this war commenced." Elizabeth knew her cousin's anguish. "Poor Peggy, how I pity her. At any rate her situation must be extremely disagreeable, she has great sensibility and I think it must often have been put to the trial."[251]

Arnold's request for a military court-martial was put off in favor of a congressional committee investigation chaired by Maryland lawmaker William Paca, a signer of the Declaration of Independence who was married to one of Peggy's friends.

Reed and his allies offered evidence on the misuse of government wagons but otherwise refused to cooperate with the committee, suggesting that Paca was meeting secretly with Arnold. The general actively defended himself before the committee, stretching the truth in several instances, such as when he declared "upon my honor" that he had made no purchases while Philadelphia's shops were closed. Technically, that was true, since one of Arnold's partners had done the dealing, but Arnold was in line for the profits.

The Paca committee cleared Arnold on six charges and referred two others to a court-martial—the wagon use and the barber incident. Arnold claimed victory, confident that he could quickly dispatch those two charges later. But Arnold's triumph was temporary. The full Congress feared that the Paca findings would widen an already dangerous split with the state of Pennsylvania, a division so sharp that there was even talk of Congress leaving Philadelphia. Congress decided to cast aside the Paca committee's findings altogether. Instead, Continental lawmakers reached a compromise with Reed to refer four charges to a court-martial. Arnold would face a military trial over the wagons, the barber, the *Charming Nancy* pass, and purchases while shops were closed.[252]

Arnold was furious. The clarity of victory or defeat that he had experienced on the battlefield was unattainable in the murky chaos of American politics. But at least Peggy was constant. With the New York land opportunity unpursued, Arnold set about finding another way to demonstrate his prosperity to the Shippen family. He purchased an impressive gift for his bride-to-be: Mount Pleasant, an elegant Georgian mansion on the banks of the Schuylkill River.

The home was built in the early 1760s by Scottish-born ship captain John Macpherson, whose firstborn son served under General Montgomery and was killed in the failed storming of Quebec, the same battle where Arnold was first wounded. John Adams, who dined with Macpherson at Mount Pleasant in 1775, called the ninety-six-acre estate "the most elegant seat in Pennsylvania."[253]

Mount Pleasant was rented to a Spanish diplomat at the time that Arnold made the purchase. It appears that he and Peggy never got a chance to move in—that for Peggy, Mount Pleasant was a grand opportunity barely missed, like the Meschianza (and like the conspiracy yet to come).

Arnold's purchase of Mount Pleasant only increased his enemies' suspicions about his sources of income. He is believed to have made the down payment with proceeds from the *Active* deal and a twelve-thousand-pound loan from French shipping agent Jean Holker. This enormous French loan not only increased his financial and psychological insecurity but also created yet another potential conflict of interest, since Arnold had to deal with the French on official military business.[254]

But Mount Pleasant won over the Shippen family. It was no fleeting promise—it was an estate that might keep Peggy in Philadelphia, a tangible asset that she could build a future on.

On the evening of Thursday, April 8, 1779, General Benedict Arnold and Miss Margaret Shippen were married. Neither the family finances nor the political atmosphere made a lavish public ceremony advisable. Instead of following her sister's lead with a gala featuring twenty-five bridesmaids, Peggy was married quietly in her Fourth Street home with relatives on both sides of the family serving as witnesses. An aide helped the blue-uniformed Arnold stand up during the ceremony. When he could be seated, Arnold propped his lame leg on a stool.

A witness described the bride as lovely, but the event was a long carriage ride away from the nights of high-haired glory when Peggy had been the object of admiration, lust, and jealousy among entire roomfuls of prominent people. Peggy was a married lady now, newly won by a proud and increasingly besieged man. The gossip against Arnold extended even to his wedding behavior. An Englishman who was privy to the rumors reported that the "miscreant" Arnold "made the mysteries of the nuptial bed the subject of his coarse ribaldry to his companions the day after his marriage."[255]

Elizabeth Tilghman, noting Arnold's fame as the general who had defeated Britain's Burgoyne, wrote after the wedding that Peggy had been "Burgoyned."[256] But Peggy was no mere conquest. She was nothing like her own mother, who made hardly a dent in the written record of her time despite being surrounded by literate relatives in a famous family. Peggy would prove herself to be an adviser, a strategist, and a true partner.

The bride moved into the Penn Mansion to live with her husband, his sister Hannah, and his youngest son. Arnold's older two boys were soon sent off to further their education in Maryland. The general told the boys' new schoolmaster that he had decided Philadelphia was a "bad school," and indeed Arnold was learning his own bitter lessons here.

Arnold had resigned his military governorship of the Philadelphia area, not because of pressure from Reed but because of a previous arrangement with Washington to allow the hero of Saratoga to restore his leg to vitality. Now Arnold had a twofold mission: the recovery of both his reputation and his health. Demanding that his court-martial proceed immediately, Arnold was disappointed to learn that Reed had succeeded in gaining an indefinite postponement so that he could gather evidence. Such a delay felt like extended torture to Arnold, and he penned a furious rant to Washington. "If your Excellency thinks me criminal," he wrote, "for heaven's sake let me be immediately tried and, if found guilty, executed."[257] He warned Washington that if Reed and his followers were allowed to get away with falsely accusing him, they might go after

Washington next. Arnold's letter was emotional, almost hysterical, and expressed disbelief that his bravery and physical suffering had been so carelessly discarded. "Having made every sacrifice of fortune and blood, and become a cripple in the service of my country, I little expected to meet the ungrateful returns I have received from my countrymen," he wrote. Arnold's point was as sharp as the end of his sword: "Delay in the present case is worse than death." His breaking point had come, but Arnold wasn't alone. He had Peggy, a smart and savvy ally willing to help him maneuver through the bedlam that the American Revolution had become. As one of the "Meschianza ladies" subject to ridicule and condemnation from the likes of Reed, Peggy had her own set of grievances. Her friends and their families had been harassed, arrested, and banished. Her family's wealth had been drained.

And so, just a month after their wedding, Mr. and Mrs. Arnold made a decision. The bravest and most brilliant general in the revolutionary army—and his astute, awe-inspiring wife—would offer their services to the enemy.

CHAPTER 8

Spymaster

WHO GAVE BIRTH TO THE ARNOLDS' PLOT against the American Revolution? Was it the general? Was it his wife? Was it the two of them together in a private moment of bitter realization and resolve? In some measure, the plot was a creation of Joseph Reed. His unrelenting pressure undoubtedly weighed heavily in the general's decision to turn against the country he had pledged to defend. But was that decision fully formed before Arnold took Peggy into his confidence and took her as his wife? Did Peggy try to argue with him? Did she encourage him? Or did she plant the idea in the first place?

Some facts are evident. Once the decision was made, Peggy was a full partner, a coconspirator. A key difference between Mr. and Mrs. Arnold was the extent of their betrayal. Arnold had taken a loyalty oath the previous year at Valley Forge, swearing to "support, maintain, and defend the said United States against the said King George the Third, his heirs and successors, and his or their abettors, assistants, and adherents . . . with fidelity, according to the best of my skill and understanding."[258] Peggy had made no such pledge. Her only promise was to support her husband, and indeed she did so with fidelity. Both Arnold and his wife were treacherous, but only Peggy was true.

The timing of their conspiracy, set in motion only a month after their wedding, suggests that Peggy was the catalyst. Most of the players in the plot came from her world, not her husband's. The man who would be Arnold's British counterpart in the plot, John André, was a close friend of Peggy's who had never met Arnold. The man who would carry Arnold's

92

messages to the British was a Loyalist gadabout from Philadelphia who was more familiar with the Shippen family than with Arnold.

When the Arnolds' scheme began in early May 1779, the outcome of the war was very much in doubt. And in the plot's sixteen months of gestation, the political and military situations in America remained in flux. It was impossible for the Arnolds to predict whether they were joining the winning side or leaving it. But perhaps they were confident enough to believe that their defection to the British might be the decisive action that settled the issue in North America.

While the Arnolds nurtured their ambitions, pessimism was in strong supply on both sides. For the rebels, the freefall in the value of their paper money was potentially disastrous. Congress—in a practice that has survived to modern times—found it politically expedient to spend more money than it took in. If Continental lawmakers needed cash, they simply printed more. Meanwhile, the British found it easy to counterfeit Continental currency, enriching themselves and destabilizing their enemy.

Many traders refused to accept anything but metal coins, known as specie. When a person wanted to dismiss the value of something, he would compare it to paper money, saying it was "not worth a Continental." There were stories about a barber papering his shop with money, a soldier dressing his wound with it, and even a dog being tarred and covered with the near-worthless cash.[259] It was a terrible time for an "old money" woman like Peggy to have married a "new money" man like Arnold. Their need for a trustworthy income was immediate.

Meanwhile, on the battlefield, the rebels' strategy often was not worth a Continental. The defense of the South was in ruins. Having lost the city of Savannah, Georgia, the rebels attempted to recover it with French help in September and October 1779. The siege failed with heavy losses, including the mortal wounding of famed Polish nobleman Casimir Pulaski as he led a cavalry charge for the rebels. Then in May 1780 the Continental Army suffered an even more excruciating defeat: the fall of Charleston, South Carolina, the South's most populous city.

Meanwhile up north, the Patriots' battle for hearts and minds was turning into a rout. "There is a terrible falling off in public virtue since the commencement of the present contest," General Nathanael Greene wrote. "The loss of morals and the want of public spirit leaves us almost like a rope of sand."[260] Greene was embarrassed and distressed by the indulgent atmosphere in Philadelphia. "I dined at one table where there were a hundred and sixty dishes; and several others not far behind," Greene wrote. "The growing avarice and a declining currency are poor materials to build an independence upon."

French diplomat Conrad Alexandre Gérard wrote to his government that America's cities were repudiating the idea of independence: "Scarcely one quarter of the ordinary inhabitants of Philadelphia now here favor the cause. Commercial and family ties, together with an aversion to popular government, seem to account for this. The same feeling exists in New York and Boston, which is not the case in the rural districts."[261]

While the words "Valley Forge" bring to mind the supposed low point for Washington's army in the winter of 1777–78, the army's winter bivouac two years later in the Morristown, New Jersey, area was worse in some ways. By all accounts, the weather was more severe. Some historians believe the winter of 1779–80 was the coldest of the eighteenth century. The rebel camp was buried under twenty-eight separate snowstorms, by one count.[262] The snowbound troops suffered through a continual food supply crisis, their most severe yet, according to Washington. The general wrote to Joseph Reed in December that the troops had been on half rations for more than a month and added: "There is every appearance the army will infallibly disband in a fortnight."[263]

Yet the British were disappointed and disgusted with their own war effort. General Howe's nine-month stopover in Philadelphia had proved nothing except that the British army's leadership was irresolute and its strategy unclear. The defeat at Saratoga would sting for years. France's entry into the Revolutionary War greatly complicated the picture for Great Britain. Following up on the signing of an alliance with the new nation in February 1778, the French menaced the British on the high seas, threatened their investments in the Caribbean, and forced them to keep sufficient forces guarding the home islands. The Spanish declaration of war against Britain in May 1779 imperiled the king's outposts along the Gulf Coast.

Though many Americans, both Patriots and Loyalists, viewed the Revolutionary War as a battle to the death, some politicians back in Britain considered it a sideshow. They fixated on the Caribbean, a sugar-producing area that was more profitable than the thirteen colonies at the time—though with far less potential, as it turned out. The British Empire so valued its sugar-related holdings that it sent five thousand troops to the Caribbean to fend off the French and three thousand more to Florida to ward off the Spanish. Such actions sapped the forces available to General Clinton and encouraged him to maintain a timid, largely defensive posture in New York City while the Continental Army recovered from its near-fatal wounds.[264]

Meanwhile, Continental naval hero John Paul Jones captured the British man-of-war *Serapis* off the English coast, an exploit that had little strategic importance but served as a propaganda coup both for the Continental government and for opposition members of Parliament.

British opinion makers were increasingly questioning the war strategy of King George and the parliamentary majority. In early 1779, radical preacher Richard Price declared in a sermon: "A third of our empire is lost. . . . We see powerful enemies continuing against us, our commerce languishing, and our debts and taxes . . . likely soon to crush us."[265] America was no longer an impudent child to be punished. It was "a distant country, once united to us," a place where every citizen owned "a book on law and government, to enable him to understand his civil rights" as well as "a musket to enable him to defend these rights."

The war increasingly became a struggle for the British to save face rather than a mission to quash a rebellion. British politician Horace Walpole assessed the stakes if his nation lost the war: "We shall be reduced to a miserable little island; and from a mighty empire sink into as insignificant a country as Denmark or Sardinia!"[266]

No matter the downcast feelings among many subjects of the king, the times were propitious for John André. The man who had risen steadily on the strength of his charm and abilities had made amazing leaps in his career since saying goodbye to Peggy Shippen and her friends in Philadelphia.

Returning with the British army to New York, André seemed to have dim prospects at first. His hero, General Howe, had gone home to England, replaced by a Howe rival, General Clinton. André's commander, "No Flint" Grey, was rumored to be leaving for the Caribbean, inspiring André to write to his uncle that he was "on the fidgets and not without anxiety."[267] Grey did indeed leave, but for England, and André was assigned as an aide to Clinton, a job where he could be expected to languish.

Clinton, the son of an admiral, showed skill at military strategy but often feuded with the colleagues he most needed to charm, such as Howe and the leading naval commanders. Standoffish, jealous, insecure, and easily offended, Clinton took a surprisingly warm interest in André, a Howe loyalist.[268]

The two became close friends. At lunchtime they would leave the British military headquarters at the Archibald Kennedy mansion at One Broadway and ride their horses to a handball court for a game. They also enjoyed billiards and bowling, as well as foxhunts and horseback rides in the country.

As other aides fell out of favor, André gained increasing trust and responsibility until he rose to the rank of major and served as acting adjutant general, Clinton's chief of staff. Writing home, he took stock: "You may well conceive how much I am flattered at being called in the space of three years from a subaltern in the Fusiliers to the employment I hold and the favor in which I live with the commander in chief."[269]

Though André was generally well liked, his ascent was not well received. Lieutenant Colonel Stephen Kemble, a Loyalist who stepped aside to avoid the prospect of serving under André, complained in his journal about Clinton's "unheard-of promotion to the first department of boys not three years in service, his neglect of old officers, and his wavering, strange, mad behavior."[270] Some Loyalists speculated that André's career advances were helped by sexual advances—that he was having an affair with Clinton. Historians have sometimes sought to identify the "closeted" gays among the bright lights of the past, and André's name has come up. But it's a tough case to make. Certainly, descriptions of him seem to lend some evidence. While a young man in Germany, André was praised by German scientist and satirist Georg Christoph Lichtenberg as "a man of nearly womanlike modesty and gentleness."[271] Later, a key figure in the Arnold conspiracy, Joshua Hett Smith, said André impressed him with "the softness of his manners."[272] But there is no solid evidence that André was gay, or that his relationship with Clinton was sexual.

André, who was circumspect in his love life, was linked at this time to a New York woman known as "Miss K," who may have been the much-admired Kitty Van Horn. Peggy Shippen's friend Becky Franks, who had moved to New York, observed that Van Horn had "the finest hair I ever saw" but that "her teeth are beginning to decay, which is the case of most New York girls after eighteen."[273]

Meanwhile Clinton, a widower, had a longtime mistress who served as his housekeeper and bore his children. She was an Irishwoman married to a British soldier who benefited from his wife's services to Clinton—an arrangement similar to General Howe's with Mrs. Loring.[274]

There is a simple explanation for André's rise that has nothing to do with sex: He was an energetic administrator who knew how to charm those above him and who found, in Clinton, a superior who was desperate for an aide he could trust. André wasn't a scheming sycophant—he was a bright young man dedicated to the cause who could be counted on to get things done in difficult circumstances. And indeed, there was no manual for the present situation in New York.

With Philadelphia and Boston both in rebel hands, Loyalists from across the North fled to New York and the protection of Clinton's army. The families of arriving British soldiers also swelled the population, as did runaway slaves lured by British promises of freedom. The city's population, which was as low as five thousand after Patriots fled the British invaders in 1776, grew to at least twenty-five thousand with the Loyalist and slave arrivals.[275]

Up to a quarter of the city's housing was destroyed in a fire shortly after the British occupation began, leaving many residents living in the squalor of tent cities. The influx of the moneyed classes caused prices for food and other essentials to skyrocket, adding to the misery of the poor. Profiteering and graft pushed the people further into desperation.

Clinton tried to impose price controls with limited success, but his sympathy did not inspire any personal sacrifices of note. The commander in chief had four New York residences, perhaps in part to thwart would-be kidnappers, and he kept his kitchens well-stocked with beef, veal, turkey, mutton, crabs, tripe, eggs, and sweetbreads. He ordered brandy in ten-gallon lots.[276]

André also found New York hospitable. When he first arrived, he stayed with other soldiers in the home of a Dutch family whose daughters gossiped about them. André surprised the daughters by delivering a lecture—in Dutch—about good manners.[277] Moving on to more luxurious quarters, André found himself a welcome guest at dinners, dances, concerts, and card games hosted by Loyalists and high-ranking officers. He once regaled a dinner party with his description of a dream in which various rebels showed up as animals. The judge who had ordered the execution of the two Philadelphia Quakers was a bloodhound, while one enemy politician was a monkey and another was a serpent. The entire Continental Army was a timid hare.

While André was making new friends in New York, he had not forgotten about the ladies of Philadelphia. Despite the battle lines, André and his friends managed to correspond regularly with the Meschianza ladies—just one illustration of how "talking to the enemy" was a well-practiced art in this war. Such flirtations with single men would have been improper for Peggy Shippen as a married lady, but her friend Peggy Chew was certainly involved in a sort of "birthday club" with André and company.

Peggy Chew and her sister Nancy described the long-distance dalliances while having tea with Grace Galloway, an in-law of the Shippens who was the wife of leading Loyalist Joseph Galloway. The sisters said André and five other British officers "sent them cards and messages and that they kept the birthdays of six of them by meeting together and drinking their healths in a glass of wine, and that the gentlemen kept theirs in the same manner." Grace Galloway, who recorded the conversation in her diary, added: "They bragged so much of their intimacy that I was sick of it."[278]

André continued another of his favorite pursuits from Philadelphia. Though short of time, he volunteered at the Theatre Royal, where fellow officers put on such plays as Shakespeare's *Richard III* and *Macbeth* and Oliver Goldsmith's *She Stoops to Conquer.* André painted backdrops, wrote prologues, and took minor roles.

But his role in real life was quite major, and often all-consuming. Praised for his diplomacy in a politically poisonous atmosphere, André maintained an aggressive attitude about prosecuting the war while holding fast to civilized norms. In a report about plundering by British and Hessian troops, André pointed to the sorry sight of "soldiers loaded with household utensils which they have taken for the wanton pleasure of spoil and have thrown aside soon afterwards." While some soldiers were following the rules and suffering privation, others were feasting on what they stole, creating a morale problem in the army. And the king's troops were stealing not only from suspected rebel sympathizers but from Loyalists as well. André denounced this, but showed himself to be practical: He recommended that a board consider restitution—for the Loyalists only.[279]

André's efficiency at correspondence made him the go-to person at the One Broadway headquarters—"the only man of abilities," according to one Loyalist—but the work took a toll on him.[280] André, who explained his illness only as a "treacherous complaint," was twice sent off for rest, once to Oyster Bay on Long Island and another time to one of Clinton's country houses closer to the city.

Despite his physical problems and crushing workload, André retained an optimism about the war. While Clinton's correspondence was bluntly negative about how the war was going, André wrote that the Americans seemed ready to sue for peace and were already sick of their alliance with the French.

In April 1779, André received the assignment that would end him. Clinton appointed him director of his secret service—his spy chief. André had virtually no training in such activities, and no particular qualifications except a resourceful mind and a gift for stagecraft. Two weeks after he became spymaster, he received two visitors at One Broadway. They carried a message from Philadelphia, from the spouse of a friend of his.

Peggy Shippen's new husband, the Continental Army's most ferocious warrior, was ready to betray the cause of independence, if André was interested in helping him and his wife.

CHAPTER 9

The Dance of Deceit

AT FIRST THEY DIDN'T KNOW HOW, where, or whether they would strike. But all three saw tremendous potential in their secret partnership, so much potential that they were willing to risk their lives. Three of North America's most prominent people transformed themselves into shadowy conspirators known by a variety of code names. André would be called Lothario, Joseph Andrews, or John Anderson. Arnold was Monk, Gustavus, or Mr. Moore. Peggy was simply the Lady, or Mrs. Moore.[281]

The three of them enlisted the help of confederates both intentional and oblivious, and in May 1779 they set about to deal a death blow to the American Revolution.

Arnold took the first step when he summoned Joseph Stansbury, a Philadelphia china dealer who had helped furnish the Penn Mansion after the general became military governor. A London-born Loyalist known for his fashionable clothes and his poetry, Stansbury used his social skills to avoid persecution by the rebels despite his firm friendship with the British general Howe. In 1776 Stansbury had gone so far as to pen a bit of verse welcoming Howe to America:

> He comes, he comes, the hero comes
> Sound, sound your trumpets, beat your drums
> From port to port let cannon roar
> Howe's welcome to this western shore.[282]

Later, when the British occupied Philadelphia, Stansbury helped supervise the policing of the city and ran Howe's lottery to benefit the poor. But when the British left, Stansbury took an oath of allegiance to the rebels. Somehow that was considered enough.[283]

The Shippens knew Stansbury, and it seems likely that Peggy recommended that he be approached. The Arnolds' faith in the china dealer was well founded: Stansbury enthusiastically embraced their plot, even if he didn't always embrace their rules. Whether Peggy attended that first meeting with Stansbury and Arnold is unclear. Describing the encounter fifteen years later, Stansbury left Peggy out of it, as her allies and admirers often seemed to do. "General Arnold sent for me," Stansbury wrote, "and, after some general conversation, opened his political sentiments respecting the war carrying on between Great Britain and America, declaring his abhorrence of a separation of the latter from the former as a measure that would be ruinous to both."[284]

Arnold said he was ready to take any action necessary to bring down the "then usurped authority of Congress," either by defecting immediately to the British or embarking on "some concerted plan" with the British commander Clinton. Although finances were a vital concern to Arnold, he soft-pedaled his monetary interest at this time, asking Stansbury to inquire about what the British would pay him but making no firm demands. The question that Arnold said he most wanted answered was whether the British were in America for the long haul—whether they were committed to fight until victory. He asked Stansbury to put nothing in writing, and to take his entreaty directly to a British officer in New York named John André.

Why André? Peggy may not have yet learned that he was Britain's spymaster, but she almost certainly knew that he was highly placed with Clinton. And she knew that the days of parlor games and dances and friendship in Philadelphia had forged a trust that would be vital if the plot was to come to fruition.

Arnold had another instruction for Stansbury: He was to share his secret with no one but André. Stansbury promptly ignored that by confiding in a New York–based Anglican minister and physician, the Reverend

Jonathan Odell, who, like Stansbury, enjoyed penning Loyalist poetry, such as:

> Long as sun and moon endure
> Britain's throne shall stand secure
> And great George's royal line
> There in splendid honour shine
> Ever sacred be to mirth
> The day that gave our monarch birth![285]

What gave Stansbury and Odell mirth was the opportunity to demonstrate their loyalty to the crown and dabble in cloak-and-dagger intrigue at the same time. The two showed up at British headquarters in New York on May 10, 1779, and asked for a private audience with André.[286]

The spy chief was surprised by their news, to say the least. Surprised, and intensely interested. André wrote a memorandum to Stansbury, to be shared with Arnold, explaining what the British were willing to promise and what they most desired. First of all, André wrote, royal forces had no intention of leaving America; "on the contrary, powerful means are expected for accomplishing our ends." Second, Arnold could feel confident that if he helped the British, "our liberality will be evinced." André avoided numbers, though he said vaguely that there would be "rewards equal at least to what such service can be estimated at."[287] André said the rewards would be especially sweet if Arnold helped the British "defeat a numerous body" or assisted them in "seizing an obnoxious band of men." The use of the word "obnoxious" has prompted modern speculation that André may have referred to the group most annoying to the British, that is, Congress. But perhaps André only meant the word in the purely Latin sense, describing any group that was "harmful."[288]

Also on André's wish list were details on troop deployments and movements, locations of gunpowder, original military dispatches, recruitment of other defectors, and efforts to secure prisoner exchanges. André was especially interested in recovering the thousands of British soldiers who had surrendered at Saratoga—troops whose capture was largely a result of Arnold's bravery. Conspicuous by its absence was any suggestion that Arnold immediately cross the lines and join the British army. For now, he was more valuable to the British while wearing a Continental Army uniform.

This first message from André referred to Arnold as Monk, a code name chosen by the general to compare himself to George Monk, a seventeenth-century British general under Oliver Cromwell who had turned against Parliament and helped restore the monarchy. Peggy was the Lady, whose meaning seems innocent enough, despite the temptation to note that one of André's theater productions in New York featured Lady Macbeth, another woman with elaborate schemes.

André would communicate with the Arnolds through Stansbury, using a code. As a key, each side would have a copy of the same edition of the same book—Blackstone's *Commentary on the Laws of England*—and they would use three sets of numbers as code for every word they wanted to use. The first number would signify the page on which the word appeared, the second would signify the line, and the third would signify the placement of the word on the line. They also would use invisible ink to write messages "interlined" between the lines of a normal-looking letter. If the invisible ink was meant to be revealed by being heated over a fire, the letter F would be on the message. If the ink was to be revealed by acid, the letter A would be used. André suggested that such letters contain innocuous information. For example, "an old woman's health may be the subject."

This very first correspondence made clear that André knew, without talking to either Arnold or his wife, that Peggy Shippen was important to the plot, and that she could be counted on if a second channel was needed. "The Lady might write to me at the same time with one of her intimates," he instructed them. "She will guess who I mean, the latter remaining ignorant of interlining and sending the letter." That intimate was Peggy Chew. "I will write myself to the friend to give occasion for a reply," André explained. "The letters may talk of the Meschianza and other nonsense."

Odell and Stansbury left British headquarters, with the china dealer in possession of André's script for treason. And thus was born the plot of the poets—Stansbury, Odell, and André, three men of confident verse, all of them rookies in the spy trade, trying to write an end to American independence.

Before his absence from Philadelphia could be noticed, Stansbury hurried back, a difficult journey that included rides on a sloop and a whale boat and then a trip across New Jersey on back roads.

Meanwhile, André wrote to Peggy Chew as promised. "I would with pleasure have sent you drawings of headdresses had I been as much of a milliner here as I was at Philadelphia in Meschianza times," he wrote, "but from occupation as well as ill health I have been obliged to abandon the pleasing study of what relates to the ladies."[289] Then he got to the point as overtly as he dared—he wanted this letter shown to Peggy Shippen: "I trust I am yet in the memory of the little society of Third and Fourth street and even of the other Peggy, now Mrs. Arnold, who will I am sure accept of my best respects and with the rest of the Sisterhoods of both streets peruse not disdainfully this page meant as an assurance of my unabated esteem for them." But the André-Chew correspondence yielded nothing.

Curiously, a signed draft of André's letter survives in General Clinton's records, but it is unknown whether the draft is a copy of a sent letter or the unsent original. It was marked A for acid, but researchers have determined that it contains no interlining with invisible ink.[290] Did André decide against sending the letter and involving Chew? Did he send it and get no response? Did Peggy Shippen decide that the Chew channel was unworkable and intervene, either to protect her friend or because she didn't trust her?

Peggy Chew, to her good fortune, would remain out of the plot.

Arnold, on the other hand, received and answered his message from André. But he told Stansbury he was changing the ground rules a bit. He would use *Bailey's Dictionary* rather than Blackstone's *Commentary on the Laws of England,* and he would add one to each number in the code. For example, the first word on the second line of the third page would be 2.3.4, not 1.2.3.

Arnold also moved on to another code name, Gustavus, believed to be a reference to Gustavus Vasa, who led Sweden to independence from

Denmark in the 1500s. Gustavus's story included an escape in which he hid in a wagon of hay while Danish soldiers poked it with their weapons. The soldiers pierced Gustavus's skin, but he did not cry out, and he passed through the Danish lines to lead the revolt that made him king. Arnold, too, intended to quietly endure the pain and prevail.[291]

Stansbury smuggled Arnold's response out of Philadelphia and sent it to Odell in Manhattan so he could forward it to André. But Odell got curious. He opened the letter, noticed that it was marked F for fire, and held it over a candle to heat it up and reveal the message. What appeared was "one indistinguishable blot, out of which not the half of any one line can be made legible," according to Odell. The letter had become wet, thereby spreading its invisible ink. Odell was forced to write a confessional letter to André explaining that he was "mortified to death" about his unauthorized peeking. But he offered to decipher future letters, and indeed most of the André-Arnold correspondence that survives today is decoded in Odell's handwriting.[292]

The inky mess was an apt metaphor for the blots on Arnold's career that were multiplying and spreading. Shortly after volunteering to commit treason, Arnold wrote Washington asking to be given a new assignment. He secretly wanted to be in a better position to help the British inflict pain on his own army. Washington turned Arnold down, urging him to concentrate on his court-martial, which had been rescheduled to begin on June 1. Arnold was in no shape for warfare anyway. His wounded left leg was causing him great pain, and his good right foot was wracked by gout. He was lifted into his carriage for the trip to army headquarters in Middlebrook, New Jersey, where the court-martial would take place.

Peggy stayed in Philadelphia while Arnold settled in at headquarters to prepare his case. He could have used her diplomatic advice. Talking openly in camp about the charges and even trying to lobby the scrupulously impartial Washington, Arnold earned rebukes. And when the court-martial opened, Arnold made matters worse by complaining that there were too many Pennsylvanians sitting in judgment of him.

The court-martial lasted one day before it was suddenly postponed by Washington so that he and his officers could respond to a British offensive north of New York City. Arnold waited three weeks for the court-martial to resume. Then he gave up and went home.[293]

In the offensive that preempted Arnold's court-martial, the British seized two rebel outposts along the Hudson River, at Stony Point and Fort Lafayette. And André seized a bit of melodramatic glory that annoyed his comrades. He personally accepted the surrender of the tiny Fort Lafayette, a blockhouse with about seventy-five men, by staging a showy event as if he had just knocked down the walls of Jericho. The surrender ceremony, held on the ramparts and visible from both shores, occurred on the king's birthday, providing an excuse for salutes to be fired off and soldiers to cheer in a manner far out of proportion to the significance of the victory.[294] "No display of ostentatious arrangements was overlooked on this occasion," a critic wrote in a public letter to Clinton. "What, Sir Henry, could you intend by this farce? What excuse will a person of Mr. André's reputed sense find for this parade?"[295]

About six weeks later, rebel forces recovered the position, but André's confidence and ambition were nonetheless swelling. He hungered for a more dramatic triumph, the kind that Arnold might provide. And he wanted an answer from Arnold right away. Odell wrote to Stansbury, "Lothario is impatient." As a code name for André, Lothario was an interesting choice, as it referred to a character in Nicholas Rowe's 1703 play *The Fair Penitent* who was a womanizer.[296]

But this Lothario was not impatient for long. A second letter arrived from Arnold, and this one was unblotted. The general shared the intelligence that no action had been taken to prevent the depreciation of currency, and that the Continental Army was poorly supplied in Charleston and would give up the city if pressed. Simply by divulging that information, Arnold was acting as a spy and risked the hangman's noose. But the intelligence served as a sign of good faith as Arnold brought up his chief concern: "I will cooperate when an opportunity offers, and as life and everything is at stake, I will expect some certainty—my property here secure and a revenue equivalent to the risk and service done." Arnold wrote, "I cannot promise success; I will deserve it."[297] He added a personal note indicating that the negotiations would be friendly: "Madam Ar presents you her particular compliments." A second letter from Arnold, with valuable intelligence about the Hudson defenses, arrived too late to assist the British offensive.

André responded promptly, but Stansbury could not get an audience with Arnold and left the letter with Peggy—yet another indication that the British and Loyalists trusted her in the plot. The letter did not fill Mr. and Mrs. Arnold with joy.

André knew about Arnold's legal struggles, and knew he had the upper hand in any negotiations. Responding to a request by Arnold that Clinton disclose his military plans so that Arnold could tailor his intelligence, André wrote brusquely: "His Excellency wishes to apprise you that he cannot reveal his intentions as to the present campaign, nor can he find the necessity of such a discovery."[298] As his primary goal, André pushed for Arnold to arrange for the capture of a huge Continental force. But the twenty-nine-year-old soldier-poet's instructions to the thirty-eight-year-old wounded war hero came across as a haughty lecture: "Join the army, accept a command, be surprised, be cut off—these things may happen in the course of maneuver."

Even so, the lecture came with some words Arnold wanted to hear: "A complete service of this nature involving a corps of five or six thousand men would be rewarded with twice as many thousand guineas." Again, André was pushing for Arnold to arrange for the prisoners of war from Saratoga to be exchanged. "It could be urged by none with more propriety," wrote André, ironically mentioning "propriety" while discussing bribery.

After a wait of four days, Stansbury was finally allowed to meet with Arnold on July 11, 1779, and that same day the china dealer wrote a note conveying his impressions to be sent to André via Odell. There was no new letter from Arnold, but the packet included a request by Peggy for sewing supplies from New York, perhaps her way of offering encouragement to her friend André. Included was a shopping list—in Arnold's handwriting—that asked for pale pink mantua with matching ribbon, black satinet for shoes, diaper cloth, and a pair of "neat spurs." Why was the list in Arnold's handwriting? Perhaps it was to provide a sample that might be used for verification later.

Odell passed those items on to André, and included a letter describing his own communications with Stansbury and assessing the state of negotiations. While the shopping list indicated a willingness to do business, the Stansbury and Odell messages were not sanguine. "I delivered Gustavus your letter," Stansbury wrote André. "It is not equal to his expectations."[299] In his talk with Stansbury, Arnold had gone straight to the bottom line. "He expects to have your promise that he shall be indemnified for any loss he may sustain in case of detection and whether this contest is finished by sword or treaty that ten thousand pounds shall be engaged him for his services."

Odell, in his own note, said Arnold appeared unimpressed with André's level of enthusiasm. Arnold told Stansbury that "he had carefully examined the letter, and found by the laconic style and little attention paid to his request, that the gentleman appeared very indifferent respecting the manner."

Two days after meeting with Stansbury, Arnold wrote to General Washington to urge that the court-martial resume or that he be given a few months' leave to pursue personal business. He also suggested to Washington that his best general might be up to fighting soon. "My wounds are so far recovered that I can walk with ease, and I expect soon to be able to ride on horseback," Arnold wrote.[300] Was he giving up on the conspiracy, or was he merely trying to gain a command that would improve his bargaining position? In either case, a return to service made all the sense in the world.

Odell refused to write off Arnold, and urged André not to give up on him either. "If I might take the liberty to suggest my own opinion," Odell wrote, "I could wish you to write once more at least, as it cannot do any harm and may possibly still be worthwhile." André did indeed write again, but it's clear he had no intention of haggling like a rug merchant for Arnold's services. And he was unwilling to guarantee payment regardless of outcome, as Arnold demanded. André explained this officiously to Arnold, as if the general's claim was just a line on an expense-account form. "Such sums as are held forth must be in some degree accounted for, real advantage must appear to have arisen from the expenditure or a generous effort must have been made," André wrote.[301]

But if any accounting was being done, André already owed Arnold. The general had supplied intelligence—for free—and André was asking for more. "We are thankful for the information transmitted and hope you will continue to give it as frequently as possible," he wrote. And then the haughty tone: "Permit me to prescribe a little exertion." He wanted Arnold to give him details about Washington's headquarters. He wanted to know more about rebel ships in the Hudson River. He wanted a map of West Point, a rebel-built collection of fortresses on the Hudson, north of where André had done his victory dance at Fort Lafayette. And he wanted to meet Arnold face-to-face. "The only method of completing conviction on both sides of the generous intentions of each and making arrangements for important operations is by a meeting," André wrote. "Would you assume a command and enable me to see you, I am convinced a conversation of a few minutes would satisfy you entirely, and I trust would give us equal cause to be pleased." André said the intelligence was welcome but "so much greater things may be done."

Arnold was unimpressed. Stansbury reported that Arnold showed him André's letter and "remarked that it contained no reply to the terms mentioned in my last. . . . There was no assurance given that his property in this country should be indemnified from any loss that might attend unfortunate discovery."[302] Therefore, Arnold told him, it would be unfair to his family for him to enter into a risky deal.

And so André and the Arnolds were at an impasse. A few weeks later, André reached out to Peggy, sending a letter through a friend of hers named Major Aquila Giles, a rebel officer who was a prisoner in New York and had been willing to help secure sewing supplies for her in the past. (Giles, grandson of Maryland governor William Paca, was in a situation similar to André's in the early days of the war: He was on parole in enemy territory, a prisoner without bars.)[303]

Despite the fact that André had not acted on Peggy's previous request for sewing supplies, he pretended that such supplies were his primary concern. His message to Peggy would later gain notoriety and be known by some as the "Millinery Letter":

Madame—Major Giles is so good as to take charge of this letter, which is meant to solicit your remembrance, and to assure that my respect for you, and the fair circle in which I had the honor of becoming acquainted with you, remains unimpaired by distance or political broils. It would make me very happy to become useful to you here. You know the Meschianza made me a complete milliner. Should you not have received supplies for your fullest equipment from that department, I shall be glad to enter into the whole detail of capwire, needles, gauze, etc., and to the best of my abilities render you in these trifles services from which I hope you would infer a zeal to be further employed. I beg you would present my best respects to your sisters, to the Miss Chews, and to Mrs. Shippen and Mrs. Chew. I have the honor to be, with the greatest regard, Madam, your most obedient and most humble servant.[304]

It seems safe to assume that André's "zeal to be further employed" did not extend to gauze and diaper cloth. Nor was he trying to supplant the dutiful Major Giles, though by involving Giles in the plot he was doing the major no favor. In fact, Giles was violating his parole by carrying such a message, and could have paid with his life.[305]

André waited two months for a response from his beautiful Philadelphia friend, who politely referred to herself in the third person:

Mrs. Arnold presents her best respects to Captain André, is much obliged to him for his very polite and friendly offer of being serviceable to her. Major Giles was so obliging as to promise to procure what trifles Mrs. Arnold wanted in the millinery way, or she would with pleasure have accepted of it. Mrs. Arnold begs leave to assure Captain André that her friendship and esteem for him is not impaired by time or accident. The ladies to whom Captain A wished to be remembered are well, and present their compliments to him.[306]

In other words, she was telling him thanks but no thanks.

General and Mrs. Arnold would turn their efforts toward getting the general back into Washington's good graces. They would hope for the court-martial to resume and clear him. They would seek a proper command in the Continental Army, or an honorable release so the general could pursue his private business. They were ready to build their life together, to prosper in bad times, to grow. Their family was indeed growing—Peggy had recently shared the good news with Arnold that she was pregnant, with the baby due the following spring.

The conspiracy with André seemed like a thing of the past, a sideshow, a dream. The Arnolds were now thinking of their future. They were strivers. They were optimists. And it was an optimism unimpaired by time or accident.

CHAPTER 10

The Way to West Point

EVEN WITHOUT INVISIBLE INK, PLOTTING POETS, and code names, the first year of the Arnolds' marriage would have been a complicated challenge. Peggy, pregnant within a couple months of her wedding, was going through all the pressures of an expectant mother. Like the institution of marriage itself, motherhood was a "dark leap." Though Peggy could count on the best of medical care, the best was not very good at that time, and pregnant women were terrified both for themselves and their babies.

Married women of the era were likely to be pregnant five to ten times, with three to eight of their offspring surviving and the rest lost to miscarriage, stillbirth, or death in infancy. Women were at greater risk than men of dying in the prime of their lives, partly because of the dangers of childbirth.[307]

The crude conduct of midwifery brought a host of horror stories. Reformist Dr. William Shippen, Peggy's relative, recalled arriving at a home where there were "two grandmother midwives, one of whom . . . had borrowed a sharp knife and scissors and took off one arm [of the baby]. . . . The other was attacking like a horrible insensible the other arm."[308]

Peggy could count on her mother and the rest of her family to consult the proper professionals before any such atrocities, but the uncertainty inherent in childbirth must have weighed heavily on her. One of her few comforts was the fact that she could share the uncertain adventure with her sister Betsy, who had become pregnant three months before Peggy.

While Mrs. Arnold embarked on the path to motherhood, her husband was in a legal no-man's-land—charged with serious crimes but given no prompt opportunity to refute them. And her city had become a house of horrors, where the streets were unsafe and her friends were persecuted and prosecuted. Shippen in-law Grace Galloway, who stayed in Philadelphia to protect her family's property when her Loyalist husband fled for his life, wrote in her diary: "Awoke early in a fright. Dreamed I was going to be hanged."[309] The treatment of Mrs. Galloway was a reminder to the Shippens and other elite families that they could be instantly dispossessed. Pennsylvania's radical lawmakers voted to confiscate the Galloway house to serve as the official residence of the state's president, Joseph Reed. When Mrs. Galloway refused to leave, radicals threatened to throw her clothes into the street. Arnold posted a guard at her house to try to protect her, but she was evicted and carried out in her chair by militiamen. The Arnolds sent their housekeeper to help her pack, and lent their coach to take her away in the style to which she was accustomed. To the annoyance of Peggy and her husband, no doubt, Reed moved into the house with his wife, Esther, in the summer of 1779.[310]

By the time the Arnolds gained Reed as an unwelcome neighbor at Sixth and Market Streets, the cosmopolitan, genteel atmosphere of Philadelphia seemed lost to history, replaced with barbarism, meanness, and desperation. "There are few unhappier cities on the globe than Philadelphia," Silas Deane, a former delegate to the Continental Congress, wrote to his brother.[311] To be sure, the public's anger had some basis. Many Philadelphians were struggling to pay for food with Continental money that was losing value by the day. There was enough grain, but some of it was being diverted to the Atlantic coast to feed newly arrived French forces, who were paying in gold.

At public meetings, angry radicals proposed to load the wives and children of escaped Loyalists onto ships and send them to New York City so that there would be fewer mouths to feed in Philadelphia. And fury was building against moderate businessmen such as Robert Morris who were accused of "forestalling"—holding on to food supplies—in an attempt to get hard money instead of Continentals in payment, or simply to push up prices. To keep food affordable, radicals formed committees that enforced price controls, which businessmen took as an affront to their property rights. Other radicals had less civilized ideas. Instead of committees, they preferred mobs.

On October 4, 1779, the ascendancy of street justice culminated in an incident known as the Fort Wilson Riot.[312] A group of armed militiamen, fueled by drink, seized a few suspected Tories on a Philadelphia street and paraded them through town, beating "The Rogue's March" on their drums. Outside City Tavern, the mob spotted Robert Morris and his political allies. The Morris group fled to the nearby home of one of its members, James Wilson, a lawyer who had defended men accused of antirevolutionary treason. Like Morris, Wilson was a signer of the Declaration of Independence.

Wilson's three-story brick mansion at Third and Walnut Streets, about a block from the house where Peggy Shippen was raised, was quickly dubbed Fort Wilson. Morris, Wilson, and about thirty others shuttered the windows, barricaded the doors, and prepared to defend themselves. An estimated two hundred radicals surrounded the place, while their cohorts fetched iron bars, sledgehammers, and even a cannon.

A one-armed veteran inside Fort Wilson threw open the shutters of a third-floor window and shouted something at the mob. Whether he fired first or a militiaman did so is unknown, but the veteran was shot dead and was the first casualty of the battle. A wild firefight erupted, and invaders broke into the home, bayoneting a defender before retreating under gunfire.

Joseph Reed, who had been sick in bed when he heard about the disturbances, got dressed and hurried on his horse to the scene. With help from troopers, Reed ordered the arrest of all combatants on both sides. Morris, Wilson, and others were able to make bail, while the radicals spent longer in jail before they were freed.

The one-armed veteran was the only fatality among defenders, but the bayonet victim and other comrades were injured. The mob lost four radicals killed and about a dozen wounded. A bystander described as a "black boy" also died.

Later, Reed downplayed the disturbing clash. "Our domestic tranquility has been interrupted by some unhappy commotions, to which free states in all ages have been subject," he told the state's assembly. "We trust they are rather to be considered as the casual overflowings of liberty than proceeding from avowed licentiousness, or contempt of public authority."[313]

Arnold's role in this incident remains a mystery—either he was everywhere, or he was nowhere. By one account, he arrived in his carriage and tried to stop the paraders before they reached the Wilson house, but was forced to retreat when the militiamen threw paving stones at him. Another account placed Arnold inside the house taunting a Reed supporter from a window with the words "Your president has raised a mob, and now he cannot quell it." According to yet another account, Arnold was not only inside the house but in full command of its defense. Supporting this theory is the fact that the other known defenders lacked combat experience but held out against a mob that outnumbered them about seven to one. Yet some insist that Arnold was not involved in the clash at all.

In any case, Arnold was clearly a target of the radical mobs of that time. In an incident soon after the Fort Wilson Riot, two men chased him in the street, forcing him to draw his pistols and threaten to kill them both if they did not withdraw. A mob gathered outside Penn Mansion, the Arnolds' home. Peggy, who was about four months pregnant by now, was terrified, as was the rest of the Arnold family. The general demanded that Congress supply a guard of twenty men and an officer. Congress advised him to make his request to the "proper authorities"—Reed's government.

More than two months later, Arnold was finally able to confront Reed in a quiet chamber far from the mob. After a six-month delay, his court-martial resumed on December 23, 1779, at the Norris Tavern in Morristown, New Jersey. Meanwhile Peggy stayed in Philadelphia, where her sister Betsy gave birth on Christmas Day to their parents' first grandchild. Betsy and Neddy christened their newborn son Edward Shippen Burd.[314]

At Morristown, Arnold represented himself, thrilled at the chance to state his case. But the proceedings were agonizing for his wife, who was dissatisfied with the scant details in one of his reports to her in

Philadelphia.[315] "I cannot but wish you had been more particular in letting me know how your trial goes," Peggy wrote. "You say so little about it that I am apprehensive things do not go as well as you expected and you are afraid of alarming me by letting me know it."[316]

Contrary to Peggy's fears, Arnold generally performed quite ably. He cast serious doubt on whether the owner of the *Charming Nancy* was a Loyalist when Arnold had written his controversial pass giving the ship free rein in American-held ports. Arnold did not mention, of course, that he had later obtained a financial interest in the ship's cargo. He made quick work of the militiaman who complained about being ordered to summon a barber. In that charge, Arnold found the military jury to be a friendly audience, since he was simply arguing for obedience to orders. Arnold admitted that he had arranged for public wagons to carry his private merchandise, but insisted that he always intended to pay for their use and that he did not believe they were needed for public purposes at the time. Arnold had trouble tracking down a potential witness named Mitchell, the quartermaster who had arranged for the wagons. (Back in Philadelphia, Peggy sent a servant to look for him, and she wrote Arnold: "I never wanted to see you half so much. You mention Sunday for your return [but] I will not flatter myself I shall see you even then, if you wait for Colonel Mitchell.")[317]

Eventually the quartermaster emerged, testifying that Arnold had offered to pay but also saying the wagons had been needed elsewhere. In addition, he said he didn't think he could reject Arnold's request "without incurring his displeasure as a commanding officer."

To Arnold's advantage, and Reed's vexation, Pennsylvania authorities had little proof to support their case, even though it was generally on target and in some cases understated the breadth of Arnold's transgressions. But on one of the most serious charges—that Arnold had made secret purchases in violation of his own order that shops be closed—Reed had acquired a solid piece of evidence. Colonel John Fitzgerald, who had lodged with Arnold's aide David Franks when they first reentered Philadelphia after the British left, said he had seen a paper on a windowsill that was in Arnold's handwriting and directed Franks to buy goods.

Franks tried to explain away that revelation, testifying that he was thinking about quitting the army and his friend Arnold was only seeking to set him up in business. Franks insisted that Arnold had soon seen the impropriety of such purchases and had avoided them. Like all liars, Arnold knew that his credibility depended on affecting an air of moral certitude. Arnold said that if he had indeed made illegal purchases as his foes had alleged, "I stand confessed . . . the vilest of men; I stand stigmatized with indelible disgrace. . . . The blood I have spent in defense of my country will be insufficient to obliterate the stain."

Arnold often talked too much during the court-martial, as if he had been saving up the words for these many months. He brought up accusations that were not even at issue in this proceeding, such as the pass for Hannah Levy and his alleged insult of Pennsylvania authorities. Raising the issue of Reed's petty backbiting of Washington in 1776, Arnold all but called Reed a traitor.

He predicted that his fellow officers would allow him to "stand honorably acquitted of all the charges brought against me and again share with them the glories and danger of this just war."

The court acquitted him of the barber charge and of illegal purchases while stores were shut. But he was found guilty of giving an improper pass to the *Charming Nancy*. And while the court ruled that Arnold's use of the wagons was not an attempt to cheat the government, "the request was imprudent and improper" and "ought not to have been made." The recommended punishment was not severe—a reprimand by the commander in chief. And there was no certainty that Washington would heed the recommendation, even after it was affirmed by Congress.

Arnold was pleased enough with his spirited defense that he arranged for the 179-page court record to be printed in English and French and distributed in America and Europe. The general looked to his old love, the sea, in seeking his next military command. He wrote to Washington suggesting he be put in command of a ship with up to four hundred marines. But Washington referred the idea to the admiralty board, and nothing came of it.

The Arnolds' hope for a brighter future was bolstered on March 19, 1780, when their first child, Edward Shippen Arnold, was born. The news undoubtedly pleased Edward's uncle Edward Shippen, his grandfather Edward Shippen, and his great-grandfather Edward Shippen. Peggy's happy news pleased Washington as well. He sent the Arnolds hearty congratulations. But if they harbored hopes that Washington had forgotten about the reprimand, they were soon disabused of this notion.[318]

Washington, while gentle in demeanor and remarkably tolerant of some misbehaving colleagues such as Reed, believed in military discipline and was determined to play by the rules. He aimed to be an honest broker in an atmosphere full of backstabbing and favor trading, but that did not make him lenient. He once complained that Congress had imposed a limit on the number of lashes that could be given to errant soldiers.[319] About a week after sending the Arnolds his letter of congratulations, Washington issued his reprimand. He didn't force Arnold to listen to it in person, but published it in his general orders of April 6:

> *The commander-in-chief would have been much happier in an occasion of bestowing commendations on an officer who had rendered such distinguished services to his country as Major General Arnold; but in the present case, a sense of duty and a regard for candor oblige him to declare that he considers his conduct in the instance of the permit [for the Charming Nancy] as peculiarly reprehensible, both in a civil and military view, and in the affair of the wagons as imprudent and improper.*[320]

Washington was disappointed in Arnold's self-serving actions, but there was no reason to think he was personally angry with Arnold or had lost faith in his ability to lead troops. On the contrary, Washington continued to hope that Arnold would be physically fit enough to serve under him as a battlefield commander.

Meanwhile, Arnold was still getting no satisfaction over his financial claims from the Quebec expedition more than four years earlier. After a congressional committee referred the matter to the Treasury Board, the board referred it to the Chambers of Accounts, then took it away from the Chamber of Accounts and settled on a sum on its own. But still there was no closure, and the board recommended that its numbers be reexamined by a separate group of commissioners in Albany, New York, which might take many months.

A frustrated Arnold accused former board chairman Elbridge Gerry of plotting against him. Gerry, a member of Congress from Massachusetts and signer of the Declaration of Independence with a solid record, challenged Arnold to provide evidence, which he didn't have. Arnold again found himself matching reputations with an opponent and losing—although Gerry's later efforts to draw districts for political advantage would make him the namesake of a negative political term, "gerrymandering."[321]

The Arnold family moved out of Penn Mansion and into a more modest house acquired by Peggy's father in one of his real estate speculations. Moving into the mansion, and becoming Reed's new neighbor, was Jean Holker, the French shipping agent who had lent twelve thousand pounds to Arnold and also served as France's consul general. Peggy's fine home along the Schuylkill, Mount Pleasant, was still tantalizingly unavailable, with the rent paid by the Spanish diplomat.[322]

Arnold desperately needed money. And he needed respect as well. He was getting neither from Philadelphia, but he knew he might at least get the money from his friends in New York City. Sometime in May, about six months after their negotiations had broken down, Arnold sent his favorite Philadelphia china dealer, Joseph Stansbury, back to British headquarters at One Broadway to report that "Mr. Moore" was ready to talk some more.

But "Lothario" was not. John André and General Clinton were out of town, achieving the greatest victory of their time together, the capitulation of Charleston. Laying a systematic siege to the important Southern city, the British reduced the rebels to using broken bottles and old axes as ammunition for their cannon. The British bombardment was incessant, with one cannonball bouncing off St. Michael's Church and hitting a beloved statue of British politician William Pitt the Elder, taking off his arm. Ultimately, a rebel army of about five thousand men surrendered.[323]

This was a real victory, not an inflated conquest like André's capture of the blockhouse at Fort Lafayette on the Hudson. As a key supervisor of the triumph, André found his career on a continued upward trajectory. This was crucial because another war development had put personal pressure on André. His family's investments in sugar plantations on the Caribbean island of Grenada appeared lost when the French fleet of the Count d'Estaing captured the island, and so they were now increasingly reliant on his military salary.[324]

While André and Clinton were in Charleston, British operations in New York were run by a Hessian, Lieutenant General Wilhelm von Knyphausen.[325] When Stansbury came to visit, Knyphausen and Captain George Beckwith, who knew Peggy from the British occupation of Philadelphia, found themselves dealing with an opportunity that they quickly realized was exceptional.[326] After the meeting, the two substitute spymasters wrote down Arnold's terms. He wanted "a small sum of ready money" right away and "indemnifications" of ten thousand pounds, to protect his family's future. He was willing to "take a decisive part in case of an emergency or that a capital stroke can be struck." He also expected the British to put him in command of a "new-raised battalion," presumably of Loyalists.[327] Arnold apparently still did not realize that the British had only tepid interest in a badly wounded and fractious general joining their forces; they much preferred the single, sudden act of treachery that Arnold might provide.

The American general said he was ready for the meeting that André had suggested the previous year. "He particularly desires to have a conference with an officer of confidence," the British officers wrote. Knyphausen explained to Arnold that "the affair in agitation is of so important a nature" that he could not make any commitment without consulting Clinton.[328] But he promised that a meeting with an officer could be arranged and that a little money would be provided in the meantime. He also sent Arnold one of two identical rings. Arnold might later notice the twin ring on the finger of a British operative, Knyphausen explained. George Beckwith held onto the other ring and took the code name J.B. Ring.[329]

Arnold quickly resumed supplying information to the British, but was caught up in one of Washington's sneakiest intelligence tricks of the war. Washington spread word among his staff that he planned to invade Canada with eight thousand men—something he had no intention of doing. He asked Arnold to arrange for the printing of at least five hundred copies of a proclamation to the people of Canada. There's no indication that Washington suspected Arnold; it was simply part of his plan to let the "secret" out. Arnold indeed sent the proclamation to the British, along with intelligence from a French diplomat putting the Canadian deployment at eight thousand.

By this time Arnold and Peggy also were looking north, but not quite so far. They wanted Washington to give Arnold command of the Hudson River forts at West Point, New York, which would be the perfect prize to offer the British. Located about sixty miles north of New York City, West Point serves today as home of the US Military Academy. In the eighteenth century it was a vital stronghold for the Continental Army and prevented British ships from sailing upriver to seize control of the line of the Hudson.

Both sides knew that a takeover of West Point would allow the British to cut the new nation in two by blocking the flow of soldiers, supplies, and communications from New England to Pennsylvania and the southern states—a lifeline whose value was proven the next year when French troops used the route to move south for the decisive Battle of Yorktown. If West Point's garrison fell with the forts, the British would take at least a thousand prisoners, and maybe many more if Arnold worked it right. And such an embarrassing reversal might cause the French to lose faith in the alliance—and to withhold the kind of help that would later make victory possible at Yorktown.[330]

West Point was built where the Hudson River takes two ninety-degree turns, meaning that ships must slow down and maneuver, making them especially vulnerable to shore batteries. The first fort there was equipped with artillery surrendered by Burgoyne at Saratoga, and was named after the hero of the fighting there—Benedict Arnold. Across the river from Fort Arnold was Constitution Island, and stretching between the two points was a lengthy chain to keep ships from passing. The chain lay just under the surface, supported by wooden rafts, with each link made from two-inch-thick iron and weighing at least a hundred pounds.

Though challenging to enemy ships, the rebel position was vulnerable from the land side, a weakness that the army tried to address with the help of Tadeusz Kosciuszko, a Polish officer who was a brilliant engineer. A defensive ring was constructed, and the site featured ten separate forts by the summer of 1780.

That June, Washington's chief intelligence officer, Benjamin Tallmadge, wrote to Connecticut governor Jonathan Trumbull, who was in charge of supplying West Point, and warned that the British might make "some sudden and unexpected stroke" against the forts.[331] Small wonder that Tallmadge was worried. British general Clinton wrote that the capture of West Point "would have finished the rebellion immediately."[332] Continental general Nathanael Greene said that "such an event would have been a dangerous if not a fatal wound."[333]

West Point was a smart choice for the Arnolds for a reason other than its strategic value: Peggy could be with the general, and could defect in the same instant, something that would be almost impossible if Arnold commanded an army in the field. The couple launched a concerted lobbying effort, tapping New Yorkers who were grateful to Arnold for his sacrifice at Saratoga.

The general recruited the help of General Philip Schuyler, a key figure in the region's military affairs. (This was the same Schuyler who had befriended André when he was a prisoner of war and was passing through Albany on parole.) Schuyler talked to Washington and then reported back to Arnold on the commander in chief's sentiments:

He expressed a desire to do whatever was agreeable to you, dwelt on your abilities, your merits, your sufferings, and on the well-earned claims you have on your country, and intimated that as soon as his arrangements for the campaign should take place that he would properly consider you. I believe you will have an alternative proposed, either to take charge of an important post, with an honorable command, or your station in the field.

123

Your reputation, my dear sir, so established, your honorable scars, put it decidedly in your power to take either. A state [New York] which has full confidence in you will wish to see its banner entrusted to you. If the command at West Point is offered, it will be honorable; if a division in the field, you must judge whether you can support the fatigues, circumstanced as you are.[334]

Peggy, meanwhile, worked on another New Yorker, Robert R. Livingston, a member of Congress who was one of only three to vote against the reprimand for Arnold. The married Livingston was so charmed by Peggy that he wrote a letter to Washington complaining about the current management of West Point and asserting that Arnold would be a better choice. Peggy's attentions toward Livingston were so out of the ordinary that they alarmed Arnold's sister Hannah, who was apparently unaware of the plot and suspected that Peggy was having an affair with "Chancellor Livingston," as he was known because he was New York's chancellor, or top judicial officer. A few months after the lobbying effort, Hannah wrote her brother about West Point and Peggy:

'Tis no place for me—nor do I think Mrs. Arnold will long be pleased with it, though expect it will be rendered dear to her (for a few hours) by the presence of a certain chancellor who, by the by, is a dangerous companion for a particular lady in the absence of her husband. I could say more than prudence will permit. I could tell you of frequent private assignations and of numberless billets-doux, if I had an inclination to make mischief, but as I am of a very peaceable temper, I'll not mention a syllable of the matter.[335]

Hannah's suspicions of her sister-in-law were more than likely unfounded. No further correspondence suggests any infidelity by Peggy at any time in her life, nor is there any indication that the easy-to-offend Arnold ever held jealous feelings toward her. Perhaps Arnold understood that Livingston was an important friend to keep, and felt confident that his wife's motives were the same as his.

In early June, Arnold set out for Connecticut to sell his New Haven house, whose construction was still not completed. En route, he sent information to the British.[336] From Washington's headquarters in Morristown, Arnold reported that the French were expected to land six thousand troops in Rhode Island. And he said presumptuously that "Mr. M expects to have the command of West Point offered him on his return." Washington had made no such decision. Arnold was behaving in an increasingly risky manner that made code names useless. No Patriot who intercepted Arnold's letter would have had any problem guessing who "Mr. M" was.

Arnold's next message came from Fishkill, New York, north of West Point. Arnold had just completed his first visit to the forts that he planned to surrender in his treacherous plot. Unlike some other messages, Arnold wrote this letter so that it would appear entirely faithful to the rebel cause if read by a rebel, yet would convey valuable details to the British. He was "greatly disappointed in the works and the garrison," but noted that twelve hundred men were expected to reinforce the fifteen hundred there now. "It is hoped they will arrive before the English can make an attack, which it is thought they have in contemplation. This place has been greatly neglected."[337] He went into further detail about which forts were strong and which were weak, and noted that there was a good road the British could use to bring up cannon. "I am convinced the boom or chain thrown across the river to stop the shipping cannot be depended on," he added.

His trip to Connecticut was fruitless, and the house remained unsold. When he got back to Peggy and his family in Philadelphia in early July, there was more frustration—no answers had come from either Washington or the British.

Arnold quickly asked the British for a "very explicit answer" on the terms of his service, urged a meeting with an officer, and repeated that he expected to take command at West Point soon. Only a few days later, with his impatience growing, he wrote that "a mutual confidence between us is wanting" and asked for either progress or cessation of the negotiations. But in an attempt to make his loyalties clear, he offered a bit of poetic optimism about the prospects of American independence: "The present struggles are like the pangs of a dying man, violent but of short duration."[338]

André and Clinton had finally returned to New York, and when André wrote his first note to Arnold in nearly a year, he was responding only to the general's reopening correspondence of June, not to his more anxious notes in July. While agreeing that a meeting was necessary, André did not address Arnold's financial demands.

Arnold, obviously annoyed, appeared to up his price. He wanted ten thousand pounds guaranteed for any loss of his property in the scheme, plus an annuity of five hundred pounds for life. And here was the capper: "If I point out a plan of cooperation by which Sir Henry shall possess himself of West Point, the garrison, etc., twenty thousand pounds I think will be a cheap purchase for an object of so much importance."[339]

He got an extremely bureaucratic answer in a note Odell wrote to Stansbury: "His Excellency authorizes me to repeat in the strongest terms the assurances so often given to your partner, that if he is in earnest and will to the extent of his ability cooperate with us, he shall not in any possible event have cause to complain." But, Odell wrote, "indemnification (as a preliminary) is what Sir Henry thinks highly unreasonable."[340]

In a separate note sent at the same time, André made clear that the crown would pay for success: If West Point and its garrison were put in British hands, twenty thousand pounds was a fair price.

But at this point, even though Arnold had assured the British that he had the West Point job, he didn't. Washington was short of reliable battle-field commanders and was preparing an offensive against New York City. He wanted Arnold to command his left wing. Washington was leading his army over the Hudson at King's Ferry, south of West Point, on July 31 when Arnold asked him about his assignment. "I told him that he was to have command of the light troops, which was a post of honor, and which his rank indeed entitled him to," Washington recalled. "Upon this information his countenance changed, and he appeared to be quite fallen; and instead of thanking me or expressing any pleasure at the appointment, never opened his mouth."[341]

Back in Philadelphia, Peggy appeared even more stunned. She was dining at Robert Morris's house when a visitor congratulated her on Arnold's appointment as commander of the left wing. That was the first Peggy had heard of it. She reacted with what were described as "hysteric fits," and refused to be consoled. Some of the other diners may have viewed Peggy's behavior as an understandable reaction by a wife worried about her husband's safety in battle.

Of course, it is impossible to know the meaning of Peggy's outbursts at the Morrises' dinner or at other times in her life. Were they manipulative attempts to get her way? Or were they sincere and uncontrollable expressions of emotion?

"Hysteria" was a catch-all medical diagnosis of the era, used to describe various symptoms of what the modern world might simply call mental illness, particularly when exhibited by women. The condition was known by many names: melancholy, "the vapors," bile, nerves, and "the spleen." The word "hysteria," which comes from the Greek word for womb, carried a connotation of women bedeviled by their own volatile anatomy. The now-discredited idea of "the vapors" was based on the theory that vapors rising from the uterus and other organs played havoc in the brain.[342] Some physicians believed that upper-class ladies such as Peggy were especially susceptible to hysteria because they overindulged in luxuries and were "tortured by imaginary wants."[343]

Peggy certainly accepted the notion that she suffered from episodes of severe mental distress and disorientation. Later in her life she wrote: "I have frequently in the course of every day a confusion in my head resembling what I can suppose would be the sensations of anybody extremely drunk, and very desirous of concealing their situation."[344] But it was never clear whether Peggy's fits were truly uncontrollable or were merely a convenient psychological weapon.

Peggy's hysterics at the Morris mansion, for example, buttressed a cynical argument: Hadn't Arnold given enough to his country? Was he really fit for battlefield duty? Hadn't he earned the appointment he wanted at West Point? Along the Hudson River, Arnold reacted to Washington's decision by making essentially that argument to one of the commander in chief's aides, only slightly less hysterically.

When Washington received intelligence that dissuaded him from making a thrust toward New York City, he relented. Arnold would go to West Point, and Peggy would soon join him. Their outpost in the country would be far behind the battlefront, but it would be at the center of one of the most dramatic episodes in American history.

CHAPTER 11

"The Greatest Treasure You Have"

WHILE BENEDICT ARNOLD ASSUMED HIS APPOINTMENT at West Point, Peggy Shippen held the fort in Philadelphia. Her husband instructed her to draw all the supplies she could from the commissaries and try to sell them. Every bit of cash would be helpful to a family that might have to travel on short notice.[345] Arnold's relocation to West Point made communication with the British more difficult, which in turn forced Peggy to serve as a conduit for messages. She accepted letters from New York, but at first had no safe way to get them to her husband. "Mr. Moore commands at West Point," Stansbury wrote Odell, "but things are so poorly arranged that your last important dispatches are yet in *her* hands."[346]

It would be weeks before a letter from the British reached Arnold explaining that his stated price for delivering West Point—twenty thousand pounds—had been accepted but that no payment for failure would be guaranteed. Did Peggy know the news before Arnold did? Could she have resisted the temptation to read correspondence that would determine her future and her baby's future as well as his?

Though not able to forward André's messages to Arnold promptly, Peggy found a way to receive letters from Arnold and to forward the information to the British. Written as if they were personal letters to his Peggy, Arnold's messages included the kind of military information that no general's wife would need to know unless she were planning to join the army herself—or were serving as a spy. "All the Continental troops from West Point have joined the main army," Arnold wrote. "At present there are no troops there but about fifteen hundred of the militia of

129

Massachusetts Bay, who are destitute of almost every necessity."[347] This wasn't exactly pillow talk.

Odell felt compelled to explain to André: "You will observe that the above extracts are from letters written to Mrs. Moore, but with a view of communicating information to you. . . . I wish it were possible to open a shorter road of correspondence."[348] Ultimately they were able to find other routes.

In Philadelphia, Peggy must have felt burdened with her weighty secret. She kept company with her husband's aide David Franks and her sister-in-law Hannah Arnold, neither of whom ever showed any sign that they knew about the conspiracy. Hannah, in a letter to her brother, gossiped that Peggy was too much of a gossip. "For news of any kind I must refer you to Mrs. Arnold and Major Franks," she wrote. "If they have none, they can make you a little, my word for it."[349]

Peggy planned to say goodbye to Hannah soon and take her news northward, joining Arnold at a lovely estate near West Point that had been confiscated from a leading Loyalist, Beverley Robinson.[350]

━━◦━━

Robinson, a boyhood friend of George Washington, had become wealthy through land speculation and marriage. Like Peggy Shippen's father, he had attempted to find neutral political ground, but he had been brought before a rebel Committee to Detect Conspiracies and told to choose sides. When the war came to his part of New York in 1777, he joined the British and raised a Loyalist regiment.

From New York City, Robinson had written to Arnold in early 1779, urging the general to take over the Loyalist leadership and reach a peace settlement, thereby giving the Americans the right to make their own laws and raise their own taxes—but not enjoy total independence. It does not appear that Arnold ever answered.

Robinson House, located on a high plateau across the Hudson and two miles downstream from the forts, was a poor choice for a headquarters, according to the previous commander of West Point. That officer, Major General Robert Howe (no relation to the British general William

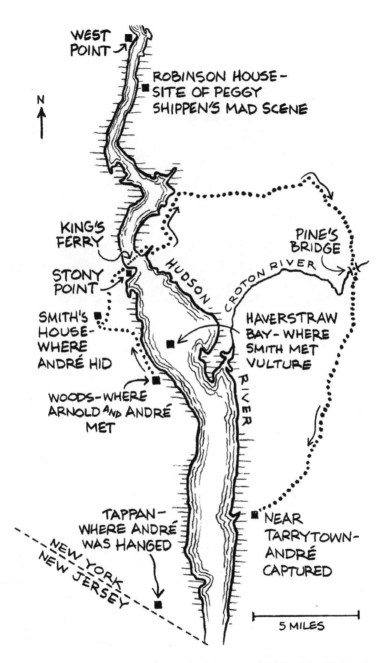

WEST POINT

ROBINSON HOUSE—SITE OF PEGGY SHIPPEN'S MAD SCENE

N

KING'S FERRY

PINE'S BRIDGE

STONY POINT

HUDSON

CROTON RIVER

SMITH'S HOUSE—WHERE ANDRÉ HID

HAVERSTRAW BAY—WHERE SMITH MET VULTURE

WOODS—WHERE ARNOLD AND ANDRÉ MET

RIVER

TAPPAN—WHERE ANDRÉ WAS HANGED

NEW YORK
NEW JERSEY

NEAR TARRYTOWN—ANDRÉ CAPTURED

5 MILES

A vital source for this approximation of André's route is Willard M. Wallace's biography of Arnold, *Traitorous Hero* (1954). ILLUSTRATION BY RICK TUMA

Robinson House, across the Hudson from West Point, was seized from a Loyalist and used as Benedict Arnold's headquarters. Peggy went mad there, and George Washington wept there. It burned down in 1892. THE BEVERLEY HOUSE, THE GEO-GRAPHIC COLLECTION; NEGATIVE #84548D NEW-YORK HISTORICAL SOCIETY

Howe), was coincidentally the president of Arnold's court-martial board. The two were cordial afterward, when Howe gave Arnold his first look at West Point in June. But Howe thought that any commander who stayed at Robinson House would be in an "exposed" position, and he told Arnold: "I leave it to you to determine whether, should accident happen, you will be held accountable."[351]

Arnold responded that his arrangements were "most convenient for an invalid." Little did Howe consider that they would also be most convenient for a traitor.[352] If the British attacked West Point, the house's distance from the forts would allow Arnold and Peggy to dash the hundred feet down to the water's edge to be picked up by their new British friends.

As commander, Arnold did not visit West Point often, even though he had a convenient mode of transportation for the two-mile commute—a barge with seats and awnings, manned by a crew of nine. The task before him would be challenging: The forts were in poor shape, and Arnold had to act as if he were improving them without actually doing so. He also had to weaken the installation's fighting strength without reducing its numbers so much that General Clinton would be disappointed in the catch.

When Arnold sent two hundred men to nearby Fishkill to cut firewood for the winter, one of his subordinates warned that he was threatening the garrison's ability to finish the defensive works and man them. In one of Arnold's messages to the British, he indicated that there were only a thousand soldiers in the garrison but that fifteen hundred more could be brought to the forts just before the trap was sprung. The goal was to keep troops from working on West Point but to have them there in time to be taken prisoner. Eventually Arnold and the British seem to have settled on a goal of three thousand captives.

From his Robinson House headquarters, Arnold certainly behaved like the fiery, impatient commander who had helped win Saratoga. He issued orders about sentry posts, the jail, the hospital, and deployment of artillery units and cavalry. He urged stricter discipline in a case that seemed to echo his own: A wagon master had been found guilty of using military transport for private commerce and was ordered to repay the army. Arnold protested the light sentence and secured a tougher punishment—twenty lashes on the wagon master's bare back.[353]

Arnold also took vigorous action to prepare Robinson House for Peggy. He ordered a feather bed shipped from Connecticut. He arranged for local farmers to provide fresh milk, meat, and vegetables, swapping his government supplies for their fresh food and incurring the wrath of West Point's provisioners, who had only Continental currency to offer the farmers.

The general seemed to love his wife deeply. It was as sincere a devotion as this traitorous man would ever have. "No sensations can bear a comparison with those arriving from the reciprocity of concern and mutual felicity existing between a lady of sensibility and a fond husband," Arnold wrote Robert Howe. "I consider the time of celibacy in some measure misspent."[354]

Arnold ordered his aide Franks to bring Peggy from Philadelphia to Robinson House, and he gave her explicit instructions: "You must by all means get out of the carriage in crossing all ferries and going over all large bridges to avoid accidents. . . . You must not forget to bring your own sheets to sleep in on the road, and a feather bed to put in the light wagon which will make an easy seat, and you will find it cooler and pleasanter to ride in smooth roads than a closed carriage—and it will ease your carriage horses."[355] He provided a list of where she would stop and under whose roof she would sleep, sometimes offering a few options.

Peggy left on September 6, 1780. While she was en route, her sister-in-law Hannah began corresponding with her: "Yesterday got a letter from your anxious husband, who, lover-like, is tormenting himself with a thousand fancied disasters which have happened to you and the family. . . . Heaven guard you safely to him, for in your life and happiness his consists."[356] Meanwhile Franks wrote to Arnold, pledging "soon to put safe into your hands the greatest treasure you have."[357]

While Peggy was traveling, Arnold worked on the final phase of the conspiracy. His task was to arrange a meeting with a top British officer to finalize all the details and set in motion the betrayal of West Point. Communication with the British was difficult, and both Arnold and André became increasingly impatient and reckless in their attempts to schedule a rendezvous.[358] To this end, Arnold tried an old trick: a shopping request from Peggy. He asked a frontline rebel commander to forward Peggy's letter seeking "trifling articles" in New York from her friend Giles. The letter was turned over to the British under a flag of truce and sent to Major Oliver DeLancey, a Loyalist who was one of André's best friends and had helped him paint theater backdrops in both Philadelphia and New York City. When DeLancey responded to Arnold's message, a path of communication was established.

But Arnold felt compelled to explain his suspicious behavior to the superior officer of the frontline commander who had forwarded the message. "I am told there is a general order prohibiting any goods being purchased and brought out of New York," Arnold wrote, "but as the goods were bought many months before the order was issued, I do not conceive they come under the intentions and spirit of it."[359] He added: "However, I would not wish my name to be mentioned in the matter, as it may give occasion for scandal."

Arnold also entrusted a letter to a woman who had a pass to travel with her children into New York City. That message got through to André. Less successful was Arnold's effort to send a message to Reverend Odell through a former Connecticut lawmaker. Instead of taking the letter into New York City, the lawmaker decided that it might involve a suspicious business scheme and turned it over to another rebel general, who put it in his desk and forgot about it.

There was some other correspondence as well, but its path remains unknown. It was clear that both Arnold and the British considered a face-to-face meeting to be essential to the success of their plot. Especially insistent was General Clinton, who was beginning to worry that the whole scheme might be a Patriot hoax. The British envisioned that Arnold would meet with André or another officer on neutral ground under a flag of truce, pretending to discuss a prisoner exchange or some other issue. But Arnold knew such a meeting would raise the eyebrows of officers who were already leery of his conduct. Arnold preferred that the British send in their emissary posing as a civilian—a notion that Clinton rejected because such a person could be hanged as a spy. The two sides' inability to reach agreement on these issues would prove disastrous in the end.

In preparation for a meeting, Arnold told the same frontline Patriot commander who had handled Peggy's shopping letter that he should expect a civilian to arrive with important intelligence from New York City. Then André took an audacious—and some might say idiotic—step. He sent a letter using one of his pseudonyms, John Anderson, to that same Patriot commander, saying, "I am told my name is made known to you" (it wasn't) and that he hoped to visit Dobbs Ferry at noon on September 11 under a flag of truce to see "Mr. G" (whom the commander also had not heard of). The confused commander contacted Arnold and, luckily for Arnold, did not inform others who would have found such a message highly irregular. Arnold knew his hand was forced, and he rode his barge downriver at the appointed day and time to see if André would appear. Instead, a British gunboat unaware of the secret meeting suddenly appeared and fired at Arnold's barge, forcing it to flee to the far shore.

André was on the opposite shore. But both "John Anderson" and "Gustavus" waited for a signal from the other, and when none came, they departed in frustration. Arnold's hopes for a meeting grew even more complicated when the frontline Patriot commander who had been vital in arranging their aborted meeting was arrested for fraud unrelated to the West Point plot. This led Arnold to contact another officer, Colonel Benjamin Tallmadge, and tell him that if a man named John Anderson arrived, Tallmadge should bring him to Robinson House. Arnold didn't know that Tallmadge was not only a field commander but also Washington's chief of spies.

Three days after the near miss at Dobbs Ferry, Arnold traveled back downriver to pick up the newly arrived Peggy, baby Edward, and Franks at Joshua Hett Smith's house in Haverstraw. Smith, a wealthy landowner whose brother was the Loyalist chief justice of New York, was friendly with Arnold and perfectly willing to assist him without question. He agreed to help arrange a meeting between Arnold and André.

Then Arnold took his wife, child, and top aide to Robinson House by barge, showing Peggy the area's impressive vistas along the Hudson. "The excursion up or down the river is truly romantic," wrote Dr. James Thacher, who worked at Robinson House when it was commandeered as a Continental Army hospital in 1778. "Nature exhibits a diversified scenery of wild mountains, craggy precipices, and noble lofty cliffs on each side the river, which at this place is about one mile wide."[360] With Robinson House's location, however, Thacher was not that impressed: "In the location of a country-seat, the judgment of Colonel Robinson is not much to be admired, unless he was guided altogether by a taste for romantic singularity and novelty. It is surrounded on two sides by hideous mountains and dreary forests, not a house in view, and but one within a mile."

To Arnold and Peggy, it was a perfect perch as they awaited a meeting with her old friend André and a well-earned prize of twenty thousand pounds. But they soon realized that the biggest threats to their plan might reside in their own house. The two top aides serving the general were stalwart Patriots, Major David Franks and Colonel Richard Varick.

Franks, while involved in some of Arnold's shady private commerce, was dedicated to the cause of liberty. He had broken with his father, a rich Canadian merchant who was a Loyalist, and once was jailed in Montreal for punching a man in the nose during a political argument. He had contributed much of his own money to defend American independence. Yet he was somewhat foppish and had his critics. Silas Deane considered Franks "mere wax, and never either too hot or too cold to receive the impression of the last application."[361]

Varick, who would later become mayor of New York City, was lured away from his legal studies to handle Arnold's correspondence at Robinson House. He had earned Arnold's notice by vigorously rounding up supplies before the Battle of Valcour Island in 1776. He also had served with Arnold at Saratoga, and had worsened Arnold's feud with General Gates through his loose talk. But he had done much for Arnold after Saratoga, and he was a frequent bedside visitor as the general slowly recovered from his devastating wound.[362]

Franks and Varick knew Arnold well, so well that they became increasingly suspicious of his secretive behavior at Robinson House. Varick, less familiar than Franks with Arnold's questionable financial transactions, objected to Arnold's attempts to profit from his government-issued provisions. When the general tried to arrange for a ship captain to sell rum for him, Varick spoiled the plan by raising questions about whether the skipper was a Tory. Varick thought he had blocked Arnold's sale of three barrels of pork in a separate deal, but Arnold managed to complete the transaction anyway.

When Franks reached Robinson House with Peggy and her husband, Varick told him that Arnold had written "in a mercantile style to a person in New York whose fictitious name was John Anderson, to establish a line of intelligence of the enemy's movements." Franks replied that he thought Arnold had "corresponded with Anderson or some such name before from Philadelphia." Both of them thought it was a business scheme, they later testified.[363]

One of Peggy's key duties was to keep Franks and Varick off the trail, a task made easier by the fact that both aides were infatuated with her. When Arnold had asked Varick to join him at West Point, he had mentioned, "As this has the appearance of a quiet post, I expect Mrs. Arnold will soon be with me."[364] Varick responded: "The presence of Mrs. Arnold will certainly make our situation in the barren Highlands vastly more agreeable, and I am persuaded will more than compensate for every deficiency of nature."[365] Franks was particularly fond of Peggy, and during her short stay at Robinson House, he went into the country with her on long picnics, accompanied by a female attendant and a guard. Franks was so attentive to Peggy's needs, including what he called her "delicate" health, that he was nicknamed The Nurse.[366] Apparently Franks was especially susceptible to female charms. "I have marked him particularly in the company of women, where he loses all power over himself and becomes almost frenzied," Thomas Jefferson wrote a few years later when Franks was his aide.[367]

During Peggy's short time at Robinson House, she had set herself up as lady of the manor, making sure that supplies were in order and servants were on task. She served as hostess at meals for Arnold, Varick, Franks, and key officers from West Point. Sometimes Arnold's friend Joshua Hett Smith would bring his wife for visits, but often Peggy was the only woman around, except for the housekeeper and other staff. Of course, Peggy was comfortable and confident in male company.

There was a servant to help her with baby Edward, and this allowed her to go picnicking with Franks when she wasn't breastfeeding her six-month-old son. Women of that era generally nursed their babies to at least ten months, and, as an attentive mother, there's evidence that Peggy observed this practice.[368]

Even though she was trying to make a home for her husband and son in the Highlands, she knew not to settle in too comfortably. Indeed, the Arnolds' plot was picking up speed. On September 16, 1780, Peggy's husband received a confidential message from General Washington that he would be crossing the Hudson River at King's Ferry the next day on his way to Hartford, Connecticut, for a secret conference with senior French commanders. Arnold responded that he would meet Washington at the crossing, which was not far from where he had attempted to meet

André only days earlier. Arnold also sent a message informing André of Washington's whereabouts, though it is unlikely that he believed the letter could travel fast enough to allow the British to try to capture the commander in chief.

The next day, before Arnold left for King's Ferry, he and Peggy were in Robinson House with Smith and his wife, Varick, Franks, and West Point guests. While they were conversing, a courier brought a letter to Arnold delivered under a flag of truce from the British sloop-of-war *Vulture*, south of King's Ferry. The message was from Beverley Robinson. He said he wanted to meet with Arnold, and added: "I did intend in order to have your answer immediately to have sent this by my servant, James Osborn." Arnold knew that "James Osborn" was a code name for another J.O., Jonathan Odell, and this indicated that someone privy to the plot was aboard the *Vulture*.[369]

Arnold's guests were curious about the correspondence, and he felt compelled to explain that the Loyalist owner of Robinson House wanted to talk with him. One of the officers then suggested that Arnold discuss its propriety with Washington that night at King's Ferry, and when Arnold did, Washington told him not to meet with Robinson. Washington had other information critical to the Arnolds' plot: He expected to stop at Robinson House on his return trip the following weekend.

While Arnold was talking with Washington at King's Ferry—the last time the two would ever meet—his aide Varick was picking a fight with Smith over dinner at Robinson House. Varick considered Smith to be a "damn Tory and snake in the grass" who was probably involved in sneaky financial deals with Arnold.[370] When Smith suggested that the rebels could have reached an honorable peace deal with the crown two years earlier, Varick argued with him, creating a confrontation that likely forced Peggy to referee.

After Arnold returned from King's Ferry, he wrote a response to Beverley Robinson, but Varick complained that it "bore the complexion of one from a friend rather than one from an enemy."[371] Instead of taking offense, Arnold simply told his prickly aide to revise it as he wished. Arnold had a trick up his sleeve—in fact, two tricks. While Varick composed the official message, Arnold wrote two secret letters that would go in the same delivery to the *Vulture*. One was a copy of one of his previous messages to André. By sending it to the British under a flag of truce from Arnold, he would confirm the authenticity of the earlier message. The second letter was what Arnold really wanted to say to Robinson: "I shall send a person to Dobbs Ferry, or on board the *Vulture*, Wednesday night the 20th instant, and furnish him with a boat and flag of truce." Arnold added another critical piece of news: "I expect His Excellency General Washington to lodge here on Saturday night next."

Was Arnold suggesting that the British try to capture Washington as part of the plot? Or was he warning them to adjust the timing of their attack on West Point to avoid the heavier security that would attend Washington on his way through? Many historians tend to believe the latter scenario, but the idea that Washington was considered as a target cannot be entirely dismissed. This would mean that those traveling with him were in peril as well. They included the Marquis de Lafayette, an intrepid French nobleman who was vital to the alliance and had been given the rank of major general by Congress before he reached the age of twenty.[372] Also with Washington was one of his most trusted commanders, Brigadier General Henry Knox, who was head of the artillery corps and would later become secretary of war.[373] And there was Washington's young aide Alexander Hamilton, who would serve as the nation's first treasury secretary.

After the conspiracy was exposed, Washington wrote that he considered West Point and not himself to have been the target, explaining in a dispassionately tactical way: "I am rather inclined to think he did not wish to hazard the more important object of his treachery by attempting to combine two events, the lesser of which might have marred the greater."[374] Even so, it is intriguing to imagine what would have played out if the British had captured West Point, Washington, Lafayette, Knox, and Hamilton at the same time. The opportunity was there. And the results could have been devastating.

Arnold slipped his two secret letters into an envelope addressed to Chief Justice Smith, which was his way of telling the British that the justice's brother, Joshua Hett Smith, would appear on the twentieth to further the plot. He then quietly sneaked this into the package that contained the Varick-approved letter to Robinson, and all three were sent to the British warship. Soon after, Smith paid a discreet visit to Arnold and agreed to pick up the mysterious "John Anderson" from the *Vulture* on the night of Wednesday, September 20. Inexplicably, Arnold did not go downriver that night. Apparently he expected Smith to take the emissary back to his own home in Haverstraw, where he would wait for Arnold's visit the next day.[375] But just after dawn Thursday, a messenger arrived at Robinson House with bad news from Smith. The rendezvous had not taken place. Smith had failed to persuade an oarsman to row out to the *Vulture* and pick up Mr. Anderson.

Arnold hurried down to his barge and headed south. He didn't explain his plans to Varick and Franks, and they suspected he was off to join Smith in an unethical scheme to trade illegally across enemy lines. Arnold's two aides told each other they would quit if this were true and went to Peggy with their complaints about her husband's activities with "the unprincipled rascal Smith." She told them she shared their feelings and that, upon her own complaints, "Arnold had made her fair promises not to countenance Smith at all," according to Varick.

Peggy was lying, of course. Smith was central to their plans as a go-between with the mysterious Mr. Anderson. Peggy was trying to keep the aides at bay long enough for her husband to line up their secret forces, and then trigger a treason that might destroy the American Revolution.

CHAPTER 12

Meeting after Midnight

THAT NIGHT, WHILE HER HUSBAND TRIED TO MEET up with his British counterparts, Peggy Shippen had a simple mission: to keep Franks and Varick from open revolt while maintaining an air of innocence and normality at Robinson House. And she succeeded.

Peggy's husband and his henchman Smith, however, had much more to accomplish, and they did it far less skillfully. Arnold, hurrying downriver to make the connection that should have been made the night before, was met by two letters from the *Vulture*. One was from Beverley Robinson, who said he was "greatly disappointed in not seeing Mr. Smith at the time appointed" and added that "my partner . . . arrived here last night."[376] The other was a protest about one of the *Vulture's* boats being fired upon while under a flag of truce. The letter, purportedly from the ship's captain but countersigned "John Anderson, secretary," was in the handwriting of John André, the "partner" aboard the ship.

Now a major serving as the full-fledged adjutant general, André was far too important to be sneaking around on risky espionage missions, but he was doing it anyway. Frustrated that his second attempt at a face-to-face with Arnold had come to nothing, André waited aboard the *Vulture* for a third chance, writing Clinton that another failure would "infallibly fix suspicions" on Robinson as a person attempting to sabotage the mission.

Clinton had very explicit orders for how his favorite protégé was to safely execute this assignment. André was not to assume a disguise. He was not to cross into American-held territory. And he was not to accept documents. Any of those three actions would turn André from an emissary into a spy.[377]

⌒

While André waited anxiously aboard the *Vulture*, a low comedy was being performed on the western shore of the Hudson by the men to whom Arnold was entrusting his life and his career. Smith, who had failed to persuade one of his tenants to row him out to get André the night before, was at his home in Haverstraw when Arnold arrived by horse. Arnold arranged for a boat to be available for him, explaining to his military underlings that Smith had a chance to obtain important intelligence downriver.

Smith and Arnold then summoned a cow tender, Samuel Colquhoun, the tenant who had refused to help Smith fetch André the night before. Colquhoun said he was afraid of gunboats and was unwilling to go by himself, so he was sent to fetch his brother Joseph. Instead, Colquhoun returned alone, explaining that his wife had forbidden him to go.[378] Arnold thundered that if he refused to row the boat, he would be considered "a disaffected man," a traitor to the cause of independence. This time Colquhoun returned with his brother. They said they were willing to perform any task for Smith and Arnold—except rowing the boat to the *Vulture*.

More wrangling ensued. Smith emphasized that they would be traveling with passes signed by Arnold. The brothers questioned why a meeting with the British under a flag of truce was happening under the cover of night. Joseph took Arnold aside and told him he would prefer to make the trip the next morning. Arnold threatened to put Colquhoun under guard if he did not go that night.

The brothers sat on the stoop of Smith's house while Arnold and Smith conferred inside. Smith came out with whiskey for the brothers and a promise of fifty pounds of flour apiece. Finally, with vital hours wasted and midnight approaching, they agreed to row Smith to the *Vulture*.

Arnold gave them pieces of sheepskin to wrap around the oars to muffle the sound. The night was clear and moonless as Smith and the

Colquhoun brothers approached the Vulture in their longboat. "I was heartily assailed with a variety of oaths," Smith recalled, "all in the peculiarity of sea language, by the officer commanding the watch on the quarter-deck, and commanded instantly to haul alongside, or he would blow us out of the water."[379]

Smith came aboard, leaving the Colquhoun brothers to float nervously alongside. André was awakened, and he and Beverley Robinson greeted Smith. Arnold's passes mentioned only Smith, two servants, and one man accompanying him, so Robinson and André agreed that both of them could not go. The adjutant general heeded his commanding officer's orders against wearing a disguise, but pulled a large blue greatcoat over his regiment's uniform, effectively cloaking his identity. Smith said later that he initially thought "John Anderson" was a civilian.

Meanwhile, one of Smith's slaves led Arnold by horse to a remote dock two miles south of Haverstraw to await André's arrival, which came around 1 a.m. on Friday, September 22, 1780. Smith escorted André to the woods where Arnold awaited. And there Peggy Shippen's husband and her old friend met for the first time.[380]

Arnold wanted André to accompany him to Smith's house for their negotiations; André insisted on staying in that secluded spot along the Hudson shore, in an area that could be considered a no-man's-land. Arnold relented. They agreed that the price for bagging West Point with at least three thousand prisoners would be twenty thousand pounds. But they were in dispute over the price of failure. Arnold wanted ten thousand pounds guaranteed even if the scheme went sour; Clinton was willing to pledge six thousand. (Arnold insisted later that André had promised to urge his commander to pay the full ten thousand, but by that time André wasn't around to confirm or deny Arnold's claim.)

Their conference under the dark treetops lasted about three hours. Undoubtedly, they discussed the logistics of an attack on West Point and reached a general agreement. It's unknown whether they found time to talk about Peggy. There is little doubt she was thinking about them.

At about 4 a.m., Smith warned them that daylight was coming. But by then it was too late to get André back to the ship. The Colquhoun brothers insisted they were too tired for a return trip to the *Vulture*, and it may have been inadvisable anyway, because day was dawning. André agreed to ride with Arnold to Smith's house, to wait out the day and go back to the *Vulture* when night fell. He would later testify that he did not know he would have to cross a rebel checkpoint. But now he was behind enemy lines, with his uniform hidden. This did not bother Arnold, and was in fact what he had suggested all along. But it would prove to be disastrous for André.[381]

Unbeknownst to Arnold, a rebel colonel who was annoyed by the *Vulture*'s presumptuous position in the river had moved artillery within range of the ship. That morning at daybreak, the enterprising colonel ordered the firing to begin. The ship suffered no major damage and only one casualty (the ship captain was cut in the nose by a flying splinter). The real casualty was André, because the attack inspired the ship to flee south, out of the range of both the rebel cannon and—as it turned out—the British army's adjutant general.

André and Arnold watched the attack from an upstairs window at Smith's house. André still hoped he might be able to reach the *Vulture*, but the odds were getting longer. Arnold wrote three passes, one allowing André to be taken by boat downriver and the other two naming Smith and Anderson individually and allowing them to travel toward the British lines by land.

Smith, who had returned home separately from Arnold and André, arranged breakfast for them in an upstairs bedroom. When André took off his greatcoat, he revealed that he was wearing a British uniform. Smith later professed to be shocked by this, but said he believed Arnold's explanation that Mr. Anderson was a civilian who had borrowed the uniform from a New York acquaintance and liked to wear it now and then purely out of vanity.

This was not entirely out of the ordinary. Because clothing was in short supply during the war, civilians sometimes wore military clothing, even the clothes of opposing armies. But it remains difficult to understand how Smith, a lawyer, could have accepted such a ridiculous story, or could have believed that a person providing vital help to the Continental Army would be delivered by a British warship. In fact, Smith's role remains murky to this day. Given Smith's ultimate acquittal in court despite his deep involvement in the Arnolds' plot, some students of history wonder whether he might have been some sort of double agent, working for both the rebels and the crown. But there is no solid proof that he was anything more than a dupe. Guilty of either stupidity or treachery, Smith pleaded stupidity, and a military court agreed.[382]

Now John André was being left in the care of the stupid. As Arnold prepared to leave, he turned over a set of papers to André, including an accounting of West Point's troops and military supplies, information about the forts' weak points, and minutes from a recent council of war held by Washington. Arnold told André he might need to return to New York City overland. "I objected much against it," André wrote, "and thought it was settled that in the way I came I was also to return."[383]

Arnold departed for Robinson House, where Peggy would be eager to hear about his meeting with her friend André. Arnold had every reason to think that their plot would proceed apace, and that he and Peggy were only days away from a triumph that would make them prosperous and heroic subjects of the king.

André's confidence, however, was waning. Despite his demand to be taken back to the *Vulture*, Smith insisted that they would travel by land to British-held territory. And while André waited for the arrival of nightfall so that they could leave, Smith proved stunningly indiscreet. When a man stopped by to drop off two cows, Smith told him he wouldn't leave the house to inspect the bovines because he was busy hiding a secret confederate of General Arnold's upstairs.[384]

André finally resigned himself to making his way back to New York City by land. But such a journey would be doomed if he were dressed as a British officer. So he tossed off his scarlet coat and replaced it with a claret-colored one borrowed from Smith, covering it with the same blue greatcoat he had worn the night before. He topped off the outfit with the kind of round hat a civilian would wear. In his boots, he hid the papers he had received from Arnold. André had now disobeyed all three of Clinton's orders: He was in disguise, behind enemy lines, and carrying secret papers.

Smith and André waited for nightfall to set out by horse, accompanied by one of Smith's slaves, the same one who had guided Arnold to the western shore to meet André. Although this slave was a key witness to a disputed series of historical events, he was never publicly identified nor officially questioned.[385]

The three crossed the Hudson by ferry. As further proof of his lack of common sense, Smith decided to visit the same colonel whose artillery had chased away the *Vulture*. André waited on the road under the cover of night while Smith paid his respects, and they soon resumed their trip.

Later that night they were stopped by militiamen who demanded to see their passes. "Mr. Anderson seemed very uneasy," Smith recalled, "but I cheered him by saying our passes would carry us to any part of the country to which they were directed, and that no person dare presume to detain us."[386] While the militia leader accepted their passes, he urged them to stop for the night. The area, he reminded them, was infested with rival bands of highwaymen—Loyalist-leaning raiders known as Cowboys, and those with rebel sympathies known as Skinners. Both groups were more likely to shoot farmers or steal their cattle than to become engaged in a debate over the rights of man.

André wanted to push on until he reached the British lines, but Smith decided to heed the warning. At a nearby farmhouse, they found a bed to share. The apprehensive André kept his boots on. "I was often disturbed by the restless motions and uneasiness of mind exhibited by my bedfellow," Smith recalled. "He appeared in the morning as if he had not slept an hour during the night."[387]

In thick morning fog they set off again, but were soon stopped by a militia captain, who suggested they seek an escort from a nearby military unit. They declined and continued on their way, passing a rebel colonel going in the other direction. André recognized the colonel as a former prisoner of war in New York City. But the colonel seemed not to recognize André, and rode on.

Smith found André sullen at times, but as they rode through the beautiful countryside and enjoyed the arrival of autumn, his worries seemed to lift. "The pleasantry of converse and mildness of the weather so insensibly beguiled the time . . . and I now had reason to think my fellow traveler a different person from the character I had first formed of him," Smith wrote.[388] While they rode, they talked about music, painting, poetry, and the prospects for peace.

They stopped at a home along the road, where they found a Dutch housewife willing to offer them a meal. A group of Cowboys had robbed the family the day before, and all she had to offer was a mush made of Indian corn. New Yorkers called the dish suppon, while New Englanders knew it as hasty pudding and the English and Irish called it stirabout. In a poem André had written that year, he had mocked suppon, but now he ate it with gusto.[389]

After paying the housewife, Smith surprised André by declaring that he and his slave would accompany him no farther. The British officer was not alarmed. After all, they were near Tarrytown, New York, close to the informal border separating territories controlled by the British and the rebels. And so they parted pleasantly, after André borrowed a few Continental dollars and offered his gold watch as a sign of good faith. Smith let him keep it, asking only that he deliver a message to Smith's brother William, the chief justice, when he got back to New York City.

André expected to be in Manhattan soon to tell his comrades about the final arrangements for Arnold's betrayal, and then to join an invasion force to seize West Point and, if all went well, to end the war.

CHAPTER 13

A Capture and an Escape

THE WEEKEND ARRIVED AT ROBINSON HOUSE with a Saturday warm and fair.[390] Joshua Hett Smith arrived there, too, and was both warmly received and fairly despised. Smith brought encouraging news for Arnold: He had escorted Mr. Anderson past hundreds of rebel soldiers and delivered him to the doorstep of British-held territory.

Peggy and her husband knew their conspiracy was coming to a head. General Washington, who was expected at Robinson House shortly, sent word that he was delayed a few days but still planned to stop by to inspect West Point. The timing of the attack on West Point was undoubtedly discussed by Arnold and André in their middle-of-the-night meeting, but the details have been lost to the ages.

Smith's visit posed a problem for Peggy, who had led Franks and Varick to believe that the general would have nothing further to do with the "scoundrel." The tension culminated at a dinner featuring all the antagonists, plus some of the same officers who had witnessed the mealtime fracas a week earlier between Varick and Smith over whether Britain had offered an honorable peace.[391]

This time, the point of argument was more petty. There was a shortage of butter on the table, and Peggy asked a servant to bring more. The servant told her they were out, but Arnold offered a solution. "Bless me," he said, "I had forgot the oil I bought in Philadelphia. It will do very well with salt fish." Arnold remarked that it cost eighty dollars. "Eighty pence," quipped Smith, suggesting that a Continental dollar was worth no more than a penny. Varick told him he was wrong, and said it in as insulting a manner as he could summon. He later testified that he had been looking for an opportunity to be "cavalier with Smith."

The two began arguing bitterly, and Franks jumped in on Varick's side. Seeing Arnold become increasingly angry, Peggy "begged that the dispute might be dropped, as it gave her great pain," a witness recalled. A truce was declared. But after Smith left, Arnold argued furiously with his aides. "He declared that if he asked the devil to dine with him, the gentlemen of his family should be civil to him," Varick recalled. The fiery Franks declared that if Smith had been at a table other than Arnold's, Franks would have thrown a bottle at his head. Franks challenged Arnold to fire him, and he stormed out of the house, saying he was off to a nearby town on business.

Varick, who was more judicious, warned Arnold that associating with Smith would hurt his reputation. "Arnold then told me that he was always willing to be advised by the gentleman of his family, but, by God, would not be dictated to by them," Varick said. Later that night, Varick and Arnold talked further and seemed to make peace. "He gave me assurances of his full confidence in me," Varick said, "of a conviction of the rectitude of my conduct, of Smith's being a rascal, and of his error in treating me with such cavalier language, and that he would never go to Smith's house again and be seen with him but in company."

Like Peggy, Arnold was stalling for time. It might have worked but for the events now unfolding about twenty-five miles south of Robinson House, near Tarrytown.

———

While it was a bad night for Peggy and Arnold, it was a far worse one for John André. After parting company with Smith and his slave that morning, André had proceeded across Pine's Bridge, only fifteen miles from the British army's outpost at White Plains. He was in the so-called Neutral Ground of Westchester County, territory that was often patrolled by roving bands of Cowboys. Such irregulars would treat a British officer well, and André later said he thought he was "far beyond the points described as dangerous." [392]

He stopped at a well and took a cup of water from a twelve-year-old-girl, giving her sixpence in exchange. He then proceeded to a wooden bridge over a small creek, where he was challenged on the other side by three young men with muskets.[393] The biggest of them was outfitted in a green Jaeger coat, the kind worn by Hessian soldiers. André apparently took him for a Cowboy and sought to confirm that the three were members of "our party." The man in the Jaeger coat asked: which party? "The lower party," André said, using the slang term for the British in New York City.

When the man indicated that was the case, André felt confident enough to identify himself as a British officer and explain that he was on important business for General Clinton. He pulled out his fancy gold watch, a possession much more likely to belong to a British officer than an American.

The man in the Jaeger coat was rebel militia sergeant John Paulding, who had escaped from a British prisoner of war camp in Manhattan earlier that month. Paulding had acquired the Jaeger coat to help him get out of the city and return to his militia. He now seemed to be using it to fool enemies he met on the road, such as André.

Paulding ordered André to get down from his horse, and André realized he had guessed wrong. "My God, I must do anything to get along!" he said, and forced a laugh as if he had only been joking about being a British officer. He showed them the pass written by Arnold, and explained that he was on that general's business, not Clinton's.

In his theater work, André was known as a better backdrop painter than actor. His performance here did not move the militiamen. The three young men searched him, taking what little cash he had borrowed from Smith, as well as his gold watch and a silver one, too. In the stocking of one of his boots, they found the papers. Paulding was the only one of the three who could read, and he quickly realized that the information was of vital importance.

There are two versions of what happened next. If André is to be believed, he offered the militiamen at least five hundred pounds (more than eighty-five thousand dollars in today's currency) for his freedom, and suggested that one of them could take a letter from André to the nearest British outpost and come back with the ransom. André said the three men considered the offer but decided that if the British got such a letter, they would return in force, rescue André, and take them prisoner. If the militiamen are to be believed, they were determined to do their duty. "No by God!" Paulding said he told André. "If you would give me ten thousand guineas, you should not stir a step!"[394] In either case, André remained a prisoner.

The captors—Paulding, David Williams, and Isaac Van Wart—would later be held up as heroes of the revolution, honored at a dinner with General Washington, awarded farmland by the state of New York, and given a congressional award of two hundred dollars apiece every year for the rest of their lives. As time passed, however, some historians questioned whether the three were merely Skinners, rebel-leaning highwaymen in search of victims and loot. According to rebel spy chief Benjamin Tallmadge, who came to admire André, the three captors' "object was to rob him." But, in fact, they may well have saved their country.

As they led André on horseback to the headquarters of dragoons at North Castle, Williams struck up a conversation with the officer. Williams said André told him: "I would to God you had blown my brains out when you stopped me."

All was not lost just yet for André, however.[395] To his captors, he was a suspicious traveler named John Anderson. None yet knew he was one of the most important British officers in America. The men delivered him to a lieutenant colonel named John Jameson, an officer under Arnold's command who was a bit confounded with how to react to the facts at his disposal. He knew Arnold had ordered that if a man named John Anderson came through the lines he was to be sent to the general's headquarters at Robinson House. But this man was going through the lines in the other direction—toward New York City. And those papers found in his stocking had highly sensitive information. And the handwriting on the papers was the same as on Arnold's pass.

It seems obvious today that Jameson should have turned over everything to Washington, but that would have been insubordination against

Arnold and could have meant serious trouble for Jameson. So he hedged his bets: He sent the papers to Washington, but he dispatched André under guard to Arnold's headquarters along with a letter of explanation. "I have sent Lieutenant Allen with a certain John Anderson taken going into New York," Jameson wrote Arnold. "He had a pass signed with your name. He had a parcel of papers taken from under his stockings, which I think of a very dangerous tendency. The papers I have sent to General Washington."[396]

If André could get to Robinson House, he and the Arnolds might be able to escape to the British lines. This seemed to be André's only chance. But about an hour after André left for Robinson House, Tallmadge arrived at North Castle and discovered what Jameson had done. Instantly suspicious of Arnold, the rebel spymaster persuaded Jameson to countermand his order and prevent the prisoner's delivery to Arnold's headquarters. Jameson sent soldiers to catch up with André and his captors. "By some circumstances I have just heard," Jameson wrote, "I have reason to fear that a party of the enemy are above; and as I would not have Anderson retaken or get away, I desire that you would proceed to lower Salem with him and deliver him to Captain Hoogland."[397] But for some reason—perhaps an attempt to stay in Arnold's good graces—Jameson hedged his bets again: "You may proceed on to West Point and deliver the letter to General Arnold," he wrote to Lieutenant Allen. "You may also show him this, that he may know the reason why the prisoner is not sent on."

Thus a most consequential prisoner was sent to South Salem while documents "of a very dangerous tendency" were sent to Washington. Yet the general associated with all this perilous conduct was to get fair warning anyway.

By the time André arrived in South Salem on Sunday morning, September 24, he was described by the duty officer as a "reduced gentleman." Still identified as a civilian named Anderson, he decided that his only remaining chance at deliverance—and a long one at that—was to own up to his scheme and argue for its legitimacy under the rules of war. André asked for a pen and paper, and composed a letter to Washington. It was an exceptional piece of writing for André because, like his initial statements to the three militiamen who met him on the road to White Plains, it was wildly disorganized and inconsistent. Writing what may have been the most important letter of his life, André was incapable of settling on a tone and maintaining it.

First he admitted lying about who he was. "I am too little accustomed to duplicity to have succeeded," he wrote.[398] Then he insisted he was not trying to save his skin but only to rescue his honor, to "vindicate my fame" by demonstrating that he had not adopted "a mean character for treacherous purposes or self-interest." Finally, he delivered the big news: "The person in your possession is Major John André, adjutant general to the British army."

Suddenly turning lawyerly, he explained that he had meant to stay on neutral ground but was misled by Arnold into entering rebel territory. At that point, he said, he considered himself a prisoner who was justified in shedding his uniform and adopting a disguise so he could escape. "I was involuntarily an impostor," he asserted. He did not explicitly ask Washington for his freedom, but only pleaded to be "branded with nothing dishonorable"—to avoid the label of spy. But after throwing himself on Washington's mercy, he then threw down a clumsy threat. Citing the thousands of Continental troops captured at Charleston, André wrote: "Though their situation is not similar, they are objects who may be set in exchange for me, or are persons whom the treatment I receive might affect."

André's suggestion—that the Charleston captives might be harmed if he were—was unlikely to play well with Washington. The American commander had survived backbiting and threats from people who were supposedly on his own side. He was unlikely to flinch at such a cheap attempt at intimidation from an enemy, especially one who was in his army's custody. The only noble aspect of André's letter was its careful avoidance of any reference either to Peggy or to Smith, a position that would remain firm in the days André had left.

The courier who was sent to deliver the suspicious papers to the traveling Washington missed him on the road. He brought the papers to

South Salem, where André's letter was added to the packet and then set off anew for Robinson House, where the commander in chief was headed.

On Sunday, Peggy and her husband made preparations for Washington's arrival the next morning. Were they planning to help the British seize Washington at Robinson House, or did they simply intend to play host to the commander in chief and then usher him out of the area to make way for a British attack?

Franks had returned, and Varick was being attentively nursed by Peggy. As Varick later recalled, "That amiable lady . . . spent an hour at my bedside while I lay in a high fever, made tea for me, and paid me the utmost attention to my illness."[399] Such kindnesses, whether calculated or instinctive, would pay tremendous dividends in the hours to come, when the friendships Peggy had made were crucial to her fate.

The Arnolds retired Sunday night, unaware that two couriers were headed separately toward them in a race that neither knew about. Lieutenant Allen carried the letters to Arnold about John Anderson's capture; the other courier intended to give Washington the incriminating papers written in Arnold's hand, plus the confession penned by André.

A cool and fair Monday dawned in the Hudson Highlands.[400] Arnold visited his office, which doubled as Varick's bedroom. His aide was still sick in bed. Arnold asked him whether he had answered routine correspondence from Jameson and Tallmadge. When Varick said he had not and could not, Arnold said he would write to Tallmadge himself.

Washington meanwhile began his day fifteen miles northeast of Robinson House, where he was expected by breakfast. Washington took his time inspecting defensive positions along the Hudson. Washington's young French aide, the Marquis de Lafayette, was apparently far more eager to inspect Peggy. According to early-nineteenth-century histories, the general said: "Ah, Marquis, you young men are all in love with Mrs. Arnold. I see you are eager to be with her as soon as possible. Go and breakfast with her, and tell her not to wait for me."[401] Lafayette, perhaps embarrassed by Washington's teasing, remained in the general's traveling party. Two other Washington aides went ahead to Robinson House instead, and breakfasted with Arnold while Peggy remained upstairs.

During this meal the first of the two competing couriers arrived. Lieutenant Allen, who had started out with André nearly two full days earlier before giving him up in South Salem, now delivered the explosive correspondence to Arnold. The general read Jameson's words, and instructed the courier not to talk about the capture of John Anderson with anyone else. Then he went upstairs to see his wife.

Their brief conversation must have been whispered, and desperate. There was no doubt that their plot was about to be exposed to all, and that Washington would act quickly when he saw the documents. Arnold must have wondered whether Washington had seen them already, though his advance party hadn't let on over breakfast.

About two minutes after Arnold went upstairs, Washington's servant rode up to Robinson House. Quite likely the servant was a slave named Billy Lee, who was described by Washington as "my mulatto man" and who was so close to the general that he was included in paintings of him.[402] The servant informed David Franks that the commander in chief would soon arrive. "I went immediately upstairs and informed Arnold of it," Franks recalled. "He came down in great confusion, and, ordering a horse to be saddled, mounted him and told me to inform his Excellency that he was gone over to West Point, and would return in about an hour."[403] Arnold, of course, was not going to West Point, and he would not return to Robinson House in an hour—or ever. Another aide said Arnold displayed "an embarrassment and agitation so unusual that I knew not to what to attribute it."[404] He rode his horse to the riverside, unsaddled the bay, and hauled his saddle and two holstered pistols onto his barge.

His crew of nine were surprised when Arnold ordered them to row downriver rather than the two miles up to West Point. He told them he had a quick errand at Stony Point and then would hurry back to meet General Washington. If they rowed quickly, Arnold said, they would earn two gallons of rum.

But when they got to Stony Point, Arnold had a different destination. He explained that he was on a mission at Washington's behest to visit the British sloop *Vulture*, and the rowers pushed the boat forward. As they approached the ship, Arnold stuck a white handkerchief onto the end of his sword. The crew of the *Vulture* took Arnold aboard—a scene in which, as Thomas Paine later put it, "one vulture was receiving another."[405] Beverley Robinson was on deck to meet the new defector, and the first question he asked was about André. The news, of course, was bad.

Arnold then announced to his bargemen that he was shifting his allegiance to the enemy and would raise a Loyalist brigade. He urged them to change sides with him, and he promised a special position for the coxswain, the man who directed the crew and steered the barge. All nine declined. "One coat is enough for me to wear at a time," said the coxswain.[406] Arnold arranged for them to be taken prisoner instead. Nine captives instead of three thousand—an ignominious result for Arnold.

And an excruciating predicament for his wife back at Robinson House. For Peggy, it would be a torture, and a test.

CHAPTER 14

The Mad Scene

THE WORST MORNING OF PEGGY'S LIFE, the morning of irretrievable disaster, was spent with her six-month-old son in a quiet bedroom upstairs as bizarre events unfolded outside.[407] She had just sent members of the staff to fetch some peaches for her when Arnold came upstairs to share the disturbing news: Their plot had been discovered.[408] They discussed their future in a desperate two minutes before he fled, leaving her to wonder whether she would ever see him again.

Washington, arriving at Robinson House soon after, was told that Arnold had gone to West Point and that Peggy would remain upstairs for a time. The commander in chief was familiar with the house, having dined there as Beverley Robinson's guest in the past and having used the home as a temporary headquarters. He and his staff enjoyed an unhurried breakfast, oblivious to the treachery around them but likely disappointed by the lack of Peggy's company.

The much-admired hostess was in no condition to entertain gentlemen with small talk. She remained quietly upstairs with her baby boy, keeping her anguish to herself and biding her time while her husband made his escape.

After eating, Washington and his staff set off to visit Arnold at West Point. It was customary for the commander of the army to receive a cannon salute when he visited a fort. But at West Point there was no such greeting. There also was no Arnold. Nor were there completed earthworks. Nor improved barracks. Nor careful deployment of the troops, as would be expected if an enemy attack seemed possible at any time. In fact, the

Peggy Shippen, traitorous American and trusted mother. This drawing is based on a painting by Thomas Lawrence circa 1783. The child is Peggy's firstborn, Edward, whom she clutched as she raved madly after the conspiracy unraveled.

soldiers at West Point seemed surprised to see Washington, and the condition of the forts was a travesty. Washington's two-hour tour began with surprise, descended into alarm, and ended in outrage. "The impropriety of his conduct, when he knew I was to be there, struck me very forcibly," Washington recalled. "But I had not the least idea of the real cause."[409]

Across the Hudson, anxiety was spiking as well. Arnold's sudden departure from Robinson House—and his instructions to the courier not to discuss what he had brought—fanned a flurry of rumors. David Franks soon heard whispers about a spy named John Anderson being captured, and he roused Varick from bed to share the news. Franks was convinced that Arnold was involved in espionage, and they speculated on whether he had fled to the enemy or gone off to kill himself. But then they decided they had reached a rash and unfair conclusion, that they did not have enough evidence to besmirch the honor of a war hero. They resolved to withhold judgment.

A few minutes later the strange atmosphere grew even more peculiar as an event that became known as the Mad Scene unfolded at Robinson House. In an era when men used the term "hysteria" to marginalize women and when women displayed various forms of "hysteria" in desperate bids for empowerment, Peggy reacted to amazing events in an astonishing way. She suddenly, inexplicably, and loudly behaved as if she had lost her mind.

Many of the details of Peggy's behavior that day come from a letter that Varick wrote to his sister Jane soon afterward. At the top of the letter Varick advised, "Read this to yourself," indicating that the contents were not suitable for polite company. At one point he wrote, "I must stop this detail until I see you," suggesting that there was even stranger behavior that he chose not to commit to paper, and that history will never know.

Peggy's hysteria began while Washington was at West Point and Varick was still in his sickbed. Peggy asked the housekeeper to see how Varick was feeling, and "no sooner had the housekeeper turned her back" than Peggy ran after her, shouting in a bizarre fashion.[410] Varick heard shrieks and got up from his bed. He said he found Peggy in great distress, "with her hair disheveled and flowing around her neck; her morning gown with few other clothes remained on her, too few to be seen even by a gentleman of the family, much less by many strangers."

With Varick's high fever, the scene must have seemed like a hallucination to him. He described no more about her attire, or the lack thereof, leaving questions about whether this beautiful woman was baring herself to twist the minds of the men in her company.

She took his hand, gave him a "wild look," and asked, "Colonel Varick, have you ordered my child to be killed?" Falling to her knees and praying at his feet, she begged him to spare the child. He tried to get her to stand up, but she refused. David Franks ran in with West Point's physician, Dr. William Eustis. Together they carried her to her bed "raving mad" and in "utter frenzy," as Varick put it.

Varick stayed with her and tried to calm her down. She told him she had no friends left at Robinson House. He assured her that he and Franks were her friends, and that Arnold would soon be back from West Point with Washington. "No, General Arnold will never return. He is gone," she replied, pointing to the ceiling. "He is gone forever—there, there, there, the spirits have carried him up there. They have put hot irons in his head." She told him that the hot irons were bedeviling her too, and that only General Washington could take them away.

Varick and Franks must have felt as if they had hot irons in their own heads as well. Even before Peggy's hysterics, they had been afraid that Arnold was involved in some evil conspiracy. Now they could hardly think otherwise. They had to alert Washington that something terrible was happening with Arnold. But what?

As it turned out, there was no need. When Washington returned to Robinson House, he finally received the incriminating documents—the top-secret information about West Point in Arnold's handwriting and the confession from André. Washington dispatched Alexander Hamilton and another aide on horseback in a futile attempt to catch Arnold, who had a headstart of a few hours. Then he ushered Lafayette into a private room. "Arnold has betrayed us," Washington said quietly. "Whom can we trust now?"[411] Showing the papers to Lafayette, he surrendered to "an ungovernable burst of feeling, fell on his friend's neck and sobbed aloud," according to an account by politician and writer Robert Dale Owen after interviewing Lafayette many years later.[412] Lafayette recalled: "I believe this was the only occasion throughout that long and sometimes hopeless struggle that Washington ever gave way, even for a moment, under a reverse of fortune; and perhaps I was the only human being who ever witnessed in him an exhibition of feeling so foreign to his temperament." Washington soon recaptured control of his emotions. When he returned to his staff, Lafayette recalled, "not a trace remained on his countenance either of grief or despondency."

There was, however, plenty of despondency upstairs. Peggy's episode of insanity showed no signs of letting up. Dr. Eustis was so alarmed by her behavior that he pleaded with Varick and Franks to fetch Arnold. In a quaint eighteenth-century diagnosis, the doctor declared that if the general didn't return immediately, "the woman would die."

Thinking that one way to alert Washington to the overall crisis—if he didn't know about it already—would be to show him Peggy's condition, Varick told the commander in chief that his old family friend from Philadelphia was in distress and that she had asked to see him. Varick escorted him to Peggy's bedroom, then told her that General Washington was paying her a visit.

Clutching her baby to her breast, Peggy responded that the man before her was not Washington.[413] Washington assured her it was him. "No," Peggy said, "that is not General Washington. That is the man who was a-going to assist Colonel Varick in killing my child." Peggy again announced that Arnold had gone up through the ceiling. "There, there, there," she said, pointing skyward.

It is not clear whether Peggy was in the same state of undress in the presence of Washington that she had been with Varick. If she was, perhaps the Father of His Country was too discreet to have ever mentioned it.

When Washington went downstairs, he resisted making a general announcement that Arnold had betrayed the country. Only a few trusted aides such as Hamilton and Lafayette knew. Varick and Franks were left to their deep suspicions. Washington simply announced, "Mrs. Arnold is sick and General Arnold is away. We must therefore take our dinner without them."[414] Even under normal circumstances, Washington had a reputation as a miserable person to eat a meal with, owing to his inability to manage small talk. This dinner, with the future of the American Revolution in the balance, was even more excruciating. As Lafayette recalled: "Gloom and distrust seemed to pervade every mind."[415]

Washington soon received word from Hamilton that Arnold had escaped. Hamilton's dispatch included letters that Arnold had written to Washington and to Peggy from the safety of the *Vulture*. The letter to Washington cast Arnold's treachery in high-minded terms:

The heart which is conscious of its own rectitude cannot attempt to palliate a step which the world may censure as wrong. I have ever acted from a principle of love to my country since the commencement of the present unhappy contest between Great Britain and the Colonies. The same principle of love to my country actuates my present conduct, however it may appear inconsistent to the world, who very seldom judge right of any man's actions.

I have no favor to ask for myself; I have too often experienced the ingratitude of my country to attempt it. But from the known humanity of your Excellency, I am induced to ask your protection for Mrs. Arnold from every insult and injury that the mistaken vengeance of my country may expose her to. It ought to fall only on me. She is as good and as innocent as an angel and is incapable of doing wrong. I beg that she may be permitted to return to her friends in Philadelphia or to come to me, as she may choose. From your Excellency I have no fear on her account, but she may suffer from the mistaken fury of her country.[416]

Arnold also threw in a good word for his aides Varick and Franks and his friend Joshua Hett Smith, saying they were unaware of his conspiracy. But near the end of his letter, Arnold became a bit presumptuous. He asked Washington to send his clothes to him, offering to pay for them if necessary. And he signed the letter in a customary but absurd manner: "your Excellency's most obedient humble servant."

Many histories have reported that Washington forwarded Arnold's letter to Peggy unopened, which would indicate good manners to some and military incompetence to others. But in fact the letter was read by Washington's staff if not by the general himself. A copy written in the hand of Washington's secretary James McHenry resides in the Library of Congress. And it's clear that Arnold expected his letter to be read by others:

Thou loveliest and best of women,

Words are wanting to express my feelings and distress on your account, who are incapable of doing wrong yet are exposed to suffer wrong. I have requested the Excellency General Washington to take you under his protection and permit you to go to your friends in Philadelphia—or to come to me. I am at present incapable of giving advice. Follow your own intentions. But do not forget that I shall be miserable until we meet. Adieu—kiss my dear boy for me. God almighty bless and protect you.[417]

Arnold then offered a postscript: "Write me one line if possible to ease my anxious heart." Peggy indeed did so, in a letter dispatched to the British commander Clinton about a week later. Its contents are unknown.[418]

With Arnold's betrayal confirmed, Washington took decisive steps to protect West Point by calling in trusted units from nearby states and appointing Nathanael Greene as the forts' commander. Even before Washington's order, Hamilton had sent a message to Greene urging him to send troops to West Point. Washington placed Varick and Franks under arrest as a precaution. The two Arnold aides asked for official proceedings to clear their names, and indeed they were ultimately found blameless. Arnold had fooled them, just as he had fooled Washington.

And Peggy had fooled them too. All the men around Peggy seemed to unite around Varick's assessment of her as a "poor distressed, unhappy, frantic, and miserable lady." But had she truly taken leave of her senses?

Peggy had certainly thrown her share of fits, and some kind of emotional reaction to her husband's news seemed completely understandable that Monday morning. But this episode was the mother of all hysterical fits, so hallucinatory and over the top that it's difficult to believe it was a condition rather than a calculated piece of theater. And the fact that it didn't start until Washington had left to inspect West Point strongly suggests that it was a distraction aimed to give Arnold time to make good his escape.

Her husband had fled with the help of a barge and nine crewmen. Peggy had no similar means. She was stuck at Robinson House with her infant son. She had no choice but improvisation, no weapons but her wits. And so she brilliantly took advantage of gender expectations: The men around her were obligated to show chivalric concern for her suffering, and to avoid any rude questions about her husband's conspiracy. She played her role, and they played theirs. For Peggy, the Mad Scene was a great achievement, a virtuoso performance.

The next morning found the wife of the traitor subdued and more or less back to her usual self. She claimed not to remember what had happened the day before. While she was busy entertaining bedside visitors such as Hamilton and Lafayette who served as witnesses to her distress, John André was taken to Robinson House by a heavy guard under torrents of rain. There is no indication that Peggy saw him or even knew he was there. He was escorted to West Point later that day.[419]

There is no documentation that a Continental Army official ever asked Peggy a single question about whether she was aware of the conspiracy or had assisted it. Lafayette's account of that morning instead hints of a certain sexual fascination:

> *The unhappy Mrs. Arnold did not know a word of this conspiracy; her husband told her before going away that he was flying never to come back, and he left her lying unconscious. When she came to herself, she fell into frightful convulsions, and completely lost her reason. We did everything we could to quiet her; but she looked upon us as the murderers of her husband, and it was impossible to restore her to her senses. The horror with which her husband's conduct has inspired her, and a thousand other feelings, make her the most unhappy of women.*
>
> *P.S. She has recovered her reason this morning and as, you know, I am upon very good terms with her, she sent for me to go up to her chamber.*

General Washington and everyone else here sympathize warmly with this estimable woman, whose face and whose youthfulness make her so interesting. It would be exceedingly painful to General Washington if she were not treated with the greatest kindness. . . . As for myself, you know that I have always been fond of her, and at this moment she interests me intensely. We are certain she knew nothing of the plot.[420]

Washington reportedly declared that he had "every reason to believe she is innocent, and requests all persons to treat her with that humanity and tenderness due to her sex and virtues."[421] The official story was established before Peggy left Robinson House: One of America's finest flowers had been betrayed by the dastardly Arnold.

While Hamilton was no master of psychology, he was adept at publicity. His letter to his friend John Laurens about Arnold's treachery was published in American newspapers, increasing Hamilton's fame while providing a prominent defense for Peggy. "It was impossible not to have been touched with her situation," Hamilton wrote. "Everything affecting in female tears, or in the misfortunes of beauty; everything pathetic in the wounded tenderness of a wife, or in the apprehensive fondness of a mother; and, till I have reason to change the opinion, I will add, everything amiable in suffering innocence conspired to make her an object of sympathy to all who were present."[422] Even in a letter to Elizabeth Schuyler, the woman he would marry in a few months, Hamilton seemed a bit too interested in Mrs. Arnold. "She received us in bed with every circumstance that would interest our sympathy," Hamilton wrote. "Her sufferings were so eloquent that I wished myself her brother to have a right to become her defender."[423]

Peggy inspired that in men. It was one of her many great gifts. Another was her resilience. The woman who shrieked about her husband flying through the ceiling with hot irons in his head was impressively down-to-earth in a note she wrote to Varick the very next day: "You will be so obliging as to receive any monies which may be due to General Arnold and transmit the same to me."[424]

CHAPTER 15

Pariah of Philadelphia

IN AN ERA WHEN FEMALE INTELLIGENCE AND TALENTS were often dismissed, women held one advantage: They were rarely suspected of elaborate crimes.

Peggy's friend and protector David Franks believed she was too nervous and flighty to be trusted by Arnold as an accomplice. "In truth," he said, "she was subject to occasional paroxysms of physical indisposition, attended by nervous debility, during which she would give utterance to anything and everything on her mind. This was a fact well known amongst us of the general's family; so much so as to cause us to be scrupulous of what we told her or said in her hearing."[425] Franks offered a second reason why Arnold wouldn't have involved her in the plot: "He was, moreover, too well aware of her warm patriotic feelings. You know . . . how completely she was an American at that important period. . . . I can aver solemnly she was totally ignorant of his schemes."

The truth was that Peggy had socialized with British officers, maintained close friendships with outspoken Loyalists such as Becky Franks, and become an enemy of Philadelphia's radical independence movement. Yet one of her intimates believed that she was such an ardent Patriot that she would have turned in her husband for talking with the British? What a testament to Peggy's powers of personal manipulation.

Others embraced the too-flighty-for-treason argument. "The surviving members of the lady's family, some of them her contemporaries, are satisfied that the texture of her mind did not qualify her to be the confidante of such perilous secrets," a journal article in 1837 declared.[426]

A century after the events, her husband's biographer Isaac N. Arnold defended Peggy with the too-virtuous argument: "If Arnold had disclosed his plans to her," he wrote, "she would have been much more likely, prompted alike by her love and her clear perception of right, to have tried to have saved him from the commission of a fearful crime and a terrible blunder."[427]

Many judged her to be innocent using even simpler logic: She was a woman; therefore, she couldn't have done it. Elizabeth Ellet, the leading nineteenth-century biographer of revolutionary women, wrote that she was "utterly rejecting" the idea that Peggy could have instigated the plot, and declared that "all common principles of human action" were opposed to it.[428]

But really, the only way Peggy could have been ignorant of the plot is if she had tried hard to be oblivious; if she had passed on secret correspondence without any thought and written to André with nothing more in mind than sewing supplies. On the contrary, Peggy wanted to know every detail of everything in her life. She upbraided Arnold for not sharing enough court-martial information with her. And in her later letters to her father, her command of financial nuances is awe-inspiring. Peggy was many things, but she was no dupe. She was, however, perfectly cast as the suffering spouse.

When the plot was exposed, American diplomat John Jay wrote from Madrid: "All the world here are cursing Arnold, and pitying his wife."[429] "Poor Mrs. Arnold!" exclaimed Robert Morris, a family friend of Peggy who now felt free to denounce her husband. "Was there ever such an infernal villain!"[430]

Washington gave Peggy the choice of crossing the battle lines with her child to join her husband in New York City or returning to her family in Philadelphia. She chose Philadelphia, a decision that cemented her admirers' view that she was true to the American cause and appalled by her husband's betrayal.

The reasons behind her decision were never explained. In many cases when Loyalists went over to the British army, they left their wives behind to try to secure their property. It didn't always work out well—Joseph and Grace Galloway were a stark example—but sometimes it did. No one can say whether finances were a factor in Peggy's decision. Her family may well have been the deciding factor. The house on Fourth Street may have seemed like the only haven left.

But in choosing Philadelphia, was she rejecting Arnold? After all, she was only twenty years old. A divorce was virtually impossible under the laws of the time, but she could have simply stayed away from the man who had abandoned her at Robinson House. She could have built a separate life, and no one in America would have judged her harshly for it. Was that her intention? In the end, her only option would be to rejoin Arnold, but she couldn't have known that on the rainy Wednesday when she left Robinson House, where her greatest hopes had died. Hamilton and the others were probably sad to see her go. "She experienced the most delicate attentions and every friendly office, till her departure for Philadelphia," he wrote.[431]

Peggy, ever conscious of the little kindnesses bestowed on her, left the residents of Robinson House "a little tea, coffee, chocolate, sugar, Madeira wine, and some salmon and old spirits, as well as some biscuits of our private stores for our use," Varick recalled.[432]

Though Franks was technically under arrest, he was assigned to accompany Peggy to Philadelphia—another sign that Washington believed the plot was isolated and Arnold's aides were uninvolved. As Peggy headed for Philadelphia with her baby, nurse, servant, and Franks, the news of her husband's treason preceded her. People along the way treated Peggy and her party as lepers, refusing to share supplies or shelter. The travelers were forced to push ahead through a rainstorm.

In Kakiat, New York, they finally encountered a man named Reed—most likely no relation to Peggy's enemy Joseph Reed in Philadelphia—who welcomed them for the night.[433] "Mr. Reed is the only man who would take us in at this place or give our horses anything to eat," Franks wrote Varick. "We got here, I very wet, Mrs. Arnold, thank God, in tolerable spirits; and I have hopes to get them home without any return of her distress in so violent a degree."[434]

Even during her miserable journey, Peggy continued to tend her relationships with powerful Patriots. Franks wrote Varick: "She expresses her gratitude to you in lively terms and requests you make her acknowledge-ments to his Excellency, to the Marquis, and to Hamilton, and indeed to all the gentlemen for their great politeness and humanity."

The next night's stop was at the Hermitage, an estate near Para-mus, New Jersey. Peggy was hosted by Theodosia Prevost (pronounced PRE-vo), a woman thirteen years her senior but in many ways strikingly similar.[435] Like Peggy, Prevost was a fifth-generation American born to privilege. The well-read Prevost spoke fluent French and proved herself the intellectual equal of the prominent men who surrounded her. Like Peggy, she had married young. At age seventeen, Prevost wed a Swiss-born lieutenant colonel serving in the British army in farflung locations such as the southern states and the Caribbean. Like Peggy, she achieved social standing with officers on both sides of the war. While married to a man loyal to the crown, she made close friends with champions of inde-pendence, such as James Madison, who would become president, and Aaron Burr, who would become both vice president and her husband. And like Peggy, Prevost was a survivor. Madison praised her "gaiety in the midst of affliction."[436]

By the time Peggy stopped at Hermitage in late September 1780, Prevost probably had started her love affair with Burr, though her mar-riage wouldn't end until the next year, when her husband died of yellow fever in Jamaica.

If Burr's memoirs are to be believed, Peggy felt comfortable enough with Prevost to unburden herself, to admit that she had been putting on a show. "As soon as they were left alone, Mrs. Arnold became tranquil-ized, and assured Mrs. Prevost that she was heartily sick of the theatrics she was exhibiting," Burr recalled. "She stated that she had corresponded with the British commander—that she was disgusted with the American cause and those who had the management of public affairs—and that, through great persuasion and unceasing perseverance, she had ultimately brought the general into an arrangement to surrender West Point to the British."[437]

Burr's memoirs, published posthumously in 1836 based on his recol-lections conveyed to longtime friend Matthew L. Davis, would renew a controversy over Peggy's role that many thought had been settled. Burr said that Prevost told him about the conversation with Peggy, but members of the Shippen family denounced it as a falsehood by Burr, and responded with a story of their own.

A Shippen family account, published six decades after Burr's memoirs, accused him of making a crude sexual pass at Peggy while he offered his help after Arnold's flight. "The tempter moved in serpent circles, ever smaller, around the intended victim," and when Peggy rejected him, he invented his story as revenge, the family claimed.[438]

Except that now we know that Peggy was indeed part of the plot. And the family claimed that Burr made his pass while taking Peggy to Philadelphia, but Franks was with Peggy at that time. Perhaps the Shippens' eagerness to exonerate Peggy could have turned a mere suspicion about Burr into a full-fledged tale. It's quite unlikely to be true.

Which is not to say that Burr's memoirs weren't harsh. They were, even if one believed her guilty. The memoirs concluded that Peggy's only motive was greed. "Mrs. Arnold was a gay, accomplished, artful, and extravagant woman. There is no doubt, therefore, that, for the purpose of acquiring the means of gratifying an inordinate vanity, she contributed greatly to the utter ruin of her husband, and thus doomed to everlasting infamy and disgrace all the fame he had acquired as a gallant soldier at the sacrifice of his blood." A more charitable and accurate view would be to see Peggy as a helpmate whose plot would have succeeded if all of her accomplices—including her husband—had been as cunning and efficient as she was.

When Peggy returned to Philadelphia in late September 1780, endorsements of her virtue by Washington, Lafayette, and Hamilton were fresh in the public mind. Her mad scene had established the story line of woman as wounded innocent. All would have been well, except that she was returning to a place where the politicians were writing the story lines, not reading them. To Peggy, Philadelphia was home. But it was also the epicenter of anger toward the British and all who would help them, especially Arnold.

While Peggy was en route home, Philadelphians paraded her husband in effigy. On that Thursday, a day after news of his treachery reached the city, a papier-mâché version of Arnold was marched to a gallows and hanged. Then Charles Willson Peale, the radical who painted portraits of many of the Founding Fathers and became known as the Artist of the Revolution, organized a more theatrical demonstration for the coming weekend.[439] A life-size version of Arnold was built, with two faces that rotated. He was dressed in a military uniform and seated on a cart, reflecting the image that Philadelphians had of him as a carriage rider rather than a horse rider because of his wounded leg. In one hand he held a mask and in the other "a letter from Beelzebub, telling him that he had done all the mischief he could do, and now he must hang himself," according to an account of the event in the *Pennsylvania Packet*.

Joining Arnold on the cart was another elaborately constructed character—the devil, with a pitchfork and a purse of gold to tempt the traitor. In the front of the cart was a lantern with transparent paper on which was written a description of his crimes and a picture of the devil pulling Arnold into the flames. The cartoon Arnold says, "My dear sir, I have served you faithfully." The devil responds, "And I'll reward you."

The cart was escorted by men on horseback, lines of Continental officers, militiamen with candles in the muzzles of their muskets, and "sundry gentlemen." Drummers and fife players performed "The Rogue's March." The effigy of Arnold was set aflame and reduced to ashes.

The West Point treason had vindicated the suspicions of Reed, Matlack, and the others about the general's questionable business deals and lavish spending while he was military governor of their city. William Church Houston, a member of Congress from New Jersey, reflected the common thinking that Arnold's decision was based solely on greed. "His dissipated and expensive course of living in this city has so involved and impoverished him that money was probably very necessary to him," Houston wrote.[440]

Authorities confiscated the Arnolds' property, including a "carriage almost new" and a "valuable negro man slave 22 years old."[441] Each sold for one hundred pounds sterling.

Reed, who had been embarrassingly short of evidence when he pursued charges against Arnold, had all the excuse he needed to dig deeper.

Patriots in Philadelphia hold a parade featuring a two-faced effigy of the traitor Arnold, with the devil behind him. FOTOSEARCH/GETTY IMAGES

His government directed "an immediate seizure of all Arnold's papers," the *Pennsylvania Packet* reported. "Though no direct proof of his treachery was found, the papers disclose such a scene of baseness and prostitution of office and character as it is hoped this new world cannot parallel."[442] The papers revealed details of Arnold's secret business deals, and also included a mean-spirited note that Peggy had once written to Arnold describing a concert attended by French officials and their ladies. Peggy's brother-in-law Neddy Burd, who learned of the note's contents, wrote: "She is free in her observations upon several of the ladies there and . . . has given them much offense."[443]

But the most devastating discovery in Reed's search was an innocent-sounding letter from a source suddenly bathed in guilt. It was the Millinery Letter, written by John André, currently held prisoner as an accused spy. "André, under the mask of friendship and former acquaintance at Meschianzas and balls, opens a correspondence in August, 1779, with Mrs. Arnold, which has doubtless been improved to the dreadful and horrid issue we have described," the *Packet* reported, assuming incorrectly that the Millinery Letter had been the first communication in the plot.

The newspaper argued that Peggy bore some of the blame, and denounced "the dangerous sentiments so frequently avowed in this city, that female opinions are of no consequence in public matters." The article even noted how women had influenced the history of ancient Rome, citing "the Clelias, the Cornelias, and Anias of antiquity." Peggy had no interest in becoming a famous female in history, especially not under these circumstances. The systematic destruction of her correspondence by family and friends was designed to do just the opposite—to obliterate any evidence that might incriminate her, and in essence to obliterate her story.

The Millinery Letter somehow survived and increased suspicions about Peggy, but it was hardly enough proof to justify the arrest of a woman who was so personally popular and who came from such a prominent family. It was certainly enough, however, to put tremendous pressure on that family, and to inspire demands that she be banished from the city.

"The family has been in the deepest distress, and how long it may continue I cannot foresee," wrote Neddy Burd. "If Mrs. Arnold shall be sent off to her base husband, it will be a heartbreaking thing."[444] Burd was convinced of Peggy's innocence, and adopted a version of Franks's too-flighty defense that might be called the too-timid defense. "The impossibility of so delicate and timorous a girl as poor Peggy in being in the least privy or concerned in so bold and adventurous a plan is great, and it is impossible she should be engaged in such a wicked one."

Peggy was an emotional wreck when she arrived back in Philadelphia, and surely that was not entirely an act. "Her spirits being quite exhausted, she fell into a kind of stupor from which she is not yet recovered and has not shed a tear for six days past," Burd reported. "She keeps [to] her room and is almost continually on the bed. Her peace of mind seems to be entirely destroyed."

The family tried to reach a deal with authorities: If they let her stay, she would pledge not to write to her husband, and she would turn over any correspondence from him to the Supreme Executive Council. Peggy's father made an explicit promise to the council, and submitted a paper signed by Peggy attesting to it. He even appealed to the Council to save her soul, warning that if she were forced to live with Arnold, her mind would "be debased, and her welfare, even in another world, endangered by his example."[445]

His pleas fell on deaf ears. "The Council seemed for a considerable time disposed to favor our request, but at length have ordered her away," Burd wrote.[446]

The order came on October 27, 1780:

The Council, taking into consideration the case of Mrs. Margaret Arnold (wife of Benedict Arnold, an attainted traitor, with the enemy at New York), whose residence in this city has become dangerous to the public safety; and this board being desirous, as much as possible, to prevent any correspondence and any intercourse being carried on with persons of disaffected character in this state and the enemy at New York, and especially with the said Benedict Arnold, therefore, resolved, That the said Margaret Arnold depart this State within fourteen days of the date hereof, and that she do not return again during the continuance of the present war.[447]

And so Peggy was declared an enemy of the people, and she prepared to leave Philadelphia. There was only one world that she knew, and she had been cast out of it. She had no viable option but to join her husband in New York City.

Had she intended to rejoin Arnold all along? Had her return to Philadelphia been a mere detour, an attempt to establish her innocence, with an eye toward a reunion with Arnold later? Her father, who seemed to be the closest person in her life if Arnold was not, had pleaded with her to forget about Arnold. "If she could stay, Mr. Shippen would not have wished her ever to be united to him again," Burd wrote.[448]

But she could not stay. And she would be united with Arnold. Because, in the end, Peggy really had no choice.

175

CHAPTER 16

The Three Fates

To Peggy's family, it was the bitterest of surrenders. Her mother, her siblings, and her cousins said their farewells to Peggy and her infant son. Her father endured a longer goodbye, helping his youngest daughter and his grandson into his carriage and taking them out of Philadelphia.

Peggy was an exile, and her family was crushed by this fact. "I cannot bear the idea of her reunion," wrote brother-in-law Neddy Burd. "The sacrifice was an immense one at her being married to him at all. It is much more so to be obliged, against her will, to go to the arms of a man who appears to be so very black."[449]

But Peggy was fading to black as well, at least as far as her family was concerned. She was leaving to start a new life in New York as the wife of an American traitor. Perhaps the only comfort for Peggy was the idea that her departure would make it easier on her family. Indeed, standing beside Peggy could be downright dangerous for the rest of the Shippens.

Englishman George Grieve, a gossipy writer of the era, went so far as to suggest without any apparent evidence that Peggy's two sisters—presumably the unmarried ones, Sarah and Mary—might have helped tempt Arnold toward evil. "Mrs. Arnold is said to be very handsome," Grieve wrote, "but this I know, that her two sisters are charming women, and must have been very dangerous companions for a wavering mind, in the least susceptible of the most powerful of passions. But an apology for Arnold, on this supposition, is too generous for a mind so thoroughly base and unprincipled as his."[450]

Yet the Shippen family had survived scandals in the past, and would survive this one as well. About a decade after the conspiracy was exposed, Peggy's father would be named to the Pennsylvania Supreme Court, and would ultimately serve as chief justice.[451]

The Marquis de Chastellux, a major general with the French expeditionary force, attended a high-society party with Peggy's cousin Nancy Shippen, daughter of Dr. William Shippen, less than a month after Peggy's banishment. And he remarked on Americans' lack of collective blame: "Thus we see that in America the crimes of individuals do not reflect upon their family; not only had Dr. Shippen's brother [actually first cousin] given his daughter to the traitor Arnold, a short time before his desertion, but it is generally believed, that being himself a Tory, he had inspired his daughter with the same sentiments, and that the charms of this handsome woman contributed not a little to hasten to criminality a mind corrupted by avarice, before it felt the power of love."[452]

Peggy and her father found temporary respite from the whispers and speculation as they made the lonely and grim trip across New Jersey. He delivered her to the British fort at Paulus Hook (now Jersey City, New Jersey), across the Hudson from Manhattan. Arnold was not there on November 14, 1780, to greet them, since it was too close to the front lines and the British could not risk having their new defector captured. It is difficult to imagine that Arnold would have looked forward to facing Peggy's father at that time anyway. After making her farewell, Peggy and her son crossed into New York City and were reunited with Arnold within the hour.[453]

Meanwhile, Peggy's sister-in-law Hannah had left Philadelphia for the family's house in New Haven, taking along Arnold's son Henry and summoning Arnold's two oldest sons, Benedict and Richard, from their school in Maryland.[454]

Arnold joined the British army and was charged with raising a Loyalist regiment. He was given the rank of brigadier general, a demotion from his position as major general in the Continental Army. Still, it was more than many British officers thought he deserved, though they were discreet about where they expressed that opinion. Official support for Arnold was part of the British face-saving effort in the wake of John André's capture. And there were those who believed that this brilliant tactician might prove useful to a British military leadership that sometimes seemed timid about leaving the island of Manhattan.[455]

There was yet a third reason for the British in New York to express pleasure in Arnold's arrival: To some it signaled the death throes of the independence movement. According to a common saying in the city at the time, "The ship must be near sinking when the rats are leaving it."[456] Among the pro-British officials who allied themselves with the defector was New York chief justice William Smith, whose brother Joshua had inadvertently helped derail the West Point conspiracy. Justice Smith thought Arnold's presence might prod General Clinton into a more lively pursuit of the war.

Together Smith and Arnold wrote two open letters to Americans, published in the *Royal Gazette*. The title of the second one fairly advertised its contents: "Proclamation by Brigadier General Arnold to the officers and soldiers of the Continental Army who have the real interest of the country at heart, and who are determined to be no longer the tools and dupes of Congress and of France."[457] But one thing that title didn't signal was the virulent anti-Catholic pitch he would make. Referring to members of Congress attending the funeral for Don Juan de Miralles, a Spanish envoy in Philadelphia, Arnold produced some paranoid prose: "Do you know that the eye which guides this pen lately saw your mean and profligate Congress at mass for the soul of a Roman Catholic in purgatory and participating in the rites of a church against whose anti-Christian corruptions your pious ancestors would have witnessed with their blood?"[458]

Religious appeals by a man like Arnold were unlikely to hold sway, but he also made promises of attractive pay and commensurate rank for those who joined his new Loyalist regiment, the American Legion. Arnold seemed to think other high-ranking members of the rebel army might, like himself, have a price.

Benjamin Tallmadge, whose intervention had prevented André's delivery into Arnold's hands after his capture, received a letter from the traitor inviting him to defect with "as many men as you can bring over with you."[459] "As I know you to be a man of sense," Arnold wrote, "I am convinced you are by this time fully of opinion that the real interest and happiness of America consists in a reunion with Great Britain." Tallmadge gave the letter to Washington, and described himself as "mortified" that Arnold would consider him open-minded about treason.

But Arnold was such a poor judge of character that he even thought the commander in chief could be recruited. "A title offered to General Washington might not prove unacceptable," Arnold wrote to Lord George Germain, Britain's secretary of state for the colonies.[460]

In the end, Arnold's recruitment efforts proved underwhelming. As one British officer wrote, Arnold's goal was to "raise a regiment of as great scoundrels as himself, if he can find them." But as it turned out, he couldn't.[461]

Despite doubts about Arnold's value to the British, his new government kept its side of the bargain. He was paid six thousand pounds for failure, as agreed by Clinton and André. But Arnold kept pressing his offensive by asking for ten thousand.[462] "When you consider the sacrifices I have made . . . the sum is a trifling object to the public, though of consequence to me, who have a large family that look up to me for support and protection," Arnold wrote Clinton.[463] The final sum granted was the six thousand pounds, plus 315 pounds in expenses. That is roughly equivalent to one million dollars in today's currency.[464] The British—unlike the Americans—paid their high-ranking officers with regularity, so Arnold would receive an additional 650 pounds a year in military pay, and half of that when he retired.

Arnold's three eldest sons also benefited. Benedict, age thirteen, was commissioned in November as a British ensign. The next October, twelve-year-old Richard and nine-year-old Henry won commissions as lieutenants in their father's regiment, though they were not expected to serve immediately. All three were entitled to salaries or half-pay pensions for life. Yet Arnold was never satisfied. He wrangled for nearly five years over various details, including his cockamamie claim that the British should pay him extra because his defection had cost him a chance for the rebel command in South Carolina. Arnold noted that the man who got the job instead, Nathanael Greene, had received twenty thousand pounds from Virginia and the Carolinas. Arnold thought the money should have been his, and he wanted the British to make good on it. Never mind that Greene had been Washington's first choice for the appointment anyway, and that Greene spent much of the money to supply his army. The British said no.

According to historian Carl Van Doren, Arnold made more money from the war than any other American officer. But Patriots scorned the bounty of his treason. Benjamin Franklin wrote to the Marquis de Lafayette: "Judas sold only one man, Arnold three million. Judas got for his man thirty pieces of silver, Arnold not a halfpenny a head. A miserable bargainer."[465]

Meanwhile, Peggy also was trying to track down every last cent owed to her. In mid-September, André had sent two hundred pounds in earnest money to cover "expenses" to the Arnolds in Philadelphia via a courier. But Peggy had already left for Robinson House, and the money didn't reach them. Ever the hardheaded money manager, Peggy hunted down and collected the two hundred pounds in New York City in January 1781.

Peggy, Arnold, and little Edward, who was nicknamed Neddy in the Shippen tradition, settled in a stately town house in Lower Manhattan next to British headquarters and across from Bowling Green Park.[466] The notorious couple endured stares and rude judgments, but they had their money, and they had their safety.

━ ⌒ ━

Not so for the third figure in the grand conspiracy. On the same day that Peggy left Robinson House for Philadelphia, John André was taken from West Point to Stony Point by barge, accompanied by Benjamin Tallmadge.[467] André, with his usual geniality, struck up a conversation with Tallmadge as they floated downriver. The prisoner pointed out the spot where the British would have landed, and described how he would have taken personal command of the invasion force, leading it up a mountain and around to the back of Fort Putnam to overwhelm the garrison. "The animation with which he gave the account, I recollect, perfectly delighted me, for he seemed as if he were entering the fort, sword in hand," Tallmadge wrote.[468]

After they transferred to horseback for the rest of the journey to Washington's headquarters in Tappan, New York, André asked Tallmadge how he thought he would be treated by Washington, or by a military tribunal if there was one.

By Tallmadge's written account, this is what he told André: "I had a much-loved classmate in Yale College by the name of Nathan Hale who entered the army in the year 1775. Immediately after the Battle of Long Island, General Washington wanted information respecting the strength, position, and probable movements of the enemy. Captain Hale tendered his services, went over to Brooklyn, and was taken just as he was passing the outposts of the enemy on his return. Do you remember the sequel of this story?"

"Yes," André said. "He was hanged as a spy. But you surely do not consider his case and mine alike."

"Yes," said Tallmadge, "precisely similar, and similar will be your fate."

Washington, now at Tappan, received letters from Clinton and Arnold arguing that André had operated under a flag of truce in good faith, and that all his actions had been at the direction of a senior American officer—Arnold. Hence, they said, André should be freed immediately. But Washington was not buying it. To help him determine André's fate, he appointed an advisory board that included Knox, Lafayette, and Robert Howe, the former commander of West Point who had presided over Arnold's court-martial.

No witness but André testified at the board's hearing. And the prisoner did not claim he was protected by a flag of truce. Rather, he admitted going behind enemy lines, disguising himself, and carrying secret papers, but said he had done so unwittingly.

Members of the board were impressed with his dignified manner, his straightforward answers, and the fact that he said nothing against the other suspect in custody, Joshua Hett Smith. But the board saw no alternative to recommending death. André was a spy, and death was the proper punishment for spies. Washington endorsed that view and scheduled André's execution for the next day, October 1.

André was helpless, except for one remaining weapon: his charm. During his imprisonment he became fast friends with several rebel officers, who advocated for him in his final days and praised him when those days were done. Even Tallmadge, who had told André bluntly en route to Tappan that he faced the hangman, had been recruited into the fan club: "He has unbosomed his heart to me, and indeed, let me know every motive of his actions so fully since he came out on his late mission that he has endeared himself to me exceedingly," Tallmadge wrote. "Unfortunate man! ... Had he been tried in a court of ladies, he is so genteel, handsome, polite a gentleman that I am confident they would have acquitted him."[469]

Alexander Hamilton seemed almost as fascinated with André as he was with Peggy Shippen. He wrote his fiancée, Elizabeth Schuyler: "I wished myself possessed of André's accomplishments for your sake, for I would wish to charm you in every sense."[470] Hamilton was so sympathetic toward André that he was strongly suspected of being the man who slipped a secret note into a packet that Washington sent to Clinton. The American commander was informing his British counterpart that André had been given a death sentence, but the secret note suggested that the Americans were willing to trade André for Arnold.

As tempting as that offer was for Clinton, it was also impossible. The British campaign to lure defectors would lack all credibility if they started giving them back. But Clinton did send a group of officers to meet with rebel leaders, and Washington delayed André's execution for a day so they could hear what the British had to say. Some of André's admirers thought a window had been opened by the postponement, but they were wrong. The British emissary simply repeated the argument about the flag of truce, and the Americans rejected it, while raising the idea of an André-for-Arnold swap. The British could not do that, but they said they were willing to free any prisoner in their custody. The Americans wanted Arnold or no one. The stakes were simply too high to allow any deal to be made. Threats, however, were in adequate supply. The British emissary noted that Clinton had never executed a rebel prisoner for violating the rules of war but had "many" captives in hand who might face that fate.

Peggy's husband, who had done as much as anyone to endanger her friend and set the stage for his capture, jumped into the discussion with all the subtlety of a twenty-four-pound cannon, and to much less effect. If André were killed, Arnold wrote Washington, he would personally "retaliate on such unhappy persons in your army as may fall within my power," and he also suggested that forty South Carolinians might be put to death in "a scene of blood at which humanity will revolt."[471]

By this time André knew better than to make threats. He wrote Washington a far more polite and eloquent letter, pleading to be shot to death like a soldier rather than hanged as a spy. "Buoyed above the terror of death by the consciousness of a life devoted to honorable pursuits, and stained with no action that can give me remorse, I trust that the request I make to your Excellency . . . will not be rejected," André wrote. "Sympathy toward a soldier will surely induce your Excellency and a military tribunal to adapt the mode of my death to the feelings of a man of honor."[472]

Washington, who avoided meeting or even seeing André for the four days he was in Tappan, did not respond to the request. Hamilton made his own appeal to Washington to spare André from hanging, but to no avail.[473]

André's manservant had been allowed to visit from New York City to bring linen and a clean uniform, and to shave his master's beard and powder and dress his hair. The prisoner passed the time talking with his fascinated guards and drawing sketches, including a self-portrait.

On the morning of Monday, October 2, Washington's adjutant informed André that his execution was set for noon, and the prisoner's servant fell into sobs. "Leave me until you can show yourself more manly!" André told him.

André then enjoyed breakfast from Washington's table, with the general absent. The condemned man's theater training was having a final benefit: He projected an image of calm to all those who saw him. After breakfast, André dressed and conversed with his two guards about their families until Washington's adjutant returned, ready to take the prisoner on his final walk.

FAC-SIMILE OF MAJOR ANDRE'S MINIATURE,

DRAWN BY HIMSELF, OCTOBER 1, 1780, THE DAY PRECEDING HIS EXECUTION.

Taken from the original in Trumbull Gallery, Yale College.

CERTIFICATE.

The above copy of the original portrait of Major Andre, by himself, and now in the Trumbull Gallery, appears to me to have been correctly made. B. SILLIMAN.

Yale College, August 9th, 1834.

CORRESPONDENCE.

NEW HAVEN, August 8th, 1832.

To Jeremiah Day, D. D., President of Yale College.

DEAR SIR,—It affords me pleasure, as the agent of Jabez L. Tomlinson, Esq., of Stratford, (the father of our late Governor,) and of Nathan Beers, Esq. of this city, to request your acceptance of the accompanying miniature of Major *John Andre*, Adjutant General of the British army during the revolutionary war. The melancholy fate of that accomplished gentleman excited such universal grief in the hearts of his countrymen, and such undisguised sympathy in the breasts of his foes, that it is presumed this memorial may be viewed with interest, and be deemed worthy of preservation among the historical collections of the college. Although the gift, without some explanation, might appear to be trivial, yet it possesses an *incidental value* that renders it truly interesting.

It is the likeness of Major Andre, seated at a table in his guard room, drawn by himself with a pen, on the morning of the day fixed for his execution. Mr. Tomlinson informs me that a reprieve was granted until the next day, and that this miniature was in the mean time presented to him, (then acting as officer of the guard,) by Major Andre himself. Mr. Tomlinson was present when the sketch was made, and says it was drawn without the aid of a glass.

The sketch subsequently passed into the hands of Deacon Beers, a fellow officer of Mr. Tomlinson on the station, and from thence was transferred to me. It has been in my possession several years.

While the high character of the officers who have preserved since the revolution this interesting memorial of a lamented victim to the necessary usages of war, places its genuineness beyond doubt, it may be remarked that its accuracy as a likeness is rendered probable, from the circumstance that Major Andre was accustomed to delineate, as an amusement, the outlines of his face and person.

The London edition of Joshua Smith's narrative of Arnold's treason, and of his personal connection with Andre in his attempt to escape, has a frontispiece, exhibiting the likeness of Major Andre. It is noted by the engraver as a copy from a portrait by Major Andre himself, now (or then) in the possession of his relatives in England. I have compared the sketch with that engraving, and thought that I could discern in the outlines a striking similarity.

Mr. Tomlinson and Mr. Beers were officers in the regular line of the army at the time of Major Andre's execution. I believe they severally held the rank of lieutenant.

With great respect,

Your friend and obedient servant,

EBENEZER BALDWIN.

YALE COLLEGE, August 10th, 1832.

Dear Sir,—Permit me, for myself and the guardians of the college, to express to you, and to the venerable revolutionary officers, J. L. Tomlinson, Esq., and N. Beers, Esq., my grateful acknowledgments for the miniature of Major J. Andre, generously presented to the institution. A memorial of one whose melancholy fate has long been contemplated with tender emotion, derives an additional interest from the fact that his name is associated with one of the most critical periods in the history of our glorious struggle for independence. Our possession of it at the present time will perhaps be the more highly appreciated, from the circumstance that the college is just now making arrangements for the preservation and exhibition of other monuments of revolutionary characters and events.

With affectionate regard,

Your friend and servant,

JEREMIAH DAY.

Ebenezer Baldwin, Esq.

As John André awaited the gallows, he sketched this self-portrait.
SELF PORTRAIT (THE DAY PRECEDING HIS EXECUTION), YALE UNIVERSITY ART GALLERY, GIFT OF WILLIAM S. REESE, B.A. 1977

The village of Tappan was swarming with soldiers and other onlookers—at least five hundred, and perhaps thousands. As André stepped outside the stone tavern that was his jail, he linked arms with his two guards. It was warm for October, and André was oddly sunny, flashing what one witness described as "a complacent smile."

A black coffin sat on a flatbed wagon. He was invited to ride on the wagon to the execution site, but preferred to walk. Escorted by a fife-and-drum band playing the "Dead March" and rows of soldiers four abreast, André strolled past a church and up a hill. André, ever a master of the compliment, turned to them and said: "I am much surprised to find your troops under so good discipline, and your music is excellent."

But when he reached the top of the hill and stepped into a field crowded with sightseers, he saw the gallows. "Gentlemen, I am disappointed," he said. "I expected my request would have been granted." Even so, he kept walking toward his place of death. "I am reconciled to my death but not to the mode," he said.

A freshly dug grave was covered in canvas so as not to upset the condemned prisoner. But the tenor of the crowd was soaked with emotion. Many in attendance wept, but not André.

Tallmadge stepped out of the throng at André's behest, and the two new friends shook hands. As Tallmadge later put it, "I became so deeply attached to Major André that I can remember no instance where my affections were so fully absorbed in any man."

The fatal pageantry seemed perfect for the era—it was suffused with bravery, honor, tradition, and terrible waste. For some witnesses, it was a ceremony of sad sacrifice; for others, it was a historical event with great entertainment value. Witnesses later described André in lavish terms, noting the flush of his cheek, the handsomeness of his hair, and that strange yet admirable smile.

The wagon with the coffin pulled underneath the gallows. André's death sentence was read, and he stepped into the wagon, and atop the coffin. He took off his three-cornered hat and laid it on the coffin. Then he put his neckcloth in his pocket and turned down his collar. "It will be but a momentary pang," André declared, speaking to himself as much as to anyone else.

By tradition, the hangman smeared his own face with soot in order to hide his identity. Anonymity was an especially good idea in this case: The executioner was a Loyalist prisoner who had agreed to hang André in order to earn his freedom.

André took the noose away from the man and dropped it over his own head. Then André tied a white handkerchief around his eyes. Asked whether he had any final words, André pulled up the handkerchief and replied: "I pray you to bear me witness that I meet my fate like a brave man."[474]

A presiding officer ordered André's hands tied behind his back, and the prisoner provided a second handkerchief for that purpose. Then he put the blindfold back in place. The hangman whipped the horses and the wagon moved away. The thirty-year-old adjutant general of the British Army in America was no more.[475]

American soldiers and curious civilians stood in line to view the corpse, and a few hours later André was buried on that hill in Tappan, with Tallmadge, Hamilton, and Lafayette in attendance. Four decades later, the British government disinterred his remains and reburied them in a place of high honor at London's Westminster Abbey.

The news of André's death was delivered to New York City by his distraught servant, who had witnessed the hanging.[476] Clinton was disconsolate. "The horrid deed is done," he wrote. "Washington has committed premeditated murder; he must answer for the dreadful consequences." But Clinton, who undoubtedly wondered whether he could have done more to protect his protégé, added a statement he truly wanted to believe: "I cannot reproach myself in the least."

Arnold was at Chief Justice Smith's home when the news arrived, and he was "vastly disconcerted," according to Smith. Arnold, certainly no humanitarian, was likely more distressed over the potential of being blamed for André's death than he was upset over the demise of a man he had met only once for a few hectic hours.

The news probably reached Peggy's ears when she was newly arrived in Philadelphia and had not yet been banished to New York City. She spent weeks in a state of shock, often hiding in her bedroom on Fourth Street. Was her distress based on her husband's sudden departure or her old friend's demise, or both?

Did Peggy talk to her family about André? Did she dare? After all, the discovery of his letter about millinery supplies had brought the family under a tighter and more torturous siege. Did she keep her memories and her grief to herself? Did she feel responsible for André's hanging?

There is no documentation that Peggy ever said a single word to anyone about André after his death. But there is little doubt that her friend's sad and shocking end was a wound that went unhealed for the rest of her life.

CHAPTER 17

"The Handsomest Woman in England"

FINALLY, PEGGY KNEW FOR CERTAIN WHICH SIDE of the war she was on. She was a Loyalist, with allegiance to the king of England. She was the wife of the king's newest warrior, Benedict Arnold. And within a few weeks of arriving in New York, Peggy was helping in her own small way to build the empire. She was pregnant with Arnold's second child.

Before she was too far along in the pregnancy, she sought to establish herself in New York City's high society. And she made a brilliant recovery from the excruciating weeks of dishevelment and histrionics that had followed the exposure of the plot.

A Loyalist woman described a ball at British headquarters in which Peggy was "amazingly improved in beauty and dress, having really recovered a great deal of that bloom she formerly possessed but did not bring in with her." Indeed, Peggy "appeared a star of the first magnitude, and had every attention paid her as if she had been Lady Clinton."[477] But the woman also noted: "Peggy Arnold is not so much admired here for her beauty as one might have expected. All allow she has great sweetness in her countenance, but wants animation, sprightliness and that fire in her eyes which was so captivating in [another officer's] wife. But notwithstanding she does not possess that life and animation that some do, they have met with every attention indeed, much more than they could have promised themselves."

The gossipy witness was Rebecca Warner Rawle Shoemaker, widow of a former mayor of Philadelphia, Francis Rawle. Her second husband, Loyalist Samuel Shoemaker, fled Philadelphia when Washington's troops liberated the city in 1778. Mrs. Shoemaker stayed behind, but, like Peggy, she was banished by Joseph Reed's government and went to New York City.

Mrs. Shoemaker's first husband had purchased the beautiful estate of Laurel Hill before he died in a hunting accident. Laurel Hill, in what is now Philadelphia's Fairmount Park along the Schuylkill River, was less than a mile from Mount Pleasant, the mansion that Arnold bought for Peggy but never occupied.

By marrying the widow Rawle, Samuel Shoemaker took ownership of Laurel Hill, according to the laws of the time. But when the estate was confiscated because authorities determined he had committed treason, the property was supposed to revert to her as if he had died. Reed ignored that stipulation of the law and decided it would make a fine summer estate for a government official such as himself.

Some saw divine justice when Reed's wife, Esther, took ill at Laurel Hill and died a few days later. In a letter from Philadelphia, Mrs. Shoemaker's daughter Anna shared speculation that Esther had died from eating too many of Laurel Hill's peaches.[478]

Anna Rawle also conveyed gossip about how Peggy was being remembered in her hometown: "They tell strange stories here of her, and strive to blacken her character in a way which her uncommon affection for the general renders very improbable."[479]

Though Peggy and Mrs. Shoemaker had plenty in common—their Philadelphia roots, their New York exile, their hatred of the Reeds—they didn't get along particularly well, and seemed to socialize out of obligation. "I drank a social dish of tea with Peggy Arnold today and the general came in while we were at it," Mrs. Shoemaker wrote. "You wonder, I don't doubt, at my improving an acquaintance there. I have never been in the house since the morning visit I paid her upon her first coming in." But there was a simple reason to get along, Mrs. Shoemaker said: "She is a Philadelphian."[480]

Another transplanted Philadelphian who saw little of Peggy was her saucy-tongued friend Becky Franks. "I have not seen or heard of her these two months," Becky wrote. "Her name is as little mentioned as her husband's."[481]

Peggy lived a careful and relatively quiet life in New York City while her husband tried, with limited success, to rebuild his military career under a new flag. He was befriended by Major General James Robertson, a Scotsman who had joined the British army as a private many decades earlier and had become royal governor of New York.[482] After Arnold made his narrow escape down the Hudson, he was taken in by Robertson as a houseguest at Fort George. Robertson became an enthusiastic booster of Arnold, writing to London that the defector was "the boldest and most enterprising of the rebel generals."[483]

And Robertson perhaps offered the most succinct and accurate assessment of his audacious new friend. "Arnold," he said, "does nothing by halves."[484] Arnold was quick to offer military advice, which came with the clear implication that the more the British relied on him, the greater would be their chances for success. The tone of his message was simple: Attack! He proposed to draw General Washington into a decisive battle by going on the offensive in the southern states, or by sailing up the Hudson and fulfilling the mission that André had died for—seizing West Point. He also called for driving Congress out of Philadelphia, though it's difficult to imagine that his real target wasn't Joseph Reed.[485]

Meanwhile, General Washington was so stung by Arnold's treason that he approved a bold plan to kidnap the traitor. A sergeant major named John Champe was recruited to pose as a defector to the British and to stalk Arnold. Washington was adamant that Champe must be an abductor rather than an assassin: "No circumstance whatever shall obtain my consent to his being put to death. . . . My aim is to make a public example of him."[486]

When Champe went over to the British lines, he was interrogated, given a few pounds, and invited to join their army. Champe declined, explaining that if he fought for the British and was captured, the rebels would likely hang him. Set free, Champe arranged to run into Benedict Arnold on a New York street, and he played to Arnold's vanity, explaining that he had been inspired to cast off his loyalty to the Continental Army after seeing Arnold do so. The two became friendly, and Arnold offered Champe a position as sergeant major in his Loyalist regiment. Champe accepted, and began paying careful attentions to Arnold's comings and goings.

Lurking outside the house in Lower Manhattan where Peggy was taking care of her baby, Neddy, Champe noticed that Arnold often took a midnight stroll and would stop at the outhouse before going inside to bed. He got word to his rebel commanders that he would kidnap Arnold on December 11 and take him across the Hudson to New Jersey, and then on to Washington's headquarters.[487]

Unfortunately for Champe, December 11 was the very day that Arnold mobilized a force of sixteen hundred men—including Champe—and prepared to leave New York for Virginia. Arnold's first combat mission for the British, launched less than a month after Peggy's arrival, was designed to ease pressure on Lord Cornwallis, whose army was taking a beating in the Carolinas.[488]

Some officers reportedly refused to serve under Arnold, blaming him for André's death. But one of André's best friends, Lieutenant Colonel John Graves Simcoe, apparently held no serious grudge. His Loyalist regiment, called the Queen's Rangers, joined Arnold on the mission, outfitted with black and white feathers on the horses' bridles in tribute to André. Also in Arnold's force were a company of Hessians and a regiment of British regulars under Lieutenant Colonel Thomas Dundas.

Although Arnold outranked Simcoe and Dundas, General Clinton ordered him to consult both of them before "undertaking any operation of consequence." Clinton also secretly gave the two permission to seize command upon Arnold's "death or incapacity," with the definition of incapacity left up to their judgment.

The fleet of forty-two ships was battered by the weather on the way down the coast, but Arnold managed to move up the James River in good order and surprise the rebel defenders. Arnold's orders called for the establishment of a base at Portsmouth and for raids to be conducted in the surrounding area only if they were low-risk. But Arnold was far better at raiding than at setting up bases. And risk was the fuel for his genius, so he could hardly resist some raiding.

He managed to overpower several rebel-held positions, including the state capital, Richmond. Virginia governor Thomas Jefferson was barely able to escape. Yet for all the old dash and audacity that Arnold displayed, he could not escape from his past. According to one story, Arnold interrogated a rebel prisoner who did not know who his questioner was, and when the general asked the prisoner what local residents would do with Arnold if they somehow managed to capture him, the prisoner said they would cut off the leg that had been wounded at Saratoga and bury it with honors. The rest of Arnold they would hang.[489]

Arnold also could not shake his greed. He had reached an agreement with the commodore of the fleet that had transported his army to Virginia, promising that they would split the proceeds from all enemy goods seized on land and on sea. Personal appropriation of the spoils of war was standard operating procedure back then, but Arnold seemed incapable of keeping things tidy. He and the commodore ended up in a nasty dispute, with Arnold insulting him so thoroughly that the naval officer refused to cooperate in military matters.

Clinton's best friend, Major General William Phillips, arrived at Portsmouth in March, taking over command from Arnold. Though Phillips and Arnold had been on opposite sides of the battle lines at Saratoga, they got along well in Virginia. But when Phillips came down with a fever and died in May, some of his admirers speculated that Arnold had poisoned him. Arnold never received the benefit of the doubt.

Phillips's death put Arnold back in temporary command of the force, but the harassed Cornwallis moved north and joined up with Arnold, taking over the helm. Cornwallis and Arnold discussed tactics, and the junior commander suggested that the British army move up the James River where it would not be vulnerable to the French fleet. Ignoring Arnold's advice, Cornwallis settled into a place called Yorktown. Arnold, suffering from excruciating gout and tired of such an inactive role, returned to New York in June.

—

Peggy was seven months pregnant when Arnold rejoined her, and he stayed until she gave him another son in August 1781. The boy was named

James Robertson Arnold, after New York's royal governor, who would be the last person to hold that job.

A week after James's arrival, when Peggy was still in the "lying-in" period of post-birth rest, her husband left on another military mission.[490] Peggy felt even more alone a few weeks later when she got word that her grandfather Edward Shippen, the former Philadelphia mayor who had left the city for the freer lifestyle of rural Lancaster, had died at the age of seventy-eight. In his will, he freed his slaves.[491]

Peggy was thoroughly an adult. The Meschianza must have felt as if it was a hundred years ago, though it was barely three. Now Peggy was a mother of two and a stepmother of three, and not the type to be flitting from party to party with Becky Franks. She was in a strange city, hoping that her husband would find a way to reestablish his honor. But on his new expedition, Arnold would accomplish what some thought was impossible: the lowering of his reputation even further.

He had urged a series of raids along the Atlantic coast to destroy rebel shipping, and Clinton had finally approved an attack on Connecticut's largest port, New London, which was only about a dozen miles from Arnold's hometown of Norwich.[492] Arnold's troops succeeded in destroying privateers in New London's harbor and torching warehouses full of rebel supplies. But one of the warehouses was full of gunpowder, and a huge explosion shook the town. Fires quickly grew out of control and devastated New London.

Across the Thames River, Arnold's forces tried to capture Fort Griswold. But Arnold realized that they would not be able to seize the fort before ships could escape upriver, so he sent orders calling off the assault. Those instructions did not arrive in time to prevent a vicious and bloody attack on the fort. When Arnold's forces finally entered the fort after suffering heavy casualties, the defenders attempted to surrender. But amid anger and confusion, the defending force was massacred. The fort's commander, who had turned over his sword, was bayoneted. Even though Arnold had not ordered the massacre and in fact had issued orders that would have prevented it, he was blamed.

On September 4, when Arnold was raiding New London and Peggy was caring for her newborn son in New York City, the city of Peggy's own birth was swept up in martial pageantry. French and Continental armies were marching through Philadelphia, headed south for a confrontation with Cornwallis's army in Yorktown.

The French uniforms were a dazzling white—an amazing fashion achievement after days on dusty roads—and featured colorful lapels and collars. The French also impressed the Philadelphia crowds with their brass musical instruments, a step up from the fifes and drums of the local militia. Joseph Reed hosted a dinner at which dignitaries feasted on a ninety-pound turtle, with the animal's shell used to serve soup.[493] Then the allies marched south to victory at Yorktown, capturing Cornwallis's eight thousand men and two hundred fifty cannon. Yorktown was the turning point of the war, and a bitter defeat for the Loyalists, including a young mother of two in New York City who had chosen the losing side.[494]

When the news of Yorktown reached Philadelphia, the homes of Loyalist-leaning residents were attacked by window-smashing celebrants. Anna Rawle wrote, "For two hours we had the disagreeable noise of stones banging about, glass crashing, and the tumultuous voices of a large body of men, as they were a long time at the different houses in the neighborhood."[495] It is not known whether the Shippens' home on Fourth Street was spared.

Meanwhile, in a much quieter, rather stunned New York City, Arnold prepared to take his family to London. He refused to accept Britain's ultimate defeat, and he planned to lobby the government for more vigorous conduct of the war. He was "desirous to go home," as William Smith put it in the parlance of the time, even though "home" was a place where Arnold had been only on business, and where Peggy had never been.[496]

According to William Smith, Arnold told Clinton that he would "recommend a reinforcement of twenty thousand men and promised to be back in March," but he confided in Smith that he would never return while Clinton was in command.[497] Obviously, Arnold dreamed of replacing Clinton in command of British forces in North America, a prospect that was remote at best.

On December 8, 1781, Arnold, Peggy, and their two young sons set off for London, having worn out their welcome in America.[498] "No doubt they will attract attention in England," opined Anna Rawle.[499] Peggy and the boys traveled separately from Arnold, since she wouldn't have been comfortable in a military ship and he couldn't risk traveling in a nonmilitary vessel that might be subject to capture. Arnold's traveling partner was the defeated but still ambitious Cornwallis, who had been freed in exchange for Henry Laurens, a former president of the Continental Congress captured at sea and held in the Tower of London.[500]

In a letter, Mrs. Shoemaker explained the Arnolds' travel arrangements: "The Fleet sailed from the Hook today. . . . Lord Cornwallis, his suite, and General Arnold in the *Robuste*. Peggy Arnold and her family in a private ship as more agreeable for her than a man-of-war, yet not safe for him. They give for the cabin three hundred guineas and then took in what company they chose, chiefly military I believe. I do not hear of any females but her maids."[501] Maybe Mrs. Shoemaker's comment about Peggy buying out the cabin and surrounding herself with men was innocent. But maybe not. As her own daughter had written, people told "strange stories" about Peggy.

When Peggy boarded the ship to England, she knew she might never see her Philadelphia family again. But while she may have felt lonely, she was far from alone in leaving an America torn apart by war. The fighting would officially end less than two years later, and many Loyalists would seek their fortunes elsewhere. By one count, the total diaspora from America was sixty thousand whites and fifteen thousand black slaves—one in forty residents of the thirteen colonies.[502]

Few of those refugees inspired as much anticipation in London as Peggy and her husband.[503] As had happened in New York, the Arnolds were greeted politely by top British officials, who needed the general as vindication for their policies. Arnold met with the secretary of state for America, George Germain, and visited Lord Amherst at the War Office. Jeffery Amherst and Arnold had something in common: a dicey reputation that would endure for centuries. For Amherst, lasting notoriety

195

came from his endorsement of a plan to give smallpox-infected blankets to Native Americans after the French and Indian War.[504]

The Arnolds were especially well received at the Court of St. James's. The general was presented to the British monarch by Sir Walter Stirling, a career officer in the British Navy who had married a first cousin of Peggy's father in the 1750s. Stirling had brought home the news of the British victory at the Caribbean island of St. Eustatius in 1780, and King George III had rewarded him with a knighthood.[505] The permanently limping Arnold met the king while leaning on the arm of Sir Guy Carleton, who had been his opponent in the Battle of Valcour Island and would soon replace Clinton as commander in chief of British forces in America.

Peggy was presented at court by Lady Amherst, the smallpox schemer's wife, who like Peggy was about half her husband's age. The American beauty made such an impression that Queen Charlotte urged the ladies of the court to shower attention on her.[506] British royalty showered money on Peggy, too, presenting her with a pension of five hundred pounds a year. At the time, people might have thought she was receiving the money for her unquestioning and uninformed support of her husband. But a handwritten memorandum by Clinton, found in his papers a century and a half later, stated that the money was "obtained for her services, which were very meritorious."[507] The services were not specified, but such a citation suggests gratitude from the enemy that went beyond her role as the wife of a defector. After all, Arnold had already received his financial rewards. Peggy insisted on saving this pension money, allowing her to establish some semblance of stability while married to a mercurial and financially risky man.

The Arnolds settled in Portman Square, a fairly fashionable area of London with some colorful characters, such as "authoress" Elizabeth Montague, who held a Sweeps Holiday for chimney sweeps every May 1, feeding them roast beef and plum pudding "so that they might enjoy one happy day in the year."[508]

The Rawle-Shoemaker family seemed to conduct surveillance of Peggy even on the far side of the Atlantic. William Rawle, Mrs. Shoemaker's son who was in England to continue his legal studies, described the Arnolds' entry into London society: "They have taken a house and set up a carriage and will, I suppose, be a good deal visited."[509] They were indeed a novelty. "I saw Mrs. Arnold a few days after her arrival in town," wrote Rawle, "and was really pleased she looked so well, as general expectation was raised so high by the incessant puffers of the newspapers and the declaration of Colonel Tarleton that she was the handsomest woman in England."

The purveyor of that compliment was Banastre Tarleton, a dashing British cavalry officer and playboy who had known Peggy in Philadelphia and escorted a minister's daughter, Williamina Smith, at the Meschianza. Tarleton, who developed a reputation as a butcher for his brutal warmaking in the South, surrendered along with Cornwallis at Yorktown. After he made his way back to England, he became a baronet and a member of Parliament.[510]

Initially, Arnold's advice and counsel to Britain's leaders seemed welcome. He was seen strolling in the public gardens with the Prince of Wales and reportedly attended private conferences with the king.

Benjamin Franklin, presently in Paris, was getting reports about Arnold. "Generals Cornwallis and Arnold are both arrived in England," Franklin wrote. "We hear much of audiences given to the latter, and of his being present at councils. He seems to mix as naturally with that polluted court as pitch with tar; there is no being in nature too base for them to associate with, provided he may be thought capable of serving their purposes."[511]

Yet English popular culture, with its rough-and-tumble political discourse, was rough on Arnold—as rough as any pro-Reed newspaper in Philadelphia. Even before the Arnolds reached London, common verse was ridiculing him:

> Our troops by Arnold thoroughly were banged,
> And poor St. André was by Arnold hanged;
> To George a rebel, to the Congress traitor,
> Pray, what can make the name of Arnold greater?
> By one bold treason, to gain his ends,
> Let him betray his new adopted friends.[512]

197

And soon after Peggy and Arnold reached London, a letter signed "R.M." heaped abuse on the defector in the *General Advertiser and Morning Intelligencer*, calling him a horse thief and a "mean mercenary" who found his courage in a brandy bottle.[513] It was enough to engender sympathy for Arnold, almost.

Arnold's hopes of military glory evaporated in March 1782 when the British government that supported the war in the colonies—and supported Arnold as well—bowed out. Lord North became the first prime minister in British history to be ousted by a parliamentary vote of no confidence.[514] His replacement sent a delegation to talk peace with Franklin.

Suddenly Peggy and Arnold were merely reminders of English political folly. And they soon discovered that contemporary culture was more fascinated by the noble death of John André than by the ongoing lives of either of them. André's old friend Anna Seward had written a "Monody on Major André." In this monody (elegy, or dirge), Britain is personified, and wanders the shore, distraught over André's death:

> With one pale hand the bloody scroll he rears,
> And bids his nations blot it with their tears;
> And one, extended o'er th' Atlantic wave
> Points to his André's ignominious grave![515]

Despite the overheated verse, Seward tapped into a wounded nation's thirst for nobility and pride.

King George was so taken with André's sacrifice that he gave the major's mother one thousand pounds and made his brother a baronet. The king also ordered a marble monument installed at Westminster Abbey to honor André, who "fell a sacrifice to his zeal for his king and country," according to the inscription.[516]

A book written more than a half century later recalled a New York Loyalist named Peter Van Schaack visiting Westminster Abbey one day when "his musings were interrupted by the entrance of a gentleman, accompanied by a lady. It was General Arnold, and the lady was doubtless Mrs. Arnold. They passed to the cenotaph of Major André, where they stood and conversed together. What a spectacle! . . . Mr. Van Schaack turned from it with disgust."[517]

With no war to fight, Arnold collected his half pay and struggled to find his future. In 1784 he reached out to George Johnstone, a director of the East India Company, seeking a position in the trading company. Arnold explained the West Point conspiracy in detail, and Johnstone wrote back: "Under an unsuccessful insurrection all actors are rebels. Crowned with success they become immortal patriots. A fortunate plot holds you up as a savior of nations; a premature discovery brings you to the scaffold or brands your fame with dark and doubtful suspicions."[518] In other words, Arnold had gambled with treachery and had lost. Johnstone turned him down.

⟞⟝

Peggy, on the other hand, had found a fulfilling role as wife and mother and was pursuing it with vigor. But she also encountered heartbreak. After giving birth to two sons within eighteen months, she longed for a girl. But her third child and namesake, Margaret, died six months after her birth in 1783.[519] "Poor woman, she lost her daughter last summer," an acquaintance wrote. "When we first came to London, you know how much she wished for a girl."[520]

A son named George followed in 1784, but he lived less than two months. All told, Peggy's maternal fortunes were the same as her mother's, with two of her children dying at an early age while five others survived to adulthood. The third of those five, a daughter named Sophia, arrived in the summer of 1785.

Peggy maintained contact with her saucy old friend Becky Franks, who was also in England. Becky wrote to fellow Meschianza veteran Williamina Bond in 1784 that Peggy "always behaved more like an affectionate sister than a common friend. . . . I hear every week or fortnight from her."[521]

Becky noted that in the latter stages of pregnancy, Peggy kept a low profile: "She expects to be confined the beginning of next month." Even so, "She was and is still more noticed and more liked than any American

199

that ever came over. She is visited by people of the first rank and invited to all their houses."

While charming the English, Peggy may have been most comfortable with fellow Loyalist exiles. She visited the village of Mortlake, outside London, and was welcomed by the family of Beverley Robinson, the former owner of the Hudson Highlands estate where Peggy's life had taken its sharpest turn. The Robinsons were happy to host such exiles as Peggy, Samuel Shoemaker, and William Smith.[522]

Peggy rode there on horseback, impressing Beverley Robinson's daughter Joanna. "She is grown amazingly lusty," Joanna wrote, "but it becomes her better than I thought it did when I first saw her in London."[523]

Peggy was still a striking young woman. When a London lawyer gossiped about the Arnolds, he expressed the imaginations of many men, who couldn't help wondering what might become of Peggy if she were free of the despised Arnold. "By all accounts," the lawyer wrote, "she is an amiable woman and, were her husband dead, would be much noticed."[524]

CHAPTER 18

Strangers in America

LESS THAN FOUR YEARS AFTER BENEDICT ARNOLD brought Peggy to England, he prepared to leave her there and embark on yet another hunt for treasure far from home. Peggy, who had transformed herself from public curiosity to demure mother, moved her family into smaller quarters in the same Portman Square neighborhood in London so that her husband could buy and outfit a ship called the *Lord Middlebrook* for trade across the ocean.[525] And she welcomed Arnold's son Richard, who came across the Atlantic to help his father mount his new adventure.

In October 1785, a few months after the birth of daughter Sophia, Arnold and Richard set sail for Canada, where many Loyalists had fled in hopes of building a new life after the disaster of the American Revolution. The father and son reached St. John, New Brunswick, in December during a gale. Their arrival had one similarity with every other major enterprise of Arnold's career: It gave birth to a new collection of conspiracy theories and a new set of enemies. The *Lord Middlebrook* ran aground in the harbor while Arnold was belowdecks fighting off an attack of gout, and ultimately its cargo of flour, beef, butter, and pork was looted. Arnold accused his crewmen of intentionally running it aground as part of a plot to damage the reputation of St. John as a business center.[526]

St. John had doubled in population, to twelve thousand, because of land grants in New Brunswick that attracted Loyalist refugees, including members of Arnold's own Loyalist unit. Arnold viewed St. John as a shining opportunity for a fresh start, despite the best efforts of his conspiratorial crewmen. He set up a store, bought a wharf, acquired city lots, built a house, and purchased a thousand acres of forest, which he used to supply timber for a lumber yard he constructed in St. John's Lower Cove. He also acquired property in the provincial capital, Fredericton, where Peggy had cousins.

The *St. John Royal Gazette* praised Arnold's construction of a white-oak ship named the *Lord Sheffield* and declared that his "laudable efforts to promote the interest of this infant colony have, during his short residence, been very productive to its commercial advantage."[527] But the creation of the *Lord Sheffield* also provided a fresh example of Arnold's fractious nature: He and the shipbuilder engaged in a public exchange of accusations after they wrangled over late changes and then Arnold deducted a late fee from money due the builder.

While Arnold was seeking his fortune, Peggy's time without him in London—lasting most of a year—was excruciating. She had heard a rumor that Arnold was involved in a disaster at sea, and had not received any news to contradict it even three months after his arrival in St. John. "I am still in the most unhappy state of suspense respecting the general, not having heard from him since the account of his ships being lost," she wrote her father.

Arnold had left behind plenty of serious financial problems for Peggy to contend with, including a lawsuit by Frenchman Jean Holker seeking repayment of the twelve-thousand-pound loan from Arnold's time in Philadelphia. Peggy's grasp of her family finances was exceptional: A study of more than four hundred claims by Loyalist women for British compensation after the American Revolution showed them to be profoundly ignorant about money matters in their own households, lacking details about such vital matters as their husbands' income or the price of their former homes. Peggy, on the other hand, was interested in finances, and understood them, and had no choice but to get involved, considering her husband's speculation and absence.[528] While people seemed to credit Peggy's father for her financial talents, her mother also may have had such skills, or at least interests. Many of the Shippen properties in America were held in the names of both of Peggy's parents, an unusual arrangement at the time.

Peggy, in her London exile, felt alone and burdened. In the most stiff-upper-lip manner she could manage, she described her desperate emotional state to her father:

I assure you, my dear papa, I find it necessary to summon all my philosophy to my aid, to support myself under my present situation. Separated from, and anxious for the fate of, the best of husbands, torn from almost everybody that is dear to me, harassed with an expensive and troublesome lawsuit, having all the general's business to transact, and feeling that I am in a strange country, without a creature near me that is really interested in my fate, you will not wonder if I am unhappy. But I will not distress you, my beloved papa, with my unavailing complaints, which I seldom suffer to engross either my pen or my tongue, but deprived of all domestic society, I have too much time to indulge them.[529]

Arnold, of course, was not lost at sea. To some extent, he had found himself at sea. After shipbuilding in St. John, he took the *Lord Sheffield* south to the Caribbean for more of the kind of trading that had been his livelihood in the pre-Revolution days. He returned to London in late 1786 to prepare his wife and children for a voyage to their new home in Canada. When they set off in the summer of 1787, they were in a new ship named *Peggy*.

Peggy, who was seven months pregnant when they arrived, watched moving men fill a fine rental house on King Street in the Upper Cove. She had brought along blue damask sofas and chairs, matching drapes, a mahogany table that seated twelve, Wedgwood giltware, Nankeen china, and a globe of the world.[530]

Two friends, Judge Jonathan Sewall and his wife, had taken the ocean voyage with them, and Peggy soon made other friends as well. Her manners, looks, and charm were a currency valuable across nations and continents, and she was welcome in the salons and dining rooms of her new town.

It's not clear how many servants Peggy's household required in St. John, though throughout her life she made sure they were plentiful. Many years later, when money was tight, she wrote that "our living is plain and frugal" with only two full-time servants—a cook and a maid.[531] Peggy certainly wasn't idle, though. She kept up with her reading and always monitored her children's education. She also was an avid seamstress, and even made some of her own furniture.

Arnold saw St. John as a gathering place for his far-flung loved ones. Nineteen-year-old Benedict was away in pursuit of his military career, but the rest of his family assembled—Arnold's sister Hannah, seventeen-year-old Richard, and fourteen-year-old Henry, plus Peggy and her newer branch: seven-year-old Edward, five-year-old James, and Sophia, who was nearly two.[532]

From letters, it's clear that Peggy never considered St. John her permanent home. She figured Arnold would earn his fortune and they would ultimately return to England. But for the time being, she was happy to get to know her stepchildren better and to attend dinners and horseback rides with willing members of local society.

She was not, however, prepared for the news that probably reached her ears soon after she reached St. John: Her husband had been a traitor to their wedding vows. No one has ever identified the woman who had the affair with Arnold in St. John in late 1785 or early 1786 when he came to town to establish himself. But their union led to the birth of a son named John Sage, who was described as "about fourteen years of age" in Arnold's will of August 30, 1800, less than a year before his death.[533]

There's no reason to think Peggy learned about John Sage from the will, and every reason to suppose that she learned of his existence soon after arrival, considering what a small town St. John was and how many enemies Arnold had already made.[534] The revelation must have come as a grievous blow to a woman who had already suffered many. Peggy had called Arnold "the best of husbands" back in March 1786 when she feared she would never see him again—perhaps at the very time when he was being unfaithful to her. But after her arrival in St. John, she never again used such exalted language to describe her husband, at least not during his lifetime.

In the place where Arnold had dishonored her, Peggy gave birth to a son in September 1787. He was given the same name as his brother who had died three years earlier—George, in honor of the king. But Peggy was nearly done with childbearing. The next year, she wrote her sister Betsy: "It gives me great pleasure to hear of your prudent resolution of not increasing your family; as I can never do better than to follow your example, I have decided upon the same plan; and when our sisters have had five or six, we will likewise recommend it to them."[535]

Though St. John carried bitter connotations for her, Peggy made the best of it, helping Arnold with his businesses, some of which struggled. She longed to make one last visit back to Philadelphia to see her family, and such a trip was now legal, since the banishment order had lapsed at war's end. "I am much gratified by your earnest solicitations for me to visit, and hope to accomplish so desirable an event in the fall," Peggy wrote to Betsy in June 1788. "Yet my pleasure will not be unaccompanied by pain; as when I leave you, I shall probably bid you adieu forever. Many disagreeable and some favorable circumstances will, I imagine, fix me forever in England, upon my return to it; while his majesty's bounty is continued to me, it is necessary I should reside in his dominions."[536]

Arnold was in England on business, and while he was gone, a fire destroyed his warehouse, store, and lumberyard in St. John. His son Henry was sleeping in the office and barely escaped the flames.[537]

Despite the setback, Peggy continued to think she would be able to visit Philadelphia that year. "As I have got the better of almost every obstacle to paying you a visit, I ought to anticipate nothing but pleasure," she wrote Betsy. "I feel great regret at the idea of leaving the general alone and much perplexed by business, but as he strongly argues a measure that will be productive of so much happiness for me, I think there can be no impropriety in taking the ship."[538] Arnold urged her to make the same arrangements she had during her voyage to England in the winter of 1781–82: buying out the whole cabin of the ship and then admitting only those people whom she deigned to travel with. She was especially eager to take the trip because her mother's health was failing. "She must suffer extremely from the loss of her limbs," Peggy wrote, "as she has been accustomed to so much exercise."

But Arnold did not return that year in time for Peggy to go. She had to wait another year, until late 1789, to make the voyage to her beloved Philadelphia. Traveling with her two-year-old son George and a servant, she sailed to New York City, where her ship's arrival refuted a rumor that the vessel had been wrecked. By December, she was with her family on Fourth Street.

Peggy came back to a Philadelphia that was very different from the one she had left.[539] Congress was gone, having departed to escape intimidation from hundreds of protesting Continental soldiers in 1783.[540] The city streets had been made level in 1782, leaving "many graceful undulations destroyed," in the words of one writer.[541] Luckily, most of the city's trees seemed to have survived a short-lived law that same year that ordered their removal from streets and alleys because they were deemed fire spreaders, waterway destroyers, and hazards to navigation.[542]

In 1789, when Peggy arrived with toddler George in tow, she fit in well with Philadelphia's new coat of arms, which featured pregnant women to symbolize the land's fertility.[543] Some of Peggy's enemies were dead or defeated. Joseph Reed, who had persecuted her husband and driven her out of town, had succumbed in 1785 at age forty-three after a period of paralysis.[544] Reed's ally Timothy Matlack, who had bedeviled Arnold over his militiaman son being ordered to fetch a barber, lived far longer—to age ninety-nine. But by the time Peggy came to visit, Matlack had stepped down as secretary of the Supreme Executive Council amid charges of accounting irregularities.[545]

In her absence, Peggy's family had found its equilibrium. Peggy's father was back on the judge's bench and would soon achieve appointment to the state's Supreme Court. Her mother, despite illness, had survived to see her youngest daughter again. Her sister Betsy and cousin Neddy Burd were happily married with children, and her other siblings had all married in her absence, Edward at twenty-seven, Mary at twenty-eight, and Sarah at twenty-nine.[546] All four gave their firstborn daughters the same name: Margaret.[547]

Despite the warmth she received from her family, Peggy discovered during her five months in Philadelphia that the wounds of the war—and especially the injuries to the new nation that had been plotted by her husband—were hardly forgotten. The nineteenth-century writer Lorenzo Sabine, in his biographies of Loyalists, described Peggy's homecoming: "Out of respect to her family, many warm Whigs had been to see her, though the common opinion was that, as her presence placed her friends in a painful position, she would have shown more feeling by staying away. I learn from another source that she was treated with so much coldness and neglect, even by those who had most encouraged her ill-starred marriage, that her feelings were continually wounded. She could never come again."[548]

After leaving Fourth Street, Peggy summed up the trip in downcast terms. "How difficult is it to know what will contribute to our happiness in this life," she wrote Betsy. "I had hoped that by paying my beloved friends a last visit, I should insure to myself some portion of it, but I find it far otherwise."[549]

Back in Canada, she seemed depressed by the chilly July. "Our summer fogs are just setting in, which is in fact the only thing that denotes the season, as we have not left off fires and have never slept under less than two blankets." But what distressed her most was the fact that Arnold was again sinking into financial quicksand, thereby threatening her hopes of returning to England: "From the present appearances of things, there is great reason to apprehend a disappointment in our going home this fall. For my own part, I have given up every hope of going. There has been a succession of disappointments and mortifications in collecting our debts ever since my return home."

The warehouse fire from two years earlier had consequences far beyond the actual financial loss. Arnold was insured for it, which turned out to be the problem. A former business partner publicly accused Arnold of committing arson to defraud the insurance company—an unlikely theory considering that Arnold was thousands of miles away and his son Henry nearly died in the fire. But the insurance company balked at paying. When Arnold demanded that his ex-partner apologize for accusing him of setting the fire, he instead received an insult: "It is not in my power to blacken your character, for it is as black as it can be."[550]

Arnold sued. Arriving at court in Fredericton with two lawyers and thirty witnesses, Arnold mounted an impressive case, including testimony from a Loyalist veteran that he had gone to the warehouse with Henry and had accidentally started the fire through the careless use of a candle. The jury found the ex-partner guilty of slander, but two judges awarded damages of only twenty shillings.

It was a humiliating result for Peggy and her family and suggested that Arnold's reputation was virtually worthless. As a further indignity, a mob invaded the Arnolds' home on King Street while they were away and set fire to an effigy of Arnold with the word "traitor" on its chest. British troops were called out to chase away the rabble and secure the Arnolds' possessions.

St. John could no longer be home to the Arnolds. Finally Peggy would get her wish to return to England, away from this place of speculation and resentment and infidelity. Hannah remained in Canada with Richard and Henry, but Peggy and Arnold left with the younger children in late 1791, bound for London.[551] Before their departure they held an auction for some of their goods, including the Wedgwood giltware, the Nankeen china, the globe, and "a lady's elegant saddle and bridle." The twelve chairs for the dining table were sold to one of Arnold's lawyer friends. Later known in St. John as the "traitor's chairs," they were destroyed in that city's great fire of 1877.

"We had a very rough and disagreeable voyage home," Arnold wrote to a St. John friend, "but our reception has been very pleasant, and our friends more than well attentive to us since our arrival. The little property that we have saved from the hands of a lawless ruffian mob and more unprincipled judges in New Brunswick is perfectly safe here, as well as our persons from insult. . . . I cannot help viewing your great city as a shipwreck from which I have escaped."[552]

The Arnold family moved onto Holles Street in London's Cavendish Square area, near their previous neighborhood of Portman Square. Four years earlier on that very same street, the infant who would become the poet Lord Byron was born, but his family had since moved away.[553] Now Holles Street was Peggy's home. She had left America for good. No more sideways sneers on the newly paved roads of Philadelphia. No more ruffians in the frozen lanes of a not-yet-boomtown in eastern Canada.

Peggy was happy to escape, too, but she faced a host of challenges in England—four children to raise and a husband to keep out of trouble. And not just any husband, but a proud, insecure, overreaching man who was intent on battling old enemies and making new ones.

CHAPTER 19

Unmanned

IN TWO LETTERS IN THE SUMMER OF 1792, Peggy told the story of how she was almost widowed, and how she nearly went insane with worry, and how—by her estimation, at least—it all ended splendidly for the Arnold family. "Should the public papers of a few days back reach you," Peggy wrote her father, "you will observe a paragraph mentioning that General Arnold is killed in a duel with the Earl of Lauderdale."[554]

The rumor was untrue—at least so far, Peggy wrote. But the report of Arnold's death "was for some time so generally believed that our friends were flocking to the house to console with and make me offers of service."

The dispute had begun with remarks made in Britain's House of Lords by James Maitland, Earl of Lauderdale, about a matter that had nothing to do with Arnold. Rather, Lauderdale meant to denounce the Duke of Richmond for establishing a military "flying camp" to intimidate citizens who were seeking political reform. Lauderdale said, according to Peggy's telling, "that he did not know any instance of political apostasy equal to the Duke of Richmond's, except General Arnold's."[555]

Peggy apparently heard about the comment before Arnold did, because she wrote that she tried to keep the news from her husband, an attempt that seemed to cause friction between them. "This is a subject to which of course he is to me silent," she wrote, "and all that I can obtain from him are assurances that he will do nothing rashly and without the advice of his friends." Peggy knew her place. She could argue against a confrontation, but she could not stop her fractious husband from demanding either an apology or a duel. "For, weak woman that

210

I am, I would not wish to prevent what would be deemed necessary to preserve his honor."

Dueling, which would be outlawed in England in 1819, was a reckless bit of macho political posturing that occasionally had lethal results, despite the fact that most participants had no intention of either dying or killing.[556] In 1789 a bullet fired by a duel opponent had grazed the hair of the king's second son, Prince Frederick Augustus, Duke of York, who declined to fire back.[557] The same year as Arnold's confrontation with Lauderdale, a duel in London's Hyde Park showed the ridiculousness of the ritual. The so-called Petticoat Duel pitted Lady Almeria Braddock against a Mrs. Elphinstone, who had allegedly made a disparaging remark about Lady Almeria's age. The women fired at ten paces and missed, though a ball went through Lady Almeria's hat. Swords were the next weapon of choice, and Lady Almeria punished Mrs. Elphinstone with an arm wound, after which they called it a day.[558]

Peggy was right to worry about Arnold's fate if he insisted on a duel: People did indeed die in such "trial by combat." The most famous American dueling fatality would occur a dozen years later and involve a man well known to Peggy—Alexander Hamilton, one of the Founding Fathers she had wrapped around her finger at Robinson House. Hamilton was killed by Aaron Burr, second husband of Peggy's friend Theodosia Prevost, three weeks before Peggy's own death in 1804.[559]

The complicated choreography following Lauderdale's insult was common for the times, and was outlined by Peggy in the account to her father. First Arnold asked Lauderdale whether he had uttered the insulting remark. Lauderdale said he had, and "made a kind of apology for it, but it not satisfying the general, he drew up such a one as he would accept, which his lordship refused to sign." Then they agreed to a "meeting"—a duel—at seven o'clock on a Sunday morning near Kilburn Wells outside of London, with the Arnolds' friend Lord Hawke accompanying the general and former prime minister Charles James Fox as Lauderdale's second.[560] "It was agreed that they should fire at the same time, upon a word given, which the general did, without effect," Peggy wrote. "Lord Lauderdale refused to fire, saying he had no enmity to General Arnold. He at the same time refused making an apology, and said the general might fire again, if he chose." Arnold refused to do such a dishonorable thing, but declared that he would not leave the field unless Lauderdale either apologized or fired. If Lauderdale would do neither, Arnold threatened to speak "such expressions to him as would oblige him" to shoot.

Peggy described these negotiations as if they were logical and sensible, yet they were in fact utterly absurd. First Arnold had threatened to shoot Lauderdale because of his insult. Now Arnold threatened to insult Lauderdale if he would not shoot.

The seconds met privately to discuss the next step, allowing Arnold and Lauderdale to chat by themselves. Arnold "told his lordship that he did not come there to convince the world that he dare fight, but for satisfaction for the injury done his character." Lauderdale and his second conferred, and then the lord "came forward and said he had no enmity to General Arnold—that he did not mean to asperse his character or wound his feelings, and was sorry for what he had said. General Arnold said he was perfectly satisfied with this apology, provided the seconds, as men of honor, declared he ought to be so, which they without hesitation did." Lord Lauderdale also expressed his concern for Peggy's feelings, and offered to pay a visit to offer his apologies personally. It is unknown whether that meeting ever took place.

The tension of the whole affair was too much for Peggy: "What I suffered for near a week is not to be described; the suppression of my feelings, lest I should unman the general, almost at last proved too much for me; and for some hours, my reason was despaired of. I was confined to my bed for some days after, but am now so much better that I shall go out [for] an airing this afternoon."

In the end, the whole situation was a triumph, at least in Peggy's mind. "It has been highly gratifying to find the general's conduct so much applauded, which it has been universally, and particularly by a number of the first characters in the kingdom, who have called upon him in consequence of it. Nor am I displeased," she added, "at the great commendations bestowed on my own conduct upon this trying occasion." Though driven to bed and to hysterics, undoubtedly alarming both her servants and her children, she had kept her feelings locked away inside the house on Holles Street. She had avoided "unmanning the general" in public.

The Arnolds, believing that their reputation was burnished by their honorable handling of the duel, launched an appeal to Prime Minister William Pitt to gain further recompense for their unsuccessful treason and Arnold's brief service with the British army more than a decade earlier. They realized that Pitt would consult Clinton, and began lobbying the general heavily. Arnold reanimated his argument that John André had shown a willingness to pay him ten thousand pounds rather than the six thousand that Clinton had initially agreed to. Clinton, no doubt tired of Arnold, responded with the same statement he had issued years earlier during financial wrangling: "My ideas of your services while you acted with the king's troops have been already communicated to the secretary of state. I am no longer in a situation either to notice or reward them."[561]

Peggy also wrote Clinton, in her most genteel manner: "Surrounded by a numerous little family, without the means of educating and supporting them in a style at all equal to what the former part of my life promised . . . you will not be surprised that every maternal feeling is awakened and that I am deeply interested in General Arnold's present application to Mr. Pitt. . . . From your justice I have everything to hope. May I presume to solicit your friendship?"[562] To the modern eye, Peggy's appeal for help may seem less than persuasive. There was no guarantee that, just because Peggy was born to wealth, she was entitled to it for the rest of her life. Nor was it the crown's problem that the Arnolds had gambled and lost at West Point and then had gambled and lost again in New Brunswick. Peggy and Arnold were once-affluent people who were desperately afraid of slipping into the middle class and were begging for government welfare to make them wealthy again.

When Arnold finally managed an audience with Pitt after several visits to his home and office, he made essentially the same argument as Peggy, asking that the British government restore him to "the style of the first people of America, by whom I was respected and beloved and among whom I had many friends." But the question was obvious: If his former life in America had been so desirable, why had he abandoned it in the first place?

Arnold asked Pitt for a gargantuan amount: twenty-five thousand pounds, the rough equivalent of four million dollars in today's currency.[563] He also sought to be named governor of the Lesser Antilles island of Dominica in the Caribbean. Instead, in July 1793, a year after the duel with Lauderdale, the Arnolds received a reward that seemed to address Peggy's "maternal feeling": Each of their four children would receive a government pension of one hundred pounds per year.[564]

A few months later, Peggy's last child was on the way. Mrs. Arnold had been pregnant six times in about eight years—more often pregnant than not—followed by a gap of six years before her seventh one. This time Arnold did not wait for his child's delivery before embarking on a new quest for fortune. He returned to the sea in the spring of 1794, bound for the Caribbean.

Peggy set a clear course for her four older children: They would attend school so that the boys could ultimately serve the military and Sophia could one day serve a marriage. With money tight, the family took less sumptuous quarters in the same general area of London, on Queen Anne Street in the Cavendish Square area. James Boswell had written the famed *Life of Samuel Johnson* at home on that very street only a few years earlier. Like Peggy, he had chosen Queen Anne because it was both genteel and reasonably priced.[565]

William Fitch Arnold, Peggy's youngest son, was born there in June 1794 and was named for an American Loyalist in exile who had fought on the British side at Bunker Hill and whose sisters Ann and Sarah were Peggy's closest friends in London. The Loyalist died in fighting against Maroons—descendants of runaway slaves—in Jamaica little more than a year after his namesake's birth.[566]

Peggy was determined that she was done with childbirth. Writing to congratulate Canadian friends upon the birth of a baby, she declared: "For my own part, I am determined to have no more little plagues, as it is so difficult to provide for them in this country."[567]

Around the time that Peggy's last "little plague" was born, she received sad news about the woman who had brought her into the world. Margaret

Francis Shippen was dead of a stroke at age fifty-eight. Her father wrote: "I have lost the staff of my age and care not how soon I follow her."[568] Yet her father's correspondence was reminiscent of his letter thirty-four years earlier in which he discussed a business voucher before announcing Peggy's birth. This new letter, describing how his wife's passing had broken his heart, included a postscript inquiring about an interest payment on one of Peggy's investments.

In their lifelong correspondence, Peggy and her father liked to move beyond niceties. After he sent her a painted portrait of himself, she responded that "the sight of it occasioned sensations I never before experienced," but then complained that "the eyes, particularly the right one, are very bad, and the heavy brow very much unlike yours." She told him that the painting was "invaluable" to her as long as she covered up the eyes so she didn't have to look at them.[569]

Peggy sometimes seemed to detest the very things she loved. That included her father's portrait, and it also included her husband, whose infidelity and recklessness tortured Peggy at times. As she cared for her new baby William, Benedict Arnold was engaged in the last grand adventure of his life. It was a lengthy one that would tax his wife and family.

Just after Arnold set out to seek his fortune in the Caribbean, a storm forced him to take refuge at an inn in Falmouth on England's far southwestern tip. There he encountered one of the giants of the age, the French diplomat Talleyrand, who was fleeing his nation's Reign of Terror. Talleyrand was not told Arnold's name but only that he was an American general. He asked for letters of introduction that he could use in America, and Arnold told him, "I am perhaps the only American who cannot give you letters for his own country. . . . All the relations I had there are now broken."[570] Talleyrand quickly realized he was talking to the famous traitor Benedict Arnold.

Proceeding to the Caribbean, Arnold fell into a trap as he entered the harbor of Pointe-à-Pitre, Guadaloupe, just after it had been captured from British forces by fighters loyal to France's revolutionary government.[571] Held prisoner aboard a French ship, Arnold gave his name as

John Anderson—the same pseudonym that John André used fourteen years earlier. And like André, his claim of being an innocent merchant was disbelieved.

Peggy, an astute reader of newspapers and observer of geopolitics, was fully aware of the danger in Guadaloupe. "I am now in a state of most extreme misery," she wrote her stepson Richard, "from the report of your father's being a prisoner to the French at Pointe-à-Pitre, Guadaloupe."[572] Peggy noted that another report had indicated Arnold was safe, but she concluded correctly that he indeed had been captured, since his last letter had reported that he was headed for Pointe-à-Pitre and the French took control four days later.

Yet Arnold did not remain a prisoner long. He effected a brilliant escape through bribery and sheer grit, and paddled a raft and then a boat to safety aboard the British man-of-war *Boyne,* anchored off the island.

The commander of British forces in the area was General Sir Charles Grey—the "No Flint" Grey who had commanded André on bloody missions in the American Revolution. It is unclear whether Grey fully forgave Arnold for André's death, but at least he didn't feed Arnold to the sharks. While Grey refused to allow Arnold to take a command as a brigadier general, he welcomed his efforts over a year's time to secure food for the British force. A junior officer wrote that Arnold "fastened himself onto Grey with a tenacity which the general's undisguised disgust was powerless to shake."[573] Arnold made himself indispensable in the islands, not only offering his own money up-front to buy food for Grey's soldiers but also helping British planters organize a militia to put down a slave rebellion. Disease and warfare were rampant, but Arnold seemed to be in his element. He found himself "considerably improved in fortune and infinitely more in health than when I left England, and though I have experienced the distress of burying two-thirds of my acquaintances in these islands since I came out, I had scarcely an hour's sickness."[574]

⌒⌒

Peggy, on the other hand, struggled both emotionally and physically in her husband's absence. When he returned in the summer of 1795, he found her "very much an invalid, but as her disorder is in a great measure nervous, I hope she will soon get the better of it."[575]

Peggy had complained of one ailment or another her entire adult life—indeed, her letters are full of aches and pains—but now she seemed to be getting worse. She suffered excruciating headaches, referring to "my head which is too full of blood."[576] And she told her father about the swelling of her limbs and a "general fullness."[577] Upon the advice of a doctor, she cut her food and drink intake in half. Also, she wrote, "I am to take no kind of medicine and never fatigue myself with exercise." She seemed annoyed that she didn't have more convincing symptoms. "Nobody, to look at me, could suppose I wanted the advice of medical people, as my appearance indicates the most florid health," she wrote. "My appetite is uncommonly good, and my digestion such that I never find any quantity or quality of food disagree with me."

Given all that, it's difficult not to wonder whether some of Peggy's health problems were in her head. They became one of the primary story lines of her later years—along with her careful attention to family finances and great devotion to her children and stepchildren.

Her eldest stepson, Benedict Arnold VI, was a constant cause of worry. Against the advice of his father, he assumed his military commission and went off to fight against the French. "We have not heard from poor Ben for a long time past, and have reason to fear he is a prisoner," Peggy wrote to her stepson Richard in mid-1794.[578] And indeed he was held captive in a French prison for two years. Like his father, he did not know when to quit, and he volunteered as an artillery officer in the Caribbean, again over his father's objections. Wounded in the leg while serving in Jamaica, he made the same choice as his father by refusing amputation but was less lucky. He died from gangrene.

The next few years followed the Arnolds' pattern of overreaching and underachieving. They took an aristocratic step up by moving the family to a town house featuring a wine cellar in Gloucester Place, in the Marylebone district of central London.[579] But Arnold could not follow up on the goodwill he had earned in the Caribbean. His suggestion that he lead an expedition to liberate Peru, Chile, and Mexico from

Spanish control was hardly taken seriously by Prime Minister William Pitt.[580]

There was one benefit from his Caribbean exploits, however. The Arnolds collected land grants for 13,400 acres among "the waste lands of the crown in Upper Canada," and because of the general's "gallant and meritorious services in Guadaloupe," they were exempted from the requirement that they live in the area.[581] The Canadian land certainly wouldn't bring quick money, though. So Arnold climbed into debt to finance privateers to seek fortune on the oceans. They would travel without Arnold, since his gout would not allow it. Arnold would have to trust in others.

Peggy hated the idea. As it turned out, she was right to distrust what she called "the vile privateers."[582] She believed the captains cheated Arnold out of fifty thousand pounds, leaving him and his family desperately overextended.

While the older boys were beginning their military careers and sending back reports of steady progress, Peggy's frail daughter Sophia was frightening her parents. Arnold wrote in March 1798 that twelve-year-old Sophia, "though not sick, is very delicate and we have ... to take her from school for the country air."[583] Two years later Sophia suffered what her mother called "a kind of paralytic stroke, which deprived her of the use of her legs, and extended up her back."[584] "After some severe remedies of blistering etc., she was in a degree restored to the use of her limbs, but one leg still remains without any sense of feeling," Peggy wrote. "After trying every means to restore it, the medical team ordered her to the seas, for the purpose of using the warm sea bath."

A governess helped take care of Sophia, who stayed with the Fitches in the English Channel town of Brighton and seemed to improve. Her mother, meanwhile, remained in London and worried. "I dread another attack which might prove fatal," she wrote.

Peggy's mental health was now tenuous at best. She seemed scattered and forgetful. In a letter, Arnold noted "a fullness of habits which frequently affects her head more or less with a giddiness."[585]

Arnold, on the other hand, seemed fully aware that his own world was steadily crumbling. "He is, at present, in the most harassed, wretched shape I have ever seen him in," Peggy wrote to their son Edward. "Disappointed in his highly raised expectations, harassed by the sailors who are loudly demanding their prize money, when in fact their advances have greatly exceeded anything that is due to them, . . . he knows not which way to turn himself."[586] But Peggy threw in a teaspoon of token optimism: "As we have often been extracted from difficulties, I trust we shall get over our present embarrassments."

But Arnold would not. The vigorous warrior's health collapsed, and he suffered from "a general dropsy and a disease in the lungs." Unable to swallow or speak for three days, he died at his Gloucester Place home, whose lease had been given up by him and Peggy just the week before because they could no longer afford it.[587] His wife and the Fitch sisters were with him when he passed away at age sixty on June 14, 1801.[588]

Peggy buried him at St. Mary's Church of Battersea, an unassuming suburb across the Thames. The basement crypt was reasonably priced, and she put him next to his friend William Fitch, whose name had been lent to Arnold's youngest son and who, like Arnold's eldest son, had died from combat wounds in Jamaica.

Arnold appointed his wife as "executrix" of his will, a testament to her talent for finances, which far exceeded his own. But that role also left her with a final insult, since Arnold's will provided money to the teenaged John Sage, product of his infidelity. Peggy was so wracked by emotions that she asked her friend Ann Fitch to write to her father with the news of Arnold's death. "She evinces upon this occasion—as you know she has done upon many trying ones before—that fortitude and resignation which in a superior and well-regulated mind only is capable of existing," Fitch wrote.[589]

But when Peggy's "well-regulated mind" felt capable of writing, it confessed to brother-in-law Neddy Burd that "I sometimes fear that my reason will give way."[590] And to make it crystal clear that her husband had long tortured her soul, she added: "My sufferings are not of the present moment only. Years of unhappiness have passed, I had cast my lot, complaints were unavailing, and you and my other friends are ignorant of the many causes of uneasiness I have had."

Now Peggy was a widow at age forty-one. The woman who had worried about "unmanning" her husband was now manless. But she wasn't free of his legacy, or his debts. Though she had always hated her husband's irresponsible speculation, she knew in her heart that life and love were always gambles. "Matrimony," she wrote her father, "is but a lottery."[591]

CHAPTER 20

The Keepsake

SOON AFTER PEGGY WAS WIDOWED, the crush of her husband's debts pushed her thoughts toward suicide. "At one period, when I viewed everything through a false medium, I fancied that nothing but the sacrifice of my life would benefit my children, for that my wretchedness embittered every moment of their lives," she wrote her father. "And dreadful to say, I was many times on the point of making the sacrifice."[592] However, she added: "Nothing more strongly proves to myself the deprivation of my reason; for situated as they are, my life is most valuable to them, as the remainder of my days will be devoted to them and their advancement and welfare."

And indeed the rest of Peggy's days demonstrated her determination to provide for her children, to push them forward to success. These days also demonstrated Peggy's essential contradiction, as a woman who complained of physical ailments and loss of reason but energetically and brilliantly maneuvered through complex financial straits to steer her family to safety.

Moving out of Gloucester Place to "a small but very neat house" on Bryanston Street, Peggy was forced to sell off many of her possessions, including her wine and some furniture that was "chiefly made by myself."[593] With creditors laying siege from all directions, she set a price and paid for any of Arnold's personal items that she refused to give up, including one of his old shirts. Likewise, "a little family pride" compelled her to hold on to her silver.[594]

In an irony not lost on Peggy, she acquired cheaper furniture for her Bryanston Street home through her maid, "who is now a more independent woman than her mistress."[595] Although she was a society woman, Peggy was not particularly obsessed with possessions except for sewing supplies, perhaps, and a few other items of sentimental value. Peggy understood that money and its trappings translated into social standing, and she feared the loss of that. "The want of a carriage I shall most feel, not only in point of comfort but of respectability," she admitted.[596]

Some aspects of her old life were gone forever, but she thought the important ones could be saved. "I trust that my character is so firmly established that, notwithstanding the great change in my situation, I shall not lose any rank in society, except among the gay and very fashionable part of my acquaintance, to whose pleasures I cannot administer, and with characters of this description I have no longer a wish to associate."[597]

Peggy took pains to stay in the good graces of powerful men, and indeed her sons' military careers were helped by the family's longstanding friendship with Lord Cornwallis, which had flowered when he and Arnold sailed across the Atlantic together. Peggy had a stranger relationship with Peter Moore, an up-and-coming politician who was Arnold's partner in the privateering venture. Peggy found Moore useless in helping her untangle the business—"more the man of words than deeds"—but she carefully avoided making an enemy of him.[598]

For some reason, possibly jealousy, Moore's wife became Peggy's antagonist. "A long time ago," Peggy wrote her son Edward, "he wrote me a very long and handsome letter, which she opened, and suppressed. She says she opened it by mistake, and suppressed it from the fear of my suspecting it to have been done from motives of curiosity. This is but a bad excuse, but I have thought proper to accept it."[599]

She told Moore about the incident, though, "to account for my never noticing his letter, which probably required a reply." Of Mrs. Moore, Peggy added: "With some good traits in her character, she has a great many peculiarities which render her less amiable than could be wished. But we must take the world as we find [it], and it does not do to investigate characters too closely." Peggy had no time for intrigue. At this stage in her life, her mission was financial survival.

Her sons Edward and James, serving in the British army, lived on their salaries and let her keep their pensions for the family's use. Peggy had protected herself years before Arnold's death by arranging for her father to help her invest her own British pension payments—"to preserve that money sacredly for my children."[600] When she asked her father for assistance, Peggy had made clear that Arnold, whom her father no doubt despised, would have no access to the money—that it was held "in the name of *my* agent, for which *I* am credited on his books."[601] In their letters about finding the best interest rate, the father and daughter never noted the oddity of depositing the crown's treason payments in the Bank of North America, chartered by the United States Congress.[602] Nor did the Bank of North America seem to ask any troublesome questions.

One member of the Shippen family was far from helpful. Peggy calculated that her brother Edward owed her four thousand pounds in principal and interest on an old, unpaid loan. But she never saw the money, and her father resisted her pleas to help her collect it.[603]

Another useless financial foray was Mount Pleasant, the beautiful Philadelphia estate whose purchase had proved to Edward Shippen how fervently Arnold wished to wed his daughter. The mansion was seized by authorities after Arnold's treason, but Peggy arranged for her father to buy it back for them, with their interest kept secret. In 1785, Peggy instructed her father to try to sell it, since land prices were falling and the estate might be seized again if anyone found out the real owner. But eighteen years later, in 1803, the investment was draped in confusion. The estate that had once represented Peggy's grand prospects was a symbol only of grim futility. "I presume from your not mentioning the subject that I am never to expect to derive any advantage from the Mount Pleasant estate," she wrote her father. "I should like, however, to know in what manner it has been disposed of."[604]

Peggy was looking for money wherever she could find it, including the Canadian wilderness. She wrote firmly to her stepsons Richard and Henry, prodding them to claim the family's lands: "I hope you will be able to have the lands located soon and eligibly, as I am told they are rising greatly in value."[605]

But the real weight around Peggy's neck was Arnold's privateering disaster, in which sailors and businessmen were demanding payment, whether they were owed it or not. Peggy was her best hardheaded self, refusing to pay claims she viewed as false, and finding a way to honor those that were valid. She waged a two-year legal battle with a man she referred to as The Swede, a shipowner who claimed thousands of pounds for the loss of cargo and detention of his vessel. Her lawyer triumphed in court over the Swede's, saving her family from ruin. "Had they succeeded, ten times the property I have would not have satisfied their demand," Peggy wrote.[606]

Detailing the financial "troubles and difficulties" in a note to her stepsons, she bragged: "I believe I may without vanity say that there are few women that could have so far conquered them as I have done. . . . I have not reserved for myself a bottle of wine or even a teaspoon that I have not paid for."[607] And she made clear that her primary aim had been to preserve the family honor: "To you I have rendered an essential service; I have rescued your father's memory from disrespect, by paying all his just debts; and his children will now never have the mortification of being reproached with his speculations having hurt anybody beyond his own family."[608]

Yet around the time that Peggy vanquished the Swede and tasted victory over her husband's debts, her health precipitously declined. She was suffering from what she called "the dreaded evil, a cancer."[609] Her illness put further pressure on the arrangements she had made for her children, and it is clear from her letters that she felt desperate to put them in the best possible position before she died. The children she once jokingly described as "little plagues" were her greatest pleasures. And in the end, they were her triumph and her legacy.

She treated her two surviving stepsons, Richard and Henry, with the utmost courtesy, sending them their father's locks of hair, sleeve buttons, and shoebuckles as keepsakes after his death. She admonished them for their harsh criticism of their father, and gave stepmotherly advice to Richard, advising him not to marry "till you are enabled to support her in a comfortable style."[610] Both brothers ultimately wed and had children in Canada, becoming merchants and maintaining vast landholdings as a result of the crown's grants. Peggy's attentive letters across the ocean also made sure the needs of Benedict Arnold's sister Hannah were addressed. Hannah died in her nephew Henry's home in 1803.

Peggy's letters voiced stern tolerance for "the Boy"—Arnold's other son in Canada, John Sage, who was treated like a brother by Richard and Henry. "The Boy who is with you," she wrote, "ought to be taught, by his own labor, to procure his own livelihood; he ought never to have been brought up with any other ideas."[611]

Her own offspring filled her correspondence, as they filled her heart. In the worst times, she wrote, "Such children compensate for a thousand ills."[612] All four of Peggy's sons embarked on military careers.[613] Her first-born, Edward, went to India, and his departure in 1800 was torturous to Peggy. "My darling Edward leaves me in about ten days, to try his fortune in the East," she wrote. "His death could scarcely be a more severe stroke."[614] She predicted that she would never see him again, and she was right.

⸺⸺

Edward, who at six months of age was in the same bedroom as his mad mother and George Washington on that remarkable day in 1780, experienced a short but interesting adulthood. A lieutenant in the Sixth Bengal Cavalry, he served as the paymaster of Muttra and, according to one historical account, "gave food largely and secretly to the suffering people during a famine."[615] Edward never married, but when he died in 1813 at age thirty-three, he provided in his will for "a native woman living with me."[616]

Asia must have seemed like a new and promising world to children whose parents had struggled so spectacularly on two other continents. Both Edward's brother George and his sister Sophia followed him to India. George rose to lieutenant colonel in the Second Bengal Cavalry before his death in 1828. He married a British woman and had a child with her, but like his brother he also had relations with a "native woman." His will remembered both the native woman and the daughter they had together. Peggy's half-Indian granddaughter eventually immigrated to Ireland and married a British architect.[617]

Sophia's fate was particularly surprising. Though much beloved, she was weak of constitution and possessed only "a moderate share of beauty," according to her mother. And she spent much of her time in the company of much older women. She seemed destined to become a "spinster" or "old maid." Sophia's brothers Edward and George summoned her to India so they could take care of her. She also may have been part of the "fishing fleet"—a slang term for women who came to India to hook a husband among the white soldiers and businessmen there.[618]

In India, Sophia met a young widowed officer named Pownoll Phipps, a friend of her brother Edward. According to family history, Sophia became terribly ill, seemed near death, and asked to marry Phipps before her demise. He agreed, and after their wedding she regained her health—a brilliant recovery that seemed reminiscent of her mother's sudden restoration to health back at Robinson House, though probably not as opportunistic. Sophia not only gave her husband fifteen good years of marriage but bore him five children. The Phippses brought their family to England, where they became active in Christian evangelism. She died of tuberculosis in 1828.

Peggy's second-born son, James, who bore the strongest resemblance to his father, served in the Royal Engineers in Malta, Egypt, and the Caribbean. In the South American country of Suriname, James suffered a leg wound while leading the successful storming of a fort, and for that act of heroism he was awarded a sword valued at one hundred pounds. He commanded engineers in Canada and, according to one story, visited his family's old house in St. John and wept as he entered. He rose to the rank of lieutenant general and served as an aide to King William IV. His marriage to a woman from the Isle of Wight resulted in no children, and he died in 1854.

Peggy's youngest, William, was less of a wanderer. He served as a captain in the 19th Royal Lancers and became a country gentleman and justice of the peace in Buckinghamshire, west of London. One of his sons, William Trail Arnold, seemed to inherit the bravery of his grandparents.

A captain, he was killed in 1855 while assaulting the Russian defenses at Sevastopol during the Crimean War. His nephew, Peggy's great-grandson, was Theodore Stephenson, a British major general in World War I.

If a person's descendants and friends serve as their measure in life, Peggy stands tall. And when she began showing severe symptoms of uterine cancer in 1803, she found herself surrounded and soothed by love. She told her stepsons that she suffered from "an internal complaint, under which I had long labored, increased to a degree highly alarming. For the last ten weeks I have been entirely precluded from the use of animal food, wine, beer, and any other thing that can enrich the blood—and have been almost entirely confined to a recumbent posture."[619] To Betsy, she called it a "complaint of the womb," and added, "My complaint is quite local, as my general health was never better."[620] In fact, she said, she was "restored to a perfect serenity of mind, and a degree of contentment, that some time ago I thought it impossible for me ever to regain. . . . The kindness I have and still continue to receive from my friends here is very uncommon."[621]

That June she brought seventeen-year-old Sophia and eight-year-old William with her to Chambers Farm in Epping, northeast of London, as guests of an old friend, Mrs. Shedden. "Being at a large farmhouse," Peggy wrote, "I have the advantage of a milk diet in the greatest perfection. . . . There are few places I can be so much at my ease as here, where I was brought in a coach, so fitted out as to enable me to perform the whole journey laying down."[622]

Peggy's collection of exiled Loyalist friends took turns watching out for her and offering comfortable places to stay. Chief among them were the Fitches, of course, as well as Sarah Coxe and her husband Daniel, who had been a member of the New Jersey governor's council before the revolution, and who wrote the letter to Peggy's father telling him that she was dying. Peggy wasn't rich and beautiful anymore, and she was no longer the life of the party. But her friends' loyalty in her final days went far beyond politeness, reflecting their deep and lasting love.

By November, Peggy's health had further deteriorated. "I have lately been much worse, in consequence of a very large tumor having formed which broke and discharged an immense quantity," she wrote her father.[623] A few months later she told her sister, "For nine days I lay with every appearance of a corpse."[624] She rallied slightly, but by May 1804 she was relying on opium to quell the pain and bring on sleep. She expressed "little hope of long continuing an inhabitant of this world."[625] In fact, she lasted long enough to send her son George off to India in early July, and to write a letter to her father that same month with a discussion of whether King George was more threatened by France's Napoleon Bonaparte or by his own domestic enemies.

But a letter to her son Edward the previous year served as a more lyrical coda. "Misfortunes and other circumstances have made me lay castle-building quite aside, but I sometimes flatter myself that we may yet see happier days," she wrote. "Mine has been an eventful life, and I may yet ascend nearer the top of the wheel."[626]

Peggy Shippen Arnold died in her Bryanston Street home at age forty-four on August 24, 1804. She was interred at Battersea, next to her husband. In her will she stipulated: "It is my wish that my funeral may be as plain as is consistent with the situation of my family, avoiding all superfluous expense, and that my just debts may be paid."[627]

Indeed, Peggy believed in paying her debts, even if she never answered for her perceived sins against the American Revolution, which would remain unconfirmed for more than a century. But a bit of evidence was available among Peggy's personal things. Soon after her death, her loved ones found the lock of hair that John André had given her in Philadelphia more than a quarter century earlier, when Peggy's life had been parties and poetry and balls.[628] Peggy had treasured André's keepsake all that time. By keeping his memory alive, she had paid her final debt.

Epilogue

THE STORY OF PEGGY SHIPPEN INSPIRES A NUMBER OF WHAT-IFS. What if Peggy had been exposed as a traitor on September 25, 1780? What if every fact about her participation in the plot had been known immediately after her husband fled to the enemy?

Well, for one thing, she would be more famous today. She might be considered one of the most famous characters of the American Revolution. She might be the subject of scores of biographies, instead of this single book written more than two centuries after her death.

Would she have gone on trial? Probably. She would have benefited from her social standing and the fact that, within her family and its sphere of influence, she would have had access to many of the finest legal minds in America. She also would have benefited from the fact that she was a woman. Even if all the facts had been known, many of the men sitting in judgment of her would have assumed that she acted at her husband's direction, rather than accepting a scenario that now seems equally plausible—that the plot was her idea in the first place.

Other people who were found guilty of spying or treason, such as John André and the two Quakers in Philadelphia, were hanged. But it seems extremely unlikely that Peggy would have met such a fate. Women were executed rarely in that era, especially white women.[629] The US government did not hang a woman until Mary Surratt suffered that punishment for the conspiracy to assassinate President Abraham Lincoln in 1865.[630]

Revolutionary justice differed dramatically for men and women, and sometimes the difference was set out in statute. In New Jersey, for example, treasonous men faced death but could be pardoned if they joined the Continental Navy. Female traitors did not have the naval option, of course. For a first offense, they faced a fine of up to three hundred pounds and a year in prison. Only for a second offense could they receive capital punishment.[631]

Peggy likely would have been imprisoned or exiled. The most prominent American to be labeled a traitor before Benedict Arnold was Dr. Benjamin Church, an independence activist in Massachusetts who was arrested for "criminal correspondence" with the enemy. He was imprisoned for two years before being allowed to board a ship for the British-held Caribbean. That ship was lost at sea.[632]

The Arnold treason was considered far worse than Church's, but Peggy would have been held less responsible for it because she was a woman. To be sure, female Loyalist spies faced punishment, but it was hardly by the book. When a New York woman, Lorenda Holmes, was caught spying, she was stripped naked and displayed before a mob, but then freed with a warning. When she continued her espionage and was caught a second time, a soldier forced her to take off her shoe and place her right foot onto hot coals.[633]

Peggy probably would have avoided such humiliations, since she was a family friend of General Washington. But one factor working against Peggy's exile would have been the idea that she would reunite with her husband. If leading Patriots had known Peggy was guilty, they hardly would have sought to restore her happiness by returning her to Arnold. Thus Peggy might have stayed in custody a long time.

While we're playing what-if, we might also ask what would have happened if Peggy had succeeded. Certainly a British capture of West Point might have made all the difference. As Arnold put it quite cleverly after his defection: "The supplies of meat for Washington's army are on the east side of the river, and the supplies of bread on the west; were the Highlands in our possession, Washington would be obliged to fight or disband his army for want of provisions."[634] If Peggy had helped deliver the Hudson Highlands, she might be considered the heroine who saved the colonies for the king. She and Arnold might even be honored in Westminster Abbey, alongside André. Or perhaps Arnold and André would have taken all the credit, and she would have ended up no more famous than she is now.

Of course, Peggy didn't succeed in her plot. Nor was she captured and tried. Instead she retreated to the margins of history.

So what is the proper way to remember her?

She was quintessentially American in her bravery and her improvisation. She was dogged in her efforts to preserve her family, and to build on the gains made by her ancestors.

In many ways, Peggy was a real-life Scarlett O'Hara, a woman forced by desperate circumstances to take extreme measures, a woman fighting to preserve some element of a glorious past against the ravages of an unforgiving, transformative war. She was a woman who believed that the ends justified the means, and she thought she had found the means.

Peggy's story tells us much about America's Loyalists—that they were not cartoonishly vile quislings attempting to imprison their countrymen for their own comfort. Her story also tells us about the role of women in that era—how few options they had, and how almost every bold step they took to influence events was taken outside the bounds of society's norms.

But most of all Peggy's story tells us about ourselves—how we can scheme and maneuver and fail spectacularly, and then find a way to survive, and even endure.

Acknowledgments

This book would have been impossible without the expertise and ceaseless efforts of our team of four historical researchers, whose understanding of archives and broad knowledge of eighteenth-century life were awe-inspiring. We thank them for their patience, energy, and resourcefulness. The four are Andrea Meyer (M.A., New York University and Long Island University), Stephanie Schmeling and Julianna Monjeau (both M.A., NYU), and Marie Elizabeth Stango, a doctoral candidate at the University of Michigan.

Gratitude is too modest a word to express our regard for Hugh Arnold, a descendant of Benedict Arnold and Peggy Shippen who shared a rarely seen set of Peggy's letters.

Gary Heidt, our literary agent, brought us together for this project. Holly Rubino, our editor at Lyons Press, orchestrated the effort, with expert support from Ellen Urban and Ann H. Marlowe. Paul Iwanaga tracked down the historical illustrations, and Rick Tuma created the maps.

Columbia University nurtured this project. James Neal, Michael T. Ryan, and Eric T. Wakin from the Libraries were unfailingly accommodating, and helped us assemble our research team. David Schizer and Kent McKeever from the Law School facilitated our work, as did Anke L. Nolting and Laura L. Tewksbury of the College of Physicians and Surgeons.

Maya Jasanoff of the Harvard University history faculty was generous beyond any scholarly duty in sharing her research discoveries, and Emilie Hardman of Harvard's Houghton Library helped us review Arnold documents in that collection.

Author Thomas Fleming kindly volunteered information about the Arnold family in England, and assisted us in reaching out to other experts.

Heather Meek, an assistant professor of English at the University of Regina in Saskatchewan, Canada, shared her understanding of a fascinating area of study, eighteenth-century female "hysteria."

Jean W. Ashton, Edward "Ted" O'Reilly, and Tammy Kiter, always smiling, brought us boxes and boxes of interesting documents and microfilms over many visits to the New-York Historical Society. After we requested Burd-Shippen Papers at the University of Pittsburgh Libraries, a number of them were digitized and placed on the Internet under the supervision of Wendy M. Pflug and Laura Brooks.

Librarians were heroic. We thank Lynn Favreau, the extremely knowledgeable reference librarian at the Scotch Plains (New Jersey) Public Library, plus the staffs of the Skokie (Illinois) Public Library and Northwestern University in Evanston, Illinois. We also are grateful to the staff of the William L. Clements Library at the University of Michigan in Ann Arbor, especially J. Kevin Graffagnino, Barbara DeWolfe, and Janet Bloom.

Kathy Ludwig at the David Library of the American Revolution in Washington Crossing, Pennsylvania, uncovered at least a half dozen additional sources for this project. Professor James Gigantino, a visiting fellow at the David Library, helped us check on Peggy Shippen's royal pension.

The Historical Society of Pennsylvania was a vital resource. Among those who guided us through this organization's extensive collection of Shippen Papers and provided other support were Chris Damiani, Dr. Tamara Gaskell, Steven Smith, Sarah Heim, Ron Medford, Keith Lyons, Dr. Daniel Rolph, David Haugaard, and Lee Arnold.

At the American Revolution Center in Philadelphia, Bruce Cole and R. Scott Stephenson offered always welcome encouragement and assistance.

Rhonda R. McClure and Steven Solomon and their staff at the New England Historic Genealogical Society identified as many living Arnold-Shippen descendants as world privacy laws permitted. At Davis Polk & Wardwell (London), Paul Kumleben and Jill Sterner skillfully hunted down contact data for those descendants.

The collections of the New Haven Museum include interesting Arnold-related documents, which were sent to us by the redoubtable James Campbell.

Miss Allison Derrett of the Royal Archives, Windsor Castle, invested her time to find interesting information. Elspeth Flood and Rick Stirling assisted us in understanding which Sir Walter Stirling presented Arnold to the king.

Patricia Cokines of Cortes and Hay, Inc. guided us efficiently through a 1776 real estate title search in Hunterdon County, New Jersey. Richard Stothoff of the Hunterdon County Historical Society in Flemington, New Jersey, helped us access resources there.

The authors pay tribute to the New York American Revolution Round Table, and especially chairman David Jacobs, for the help provided to our colleague Andrea Meyer. It should also be noted that Andrea's knowledge of the Arnold treason was greatly enhanced by her mentor, the late John A. Burke.

Others who chipped in: Amber McAlpine of the New Brunswick Museum; Tal Nadan, Thomas Lannon, and Richard Foster of the New York Public Library; Richard Sieber of the Philadelphia Museum of Art; Elizabeth Bennett and Gabriel Swift of the Princeton University Libraries; Patrick Raftery of the Westchester County (New York) Historical Society; Jean Solinsky of the Winterthur Museum, Garden and Library; Karen Kukil of the Neilson Library at Smith College; and Simone Munson of the Wisconsin Historical Society.

Stephen's wife, Margaret Ayres, contributed more to his efforts on this book than anyone else, offering years of unfailing good cheer, patience, encouragement, and extremely careful, thoughtful reading of multiple manuscripts. Margaret: thanks and brava!

Other people in Stephen's family have patiently listened to him talk about "the Peggy project" and have read his writings since he first learned of her story several years ago from reading the masterful four-volume biography of George Washington by James Thomas Flexner. These indulgent relatives are Daniel and Elizabeth Case, Alice Ayres, Richard Case, Megan Weiss, Richard Ayres, Francesca Ciliberti, Anne Dawson, Peg Bachmann, and Michael and Pamela Miles.

Friends of Stephen's who provided writing and research advice include Ros Avrett, Jason Berger, Richard and Paula Broude, Cindy Carlson, the Honorable Thomas Carlson, Edward C. Cerny III, Sarah Parr Cerny, Michael Cook, Ronald DeKoven, Peggy Duckett, Peter East, Nathaniel Edmonds, Dr. Kenneth Forde, Jason and Janet Kranes Fensterstock, Bertram and Diana Firestone, John Gose, L. Gordon Harriss, Bo Kirschen, Laurel Kirschen, Roger Kirschen, Kimberley Cooper Kissoyan, Margaret Kratochvil, William and Evelyn Kroener, Angus and Joanne MacBeth, Jock and Jean McClellan, Joseph Pardo, David Reading, Michael Rothwell, Claire Ruppert, James Shepard, Lori Shinseki, Robert and Roseanne Sticht, Allison Stockman, Charles S. Whitman III, Dr. Clyde Wu, and Roger Zissu.

Stephen's colleagues at Emerald Development Managers LP—Neil Cohen, Charles Collins, James Wells, Thomas Gallo, and Barbara Borer—cheerfully encouraged his efforts and, more times than he can count, covered for him while he used work hours to get things done on this book.

Mark thanks his wife, Lisa, for her wisdom and support. Also deserving of gratitude are his parents, John and Jane Jacob; his siblings, Tim, Kathleen, Paul, Matt, and Anne; his daughters Maury and Katy; his mother-in-law, Jacquelyn Hall; and his son-in-law, Greg. Mark also notes the unfailing friendship and advice of Richard and Cate Cahan, Tom and Lucy Keating, Richard and Esther Triffler, Michael Williams, Ken Kozak, Lawrence Downes, Bill Hearst, Kelly Nicholas, Alexia Trzyna, Guy Ransom, Jim Hathaway, Gael Sammartino, Gerald Koonce, and Myrna Thomas. Mark's *Chicago Tribune* colleagues provided a fine support system, especially Robin Daughtridge, John Kass, Mary Schmich, Gerry Kern, Jane Hirt, Peter Kendall, Phil Jurik, Kerry Luft, and Stephan Benzkofer.

And finally, thanks to composer Julian Livingston for his 1976 opera *Twist of Treason*, an artistic reminder of the power of Peggy's story.

Chapter Notes

Chapter 1

1 Judge Edward Shippen to Edward Shippen of Lancaster, June 11, 1760, Shippen Papers, Historical Society of Pennsylvania. For clarity, citations for these two Edward Shippens call one a judge and the other "of Lancaster" even in letters before the one became a judge and the other was in Lancaster.

2 Klein, *Portrait of an Early American Family*, 22, 70; Randall, *Benedict Arnold*, 384–385.

3 Randall, 389; Lomask, "Benedict Arnold: The Aftermath of Treason," 84.

4 R. Harvey, *"A Few Bloody Noses,"* 14; Weir, *Fatal Victories*, 133.

5 Flexner, *The Traitor and the Spy*, 189; Scharf and Westcott, *History of Philadelphia, 1609–1884*, 2:870; Randall, 390.

6 Judge Edward Shippen to Joseph Shippen, Nov. 17, 1790, in Lewis, "Edward Shippen, Chief-Justice of Pennsylvania," 31. The definition of "eye servant" is from Noah Webster's 1828 dictionary, at www.1828-dictionary.com/d/word/eye-servant.

7 Christ Church of Philadelphia, www.christchurchphila.org.

8 Lippincott, *Early Philadelphia*, 69.

9 Watson, *Annals of Philadelphia*, 1:370.

10 R. Harvey, 24.

11 Sargent, *Life and Career of Major John André*, 132–134.

12 Lippincott, 88–89.

13 Jefferson, in Illick, *Colonial Pennsylvania*, xvii.

14 Washington, *Writings*, ed. Ford, 2:438; Randall, 74, 420.

15 Isaacson, *Benjamin Franklin*, 194–200; Worner, "A Benjamin Franklin Letter," 103; Bruce, *Benjamin Franklin, Self-Revealed*, 1:129. Peggy's maternal grandfather, Tench Francis, was Franklin's cowriter of the constitution for the academy that was a forerunner of the University of Pennsylvania.

16 Danson, *Drawing the Line*, 82.

17 Illick, 242; Newman, *Freedom's Prophet*, 28–32; Jones Tabernacle African Methodist Episcopal Church, www.jtamec.org.

18 Rooks, *Midwifery and Childbirth in America*, 19; Knott, *Sensibility and the American Revolution*, 99; *Hazard's Register of Pennsylvania*, 1:438; University of Pennsylvania

biographies, "Dr. William Shippen," www.archives.upenn.edu/people/1700s/shippen_wm_jr.html.

19 Purvis, *Colonial America to 1763,* 174.

20 Lippincott, 180.

21 Moss and Crane, *Historic Houses of Philadelphia,* 30.

22 Lippincott, 280.

23 Klein, 11–27.

24 Illick, 3–5.

25 Balch, "Dr. William Shippen, the Elder," 212–213; Klein, 14.

26 Walker, "Life of Margaret Shippen, Wife of Benedict Arnold," 24:258.

27 Randall, 384.

28 Klein, 45–47, 51–56, 60–67, 69–73. Shippen's scandalous third wife was Mary Gray Nowland; her diehard husband was John Nowland.

29 Klein, 70. Rev. Aaron Burr was the father of politician Aaron Burr, whose memoirs provided one of the most prominent early assertions of Peggy's guilt.

30 Walker, 24:266.

31 Jasper Yeates in 1764, in Walker, 24:266.

32 Klein, 77–82, 150; Lewis, 11–34.

33 Judge Edward Shippen to Joseph Shippen, Feb. 25, 1749, in Lewis, 13.

34 Middle Temple, history, www.middletemple.org.uk/the_inn/History_of_the_Inn.

35 Edward Shippen of Lancaster to Judge Edward Shippen, 1749, in Walker, 24:265–266.

36 Judge Edward Shippen to Edward Shippen of Lancaster, June 8, 1750, in Lewis, 18.

37 Lewis, 20; Flexner, 188–189.

38 Flexner, 189; Walker, 24:413.

39 Peggy Shippen to Judge Edward Shippen, Jan. 5, 1803, Shippen Papers, Historical Society of Pennsylvania.

Chapter 2

40 Bingham, *American Preceptor,* 42nd ed., 104. The *Preceptor* was first published in 1794.

41 Peggy Shippen to Judge Edward Shippen, June 26, 1792, in Walker, 25:460.

42 Peggy Shippen to Edward Arnold, January 1804, in Taylor, *Some New Light,* 28.

43 Poem from *American Country Almanac for 1754,* in Lyons, *Sex Among the Rabble,* 158.

44 Norton, *Liberty's Daughters,* 55; Lyons, 163. Peggy's family was not prudish about sex. According to Lyons, Peggy's merchant uncle Tench Francis Jr. advertised bawdy books for sale, including French erotica such as Roger L'Estrange's translation of *Portuguese Love Letters.*

45 Neddy Burd, 1780, in Flexner, 190.

46 Mrs. Gibson, recalling mother's impressions, in Walker, 24:414.

47 Randall, 384.
48 Edward Shippen of Lancaster to Judge Edward Shippen, April 15, 1775, in Klein, 153.
49 Anderson, *Crucible of War*, xvii–xxiv, 714–734.
50 Jasanoff, *Liberty's Exiles*, 24–25.
51 Judge Edward Shippen to Edward Shippen of Lancaster, Sept. 10, 1765, in Walker, 24:419.
52 Judge Edward Shippen to Edward Shippen of Lancaster, Oct. 17, 1765, in Walker, 24:419.
53 Judge Edward Shippen to Edward Shippen of Lancaster, April 6, 1766, in Walker, 24:420.
54 White House, presidential biographies, "George Washington," www.whitehouse .gov/about/presidents/georgewashington.
55 Dos Passos, *Head and Heart of Thomas Jefferson*, 365.
56 Peggy Shippen to Betsy Shippen Burd, May 20, 1800, in Walker, 24:414.
57 *Pennsylvania Packet*, March 18, 1777.
58 Judge Edward Shippen to Edward Shippen of Lancaster, April 20, 1775, Shippen Papers, Historical Society of Pennsylvania.
59 Judge Edward Shippen to Edward Shippen of Lancaster, June 30, 1775, in Walker, 24:414.
60 Klein, 163.
61 Shreve, *Tench Tilghman*, 37.
62 Jasanoff, 30.
63 Judge Edward Shippen to Jasper Yeates, Jan. 19, 1776, in Lewis, 25.
64 Joyce, *Story of Philadelphia*, 148.
65 Deeds from John Gregg & Wife to Edward Shippen Jr., Hunterdon County Deed Book 1, 457–60 (June 1, 1776, recorded Sept. 22, 1791), and from Edward Shippen Jr. & Wife to Robert Shewell, Hunterdon County Deed Book 1, 461–64 (Dec. 10, 1778, recorded Sept. 24, 1791), both on file with the Hunterdon County Clerk's Office, Flemington, N.J. This rural home is often described as being in Amwell, which was a regional term used loosely for places in what is now central and southern Hunterdon County, N.J. Edward Shippen paid £3,200 for the 260 acres, house, and other buildings, located on the south branch of the Raritan River about two miles east of Flemington. That price roughly compares to more than $500,000 in the United States in 2010, according to http://measuringworth.com.
66 Judge Edward Shippen, 1776, in Flexner, 194.
67 Peggy Shippen to Judge Edward Shippen, Oct. 5, 1802, in Walker, 25:480.
68 Judge Edward Shippen to Jasper Yeates, June 5, 1776, in Klein, 165.
69 R. Harvey, 229. Burgoyne would later surrender to the "spoilt children" at Saratoga.
70 Dickinson, *Letters from a Farmer in Pennsylvania*, 33. These letters calling for appeasement were originally published in 1767–68.
71 Randall, 387; Walker, 25:29.
72 Burrows, *Forgotten Patriots*, 251–253; Musto, "Captive in Jersey," 10–12.

73 Young, Jenkins, and Seilhamer, *Memorial History of the City of Philadelphia*, 344.
74 Judge Edward Shippen to Edward Shippen of Lancaster, Jan. 18, 1777, in Lewis, 27.
75 Ibid.
76 Ibid., 27–28. 77 Judge Edward Shippen to Edward Shippen of Lancaster, March 11, 1777, in Randall, 388.
78 Flexner, 200.
79 Walker, 24:426.
80 Judge Edward Shippen to Edward Shippen of Lancaster, March 11, 1777, in Lewis, 28.

Chapter 3
81 Jackson, *With the British Army in Philadelphia*, 11; Watson, 2:180. According to reports, all but one of the church bells were removed from Philadelphia and taken to Allentown, Pa.
82 Hatch, *Major John André*, 151; Rose, *Washington's Spies*, 35.
83 Brooks, "Philadelphia Dancing Assembly"; Balch, *The Philadelphia Assemblies*, 14–82; Watson, 1:277.
84 Hatch, 88.
85 Klein, 297.
86 Sale, *Old Time Belles and Cavaliers*, 145–160; Stern, *David Franks*, 22; Watson, 3:470; Randall, 389.
87 Harland, *Some Colonial Homesteads*, 120.
88 Jackson, 214.
89 Flexner, 22.
90 Hatch, 9–13.
91 Hatch, 56–57.
92 *Notes and Queries*, 79.
93 US State Department, "The Great Seal of the United States," www.state.gov/documents/organization/27807.pdf.
94 http://measuringworth.com/, accessed Aug. 17, 2011. The Measuring Worth website, developed by economists from prominent universities in the United States, Britain, and Spain, calls itself "a service for calculating relative worth over time." Obviously, such calculations are inexact.
95 Hatch, 13.
96 Flexner, 21–22, 24–29; Hatch, 13–24.
97 John André to Anna Seward, Oct. 31, 1769, in Hatch, 22.
98 Edgeworth and Edgeworth, *Memoirs of Richard Lovell Edgeworth*, 1:238–256; Flexner, 33.
99 *Encyclopaedia Britannica*, s.v. "Göttinger Hain," www.britannica.com/EBchecked/topic/239887/Gottinger-Hain.
100 Hatch, 27–31.

101 Flexner, 35; Hatch, 32–34.
102 Hatch, 34; Flexner, 35.
103 John André to Louisa André, Dec. 1, 1774, in Hatch, 34–35.
104 John André to Mary André, March 5, 1775, in Hatch, 35.
105 Hatch, 37–51; Flexner, 73–82.
106 Sargent, 91.
107 Hatch, 50.
108 Hatch, 54–67; 82, Flexner, 137–148.
109 Flexner, 139.
110 Flexner, 148–160; Hatch, 66–67.
111 John André to mother, winter 1776–77, in Flexner, 150.
112 Hatch, 71–73.
113 Hatch, 77.
114 Bersten, *Tea*, 114; thePeerage.com, "Charles Grey, 2nd Earl Grey," http://the peerage.com/p10591.htm.
115 Jackson, 14.
116 Randall, 383; Jackson, 40–41.
117 John André to Peggy Chew, probably May 1779, Clinton Papers, William C. Clements Library, University of Michigan (hereafter Clinton Papers).

Chapter 4
118 Jackson, 120–122.
119 Richard Peters to Neddy Burd, Nov. 1, 1780, in Walker, 24:426.
120 Becky Franks to Anne (Nancy) Harrison Paca, Feb. 26, 1778, in "A Letter of Miss Becky Franks, 1778," *Pennsylvania Magazine of History and Biography* 16 (1882): 216–217.
121 Hatch, 107
122 Davis, *America's Longest Run*, 15.
123 Durang, "History," as quoted in Moses, *Representative Plays*, 1:7.
124 Randall, 390; Hatch, 90–91.
125 Seilhamer, *History of the American Theatre*, 29–30.
126 Shakespeare, *Henry IV, Part 1*, Act 5, Scene 4, in *The Riverside Shakespeare*, 880.
127 Nelson, *Francis Rawdon-Hastings*, 26–29, 63, 148.
128 Randall, 391–392; *Dictionary of National Biography*, 24:251–252. Some histories spell Hamond's last name with two *m*'s, but the University of Virginia library, which holds his papers, uses only one.
129 Allen, *Tories*, 171.
130 Ketchum, *The Winter Soldiers*, 182.
131 Becky Franks to Nancy Shippen, in Snyder and Snyder, *Woodford Mansion*, 71.
132 Lord Rawdon to uncle, August 1776, in Raphael, *People's History*, 169.
133 Jackson, 103.
134 Jackson, 229–230.

135 Jackson, 231.
136 Flexner, 209–210; Jackson, 235–249; Hatch, 98–105; Randall, 393–395.
137 André, "Major André's Story." This is André's second version of the Meschianza.
138 Jordan, *Colonial and Revolutionary Families of Pennsylvania*, 511–512.
139 Stern, 149–155.
140 André, "Particulars of the Mischianza in America." This is Andre's original account of the Meschianza.
141 Jackson, 239.
142 Andre, "Particulars"; André, "Major André's Story."
143 Walker, 24:427–428.
144 Walker, 25:416.
145 Letter of Mrs. Julius J. Pringle quoted in *Pennsylvania Magazine of History and Biography* 23 (1899): 413.
146 Kingsford, *The History of Canada*, 6:145.
147 See Nigel Slater, *Observer*, April 10, 2010, www.guardian.co.uk/lifeandstyle/2010/apr/11/nigel-slater-classic-recipe-syllabub.
148 Fabian, *Card Sharps and Bucket Shops*, 21–23.
149 Flexner, 209–210; Jackson, 235–249; Hatch, 98–105; Randall, 393–395; André, "Particulars"; André, "Major André's Story"; Bishop, "You are Invited to a Mischianza." Our description of the event is a combination of André's first and second accounts, but tends to use the second version where there are conflicts. For example, the first account says the two groups of knights each had four trumpeters; the second account provides three trumpeters per group.
150 Young, Jenkins, and Seilhamer, 2:52.
151 Jackson, 249.
152 T. Jones, *History of New York During the Revolutionary War*, 261.
153 Leckie, *George Washington's War*, 433–437.
154 R. Harvey, 290.
155 Hatch, 107; *Complete Peerage*, 4:96.
156 Hatch, 107.
157 Harland, 116–125. Peggy Chew's father sold Cliveden in 1779, but bought it back eighteen years later for nearly three times the price.
158 Randall, 615; Kranish, *Flight from Monticello*, 141.

Chapter 5
159 Intelligence report to Washington, in Jackson, 261.
160 Jackson, 260–262.
161 Jackson, 265–267; Steven Morgan Friedman, "University History," www.archives.upenn.edu/histy/genlhistory/brief.html.
162 Laurens, *Papers*, 14:31–32.
163 Sargent, 135.

164   *Respublica v. Carlisle,* 1 US 35, Pa. Ct. of Oyer and Terminer 1778 (court declines
       to dismiss indictment of one defendant and reports his subsequent execution).
165   Scharf and Westcott, 3:898.
166   Anthony Wayne to Richard Peters, July 12, 1778, in Scharf and Westcott,
       3:898–899.
167   T. Jones, 719.
168   Scharf and Westcott, 3:899.
169   Letter of Feb. 23, 1779, Wallace Papers (Bradford), Historical Society of Pennsyl-
       vania, in Brooks, 4.
170   Norton, 352; Haulman, "High Roll."
171   Kochan, *United States Army 1783–1811,* 8; Scharf and Westcott, 2:1692.
172   Graydon, *Memoirs,* 469.
173   *Notable American Women,* 665; *Genealogical and Heraldic Dictionary,* 682; Axtell
       One Name Study, www.axtell-surname.org.uk/fam12216.html#Src8314-1.
174   Young, Jenkins, and Seilhamer, 2:53; Hornor, *This Old Monmouth of Ours,* 136.
175   Watson, 3:167.
176   Frost, *The American Generals,* 216–229; Maryland state archives, "Margaret
       Oswald Chew Howard," www.msa.md.gov/megafile/msa/speccol/sc3500/
       sc3520/002200/002232/html/2232bio.html.
177   André, "Major André's Story," 685–686. Howard's words were: "He was a damned
       spy, sir! Nothing but a damned spy!"
178   Brandt, *Man in the Mirror,* 3–5; Randall, 15–17.
179   Randall, 22–31; Brandt, 5–8; L. Paine, *Benedict Arnold: Hero and Traitor,* 14; Wil-
       son, *Benedict Arnold: A Traitor in Our Midst,* 5.
180   L. Paine, 20–21; Randall, 39–40.
181   Randall, 37–53, 65–68; Flexner, 12–13; Brandt, 9–15.
182   Randall, 66–67; Brandt, 15–16, Flexner, 16–17.
183   Brandt, 16; Randall, 66; Flexner, 18–19.
184   Randall, 74–76.
185   Wilson, 33–36; Brandt, 18–25. Arnold's seizing of the gunpowder was labeled
       Powder House Day, and is remembered with annual reenacts in New Haven.
186   Randall, 132.
187   Wilson, 42, 47–77; Brandt, 42–58; Desjardin, *Through a Howling Wilderness,* 22,
       189.
188   Wilson, 101–110; Brandt, 59–76; Flexner, 85–92; Desjardin, 171–177; Gabriel,
       Major General Richard Montgomery, 154–172.
189   Wilson, 117; Brandt, 77–83; Flexner, 95–100.
190   Brandt, 91, 95–96.
191   Horatio Gates to John Hancock, July 29, 1776, in W. M. Wallace, *Traitorous Hero,*
       107.
192   Randall, 277–317; Flexner, 101–113. One of Arnold's sunken boats from the
       battle was raised in 1935 and has been exhibited in the Smithsonian Museum of
       American History in Washington, D.C.

193 Randall, 318–326.
194 Randall, 326–327, 331; Brandt, 116; Eaton, "Old Boston Families," 11.
195 Benedict Arnold to Horatio Gates, March 25, 1777, in Brandt, 118.
196 Brandt, 116–121; Randall, 327–331.
197 Brandt, 119–121; Flexner, 125–128; Randall, 332–333.
198 Randall, 334–343, Brandt, 121–125.
199 Horatio Gates to John Hancock, Sept. 22, 1777, in Randall, 359.
200 Roberts, *March to Quebec*, 127.
201 Randall, 360–368; Brandt, 126–139; Flexner, 161–184.
202 Martin, *Benedict Arnold, Revolutionary Hero*, 404.
203 Randall, 371–373; Brandt, 140–145; Flexner, 218; Martin, 404–405; Palmer, *George Washington and Benedict Arnold*, 253–254.
204 Benedict Arnold to Betsy DeBlois, April 8, 1778, in Brandt, 144.
205 Benedict Arnold to Betsy DeBlois, April 26, 1778, in Brandt, 144.
206 Brandt, 143–144; Flexner 220–221; Randall, 374.
207 Flexner, 221.

Chapter 6

208 Benedict Arnold to Peggy Shippen, Sept. 25, 1778, in I. N. Arnold, *Life of Benedict Arnold*, 229–230. The biographer Arnold was no relation to the subject Arnold.
209 Randall, 408–411; Palmer, 292.
210 W. M. Wallace, 9; L. Paine, 13. While Arnold's and Andre's heights are known, Peggy's is not. It seems safe to assume that she was shorter than Arnold; otherwise, people would have noted the fact. Descriptions of her as a "delicate" person suggest that she was rather slight.
211 Mary Morris to mother, Nov. 10, 1778, in Walker, 25:32.
212 Judge Edward Shippen to Edward Shippen of Lancaster, Dec. 21, 1778, in Lewis, 29.
213 Brandt, 163.
214 Judge Edward Shippen to Edward Shippen of Lancaster, July 3, 1778, in Lewis, 29.
215 Stern, 138.
216 Randall, 411–414; Brandt, 148–150; Wilson, 152–154.
217 Esther DeBerdt to Dennis DeBerdt, Nov. 14, 1770, in Roche, *Joseph Reed*, 29.
218 Roche, 3–131.
219 Adams, *Works*, 2:378.
220 Joseph Reed to Lord Dartmouth, Feb. 10, 1775, in Reed, *Life and Correspondence*, 1:95.
221 Freeman, *George Washington*, 4:204; Roche, 95, 240.
222 R. Harvey, 210; Chernow, *Washington*, 265–267. See also note 510.
223 Van Doren, *Secret History of the American Revolution*, 176–177; Brandt, 159–160.
224 Irvin, "The Streets of Philadelphia," 17.

225 Timothy Matlack to Benedict Arnold, Oct. 5, 1778, in Brandt, 160.

226 Benedict Arnold to Timothy Matlack, Oct. 6, 1778, in Brandt, 160.

227 Benedict Arnold to Timothy Matlack, Oct. 12, 1778, in Van Doren, 179.

228 Joseph Trumbull to William Williams, Nov. 18, 1776, in Lefkowitz, *The Long Retreat*, 60.

229 *Pennsylvania Packet,* Nov. 7, 1778, in Randall, 429. Brandt notes that the Reeds "had a good view of the party to which they were not invited."

230 Joseph Reed to Nathanael Greene, Nov. 5, 1778, in Stern, 140.

231 Benedict Arnold to Nathanael Greene, Nov. 10, 1778, in Brandt, 163.

232 George Washington to Benjamin Harrison, Dec. 30, 1778, in Scharf and Westcott, 2:899.

233 Randall, 414–416, 435–436; Brandt, 160; Van Doren, 175–176; Flexner, 303.

Chapter 7

234 Elizabeth Tilghman to Betsy Shippen Burd, April 14, 1779, Shippen Papers, Historical Society of Pennsylvania.

235 Browning, *Americans of Royal Descent,* 138.

236 Neddy Burd to Jasper Yeates, Jan. 3, 1779, in Walker, 25:36.

237 Neddy Burd to Jasper Yeates, Dec. 22, 1778, in Walker, 25:34.

238 Judge Edward Shippen to Edward Shippen of Lancaster, Dec. 28, 1778, in Lewis, 29.

239 Benedict Arnold to Judge Edward Shippen, Sept. 1778, in I. N. Arnold, *Life,* 228.

240 Elizabeth Tilghman to Betsy Shippen Burd, Jan. 29, 1779, in Walker, 25:37–38.

241 Norton, 42. Pamela Dwight Sedgwick, an upper-crust New Englander, actually wrote "dark leep," according to Norton, but this book's style corrects such jarring spellings.

242 Lyons, 15; Norton, 45–46.

243 Norton, 58.

244 Neddy Burd to Jasper Yeates, Jan. 3, 1779, in Walker, 25:35–36.

245 Randall, 431. James Duane, a member of the Continental Congress, wrote Philip Schuyler on Jan. 3, 1779, comparing the speculation over Arnold's leg to the fictional gossip over a different war wound suffered by the character Toby in Laurence Sterne's novel *Tristram Shandy.* In Duane's opinion, Arnold's leg "much resembles Uncle Toby's groin."

246 Brandt, 165–166; Randall, 462.

247 Flexner, 244; Brandt, 168.

248 Benedict Arnold in *Pennsylvania Packet,* Feb. 9, 1779, in Randall, 444.

249 Benedict Arnold to Peggy Shippen, Feb. 8, 1779, in Walker, 25:38–39.

250 Benedict Arnold to Peggy Shippen, Feb. 8, 1779, in I. N. Arnold, *Life,* 230–231.

251 Elizabeth Tilghman to Betsy Shippen Burd, March 13, 1779, in Walker, 25:39.

252 Van Doren, 188–192; Randall, 443–447; Brandt, 169–172.

253 Glenn, *Some Colonial Mansions,* 2:452–453; Flexner, 252. Today, Mount Pleasant is carefully maintained and open to the public in Fairmount Park in Philadelphia.

254 Brandt, 166, 173.

255 George Grieve in Chastellux, *Travels in North America*, 1:312.

256 Elizabeth Tilghman to Betsy Shippen Burd, April 14, 1779, Shippen Papers, Historical Society of Pennsylvania.

257 Benedict Arnold to George Washington, May 5, 1779, in *Correspondence of the American Revolution*, 2:291.

Chapter 8

258 Brandt, 147.

259 Fiske, *The American Revolution*, 2:197–199; Cooley, *Currency Wars*, 85–86.

260 Nathanael Greene to James Mitchell Varnum, Feb. 9, 1779, in G. W. Greene, *Life of Nathanael Greene*, 2:168–169.

261 Conrad Alexandre Gérard to the French government, Nov. 24, 1778, in Conway, *Life of Thomas Paine*, 1:114–115.

262 Neimeyer, *The Revolutionary War*, 155.

263 Rappleye, *Robert Morris*, 210.

264 Cogliano, *Revolutionary America*, 106.

265 Reich, *British Friends of the American Revolution*, 97.

266 Horace Walpole to H. S. Conway, Jan. 3, 1981, in Walpole, *Letters*, 7:487.

267 John André to his uncle, Sept. 12, 1778, in Hatch, 120.

268 Hatch, 113–115.

269 John André, circa October 1779, in Flexner, 295.

270 Kemble, *Journals*, 188.

271 Loewenberg, "Letter on Major André in Germany," cited in Hatch, 30.

272 J. H. Smith, *Death of Major André*, 30.

273 Becky Franks to her sister, Abby Hamilton, Aug. 10, 1781, in *Bizarre, for Fireside and Wayside* 4:264.

274 Hibbert, *Redcoats and Rebels*, 59–60.

275 Jasanoff, 32.

276 Tuchman, *The First Salute*, 250.

277 Hatch, 119–145; Randall, 460–462; Flexner, 260–269.

278 Galloway, *Diary*, 78. The book transcribes the passage in question as referring to three of the officers as "And [illegible] & Cunble & Riddle." Flexner takes "And" to be André, "Cunble" to be Campbell, and "Riddle" to be Ridsale. A list of social contacts in the diary lists John André but no other person whose name begins with "And."

279 André memorandum, 1779, in Hatch, 137; Flexner, 264.

280 Flexner, 266.

Chapter 9

281 Randall, 465; Van Doren, 439, 444.

282 Alden, *History of the American Revolution*, 304.

283 Flexner, 275–276; Hatch, 155–156.
284 Stansbury's statement in support of Arnold's claim for compensation from the crown, March 4, 1784, in Van Doren, 196.
285 Jonathan Odell, "Birthday Ode," in *Loyal Verses*, 9.
286 Clinton Papers; Van Doren, 196–200; Hatch 164–165, 168–169; Brandt, 177–178; Randall, 462–465.
287 John André to Joseph Stansbury, May 10, 1779, Clinton Papers.
288 Oxford Dictionaries Online, s.v. "obnoxious," http://oxforddictionaries.com/definition/obnoxious.
289 John André to Peggy Chew, circa May 1779, Clinton Papers.
290 Brandt, 179.
291 M. Jones, *Biographies of Great Men*, 45–48; Brandt, 182.
292 Jonathan Odell to John André, May 31, 1779, Clinton Papers; Randall, 467; Hatch, 172–173.
293 Randall, 468–471; Brandt 180–182.
294 Hatch, 141; Randall, 472; Flexner, 284–285.
295 *New Jersey Gazette,* Dec. 9, 1779, in Hatch, 141.
296 Skillion, *New York Public Library Literature Companion,* 597.
297 Benedict Arnold to John André, 1779, Clinton Papers.
298 John André to Benedict Arnold, mid-June 1779, Clinton Papers.
299 Clinton Papers; Hatch, 177–178.
300 Benedict Arnold to George Washington, July 13, 1779, in *Writings of George Washington,* ed. Sparks, 6:527.
301 John André to Benedict Arnold, late July 1779, Clinton Papers.
302 Joseph Stansbury to John André, late July 1779, Clinton Papers.
303 Guide to the Giles Family Papers, New-York Historical Society, http://dlib.nyu.edu/findingaids/html/nyhs/giles_content.html.
304 John André to Peggy Shippen, Aug. 16, 1779, Clinton Papers.
305 Randall, 477.
306 Peggy Shippen to John André, Oct. 13, 1779, Clinton Papers.

Chapter 10
307 Norton, 72, 75.
308 Knott, 99.
309 Galloway, 72.
310 Roche, 171; Randall, 428; Galloway, 47–48, 51.
311 Silas Deane to Simeon Deane, July 27, 1779, in Deane et al., *Deane Papers,* 4:23.
312 Rappleye, 188–195; Randall, 479–483; Van Doren, 252; Brandt, 183–184.
313 Joseph Reed speech, Nov. 13, 1779, *Minutes of the Supreme Executive Council,* 12:168.
314 Keith, *Provincial Councillors of Pennsylvania,* 70.
315 Brandt, 180, 185–190; Van Doren, 243–252; Randall, 484–492.

316 Peggy Shippen to Benedict Arnold, Jan. 4, 1780, Reed Papers, New-York Historical Society.

317 Ibid.

318 Randall, 492–494.

319 R. Harvey, 176.

320 Washington's general orders, April 6, 1780, from Washington, *Writings,* ed. Fitzpatrick, 18:225, cited in Randall, 494. Van Doren warns against believing a second Washington reprimand or message to Arnold as reported by French diplomat François Barbe-Marbois. The version offered by the imaginative Barbe-Marbois includes this lyrical statement: "Our profession is the chastest of all. Even the shadow of a fault tarnishes the luster of our finest achievements."

321 Van Doren, 255; Brandt, 189–190.

322 Randall, 499; Scharf and Westcott, 2:882.

323 Fraser, *Charleston! Charleston!,* 161–162.

324 Hatch, 186; Randall, 472.

325 Van Doren, 260–261; Brandt, 190–191; Randall, 502–503; Clinton Papers.

326 *Royal Military Calendar,* 2:23.

327 Benedict Arnold to John André, Aug. 30, 1780, Clinton Papers.

328 George Beckwith document summarizing negotiations, circa May 1780, in Van Doren, 261.

329 Van Doren, 261. The current whereabouts of the rings are unknown.

330 Randall, 513–515; Hatch, 201, 205; Brandt, 194, 198, 202; Flexner, 310; Richardson, *West Point,* 1–12. Fort Arnold was renamed Fort Clinton after Arnold's treachery was exposed.

331 Benjamin Tallmadge to Jonathan Trumbull, June 15, 1780, in Hatch, 201.

332 Henry Clinton to his sisters, Oct. 4 and 9, 1780, Clinton Papers.

333 Nathanael Greene's statement, Sept. 26, 1780, in Thacher, *Eyewitness to the American Revolution,* 215.

334 Philip Schuyler to Benedict Arnold, June 2, 1780, in I. N. Arnold, *Life,* 263.

335 Hannah Arnold to Benedict Arnold, Sept. 4, 1780, in Van Doren, 303–304. This letter was written after Arnold received the West Point appointment but before Peggy joined him.

336 Randall, 507–509; Van Doren, 269–275; Brandt, 195; Clinton Papers.

337 Benedict Arnold to George Beckwith or John André, June 16, 1780, Clinton Papers.

338 Benedict Arnold to John André, July 12, 1780, Clinton Papers.

339 Benedict Arnold to John André, July 15, 1780, Clinton Papers.

340 Jonathan Odell to Joseph Stansbury, July 24, 1780, Clinton Papers.

341 Schroeder and Lossing, *Life and Times of Washington,* 4:1693.

342 Meek, "Of Wandering Wombs"; Bronfen, *Knotted Subject,* 108–109.

343 Leake, *Chronic Diseases Peculiar to Women,* 141, cited in Risse, "Hysteria at the Edinburgh Infirmary," 4.

344 Peggy Shippen to Judge Edward Shippen, autumn 1801, Shippen Papers, Historical Society of Pennsylvania.

Chapter 11

345 Description of Benedict Arnold's Philadelphia papers, *Pennsylvania Packet,* Sept. 30, 1780.

346 Stansbury to Jonathan Odell, Aug. 14, 1780, Clinton Papers.

347 Benedict Arnold to Peggy Shippen, Aug. 5, 1780, Clinton Papers.

348 Jonathan Odell to John André, Aug. 24, 1780, Clinton Papers.

349 Hannah Arnold to Benedict Arnold, Sept. 4, 1780, in Van Doren, 303–304.

350 Jasanoff, 35–36; Randall, 500; Brandt, 205, 213–214. Robinson's house in the Hudson Highlands was destroyed by fire in 1892.

351 Robert Howe to Benedict Arnold, Aug. 5, 1780, in Brandt, 205.

352 Benedict Arnold to Robert Howe, Aug. 5, 1780, in Brandt, 205.

353 Brandt, 200–205; Flexner, 327; Van Doren, 470.

354 Benedict Arnold to Robert Howe, Sept. 12, 1780, in Brandt, 205.

355 Benedict Arnold to Peggy Shippen, August–September 1780, in Walker, 25:44–45.

356 Hannah Arnold to Peggy Shippen, Sept. 10, 1780, in Walker, 25:42.

357 David Franks to Arnold, Aug. 28, 1780, in Van Doren, 305.

358 Flexner, 325–326; Brandt, 208–213; Van Doren, 306–309.

359 Benedict Arnold to Samuel Parsons, Sept. 8, 1780, in *Varick Court of Inquiry* (hereafter *Varick*), 197–198.

360 Thacher, 133.

361 Randall, 407; Flexner, 221–222, 335.

362 Brandt, 140–141; Cushman, *Richard Varick,* 28–33, 65–79.

363 *Varick,* 124–125.

364 Benedict Arnold to Richard Varick, Aug. 5, 1780, in *Varick,* 82.

365 Richard Varick to Benedict Arnold, Aug. 7, 1780, in *Varick,* 83–84.

366 Mrs. James Gibson's recollection of Franks's account, in I. N. Arnold, *Life,* 318–319.

367 Thomas Jefferson to James Madison, July 14, 1783, in Burstein and Isenberg, *Madison and Jefferson,* 95.

368 Peggy Shippen to Edward Shippen, March 6, 1786, in Walker, 24:454; Norton, 91.

369 Flexner, 336–337; Brandt, 213; *Varick,* 123, 140; Van Doren, 316–319.

370 *Varick,* 149.

371 *Varick,* 133–134.

372 Chernow, 297–298.

373 Puls, *Henry Knox,* 252; J. A. Greene, *The Guns of Independence,* 105.

374 Washington to John Laurens, Oct. 13, 1780, in Schroeder and Lossing, 3:1311.

375 Brandt, 215–218; *Varick,* 126–127, 178–179.

CHAPTER NOTES

Chapter 12

376 Beverley Robinson to Benedict Arnold, Sept. 21, 1780, in Van Doren, 327.
377 Van Doren, 323.
378 Van Doren, 325–329; Brandt, 216–217.
379 J. H. Smith, 27.
380 Brandt, 216–217; Van Doren, 329–333; Flexner, 342–349; Hatch, 228–231.
381 Koke, *Accomplice in Treason,* 86–92; Flexner, 350–352; Hatch, 232–237.
382 Koke, 152–197. A court-martial acquitted Smith of treason, but he was held for possible trial on related charges. He escaped from jail, reached British-held New York City, and later went to England.
383 André statement, Sept. 29, 1780, in Koke, 88.
384 Hatch, 236; Flexner, 352.
385 Hatch, 236–241; Koke, 93–99; Van Doren, 337; Brandt, 218–219; Flexner, 352–356.
386 J. H. Smith, 40.
387 J. H. Smith, 43.
388 J. H. Smith, 46.
389 Weaver, *A Quaker Woman's Cookbook,* 337; Merriam-Webster, s.v. "stirabout," http://mw1.merriam-webster.com/dictionary/stirabout. André's poem was called "The Cow Chace."

Chapter 13

390 Brandt, 218.
391 Testimony by John Lamb and Richard Varick, in *Varick,* 150–151, 174–177.
392 André's statement, Sept. 29, 1780, in Flexner, 357.
393 Hatch, 241–246; Walsh, *Execution of Major André,* 102–114, 155; Flexner, 356–359.
394 Paulding's account, in Hatch, 245.
395 Flexner, 360–365; Hatch, 247–249; Walsh, 115–123; Van Doren, 341, 486.
396 Jameson to Benedict Arnold, Sept. 23, 1780, in Van Doren, 486.
397 John Jameson to Lt. Allen, Sept. 23, 1780, cited in Van Doren, 486.
398 John André to George Washington, Sept. 24, 1780, in *Gentleman's Magazine* 50 (1780): 611.
399 Varick to sister Jane, Oct. 1, 1780, in *Varick,* 191.
400 Brandt, 220–221; Flexner, 366–369; Van Doren, 344–346; *Varick,* 129–130; Randall, 555.
401 Irving, *Life of George Washington,* 4:137. This quotation, which may seem a bit tidy, has generally been accepted by historians since its appearance in Irving's mid-nineteenth-century biography. Statements from written materials such as letters are more reliable than spoken words during this period and form the bulk of the direct quotations in this book.

249

402 Hirschfeld, *George Washington and Slavery*, 106–111. Franks's testimony doesn't name Lee but simply says that "Washington's servant" arrived. Lee was the general's primary servant at that time.

403 *Varick*, 130.

404 Words of Major James McHenry, cited in Flexner, 367.

405 T. Paine, *Collected Writings*, 251.

406 Flexner, 369.

Chapter 14

407 *Varick*, 129–130; Jasanoff, 36; Flexner, 370; Brandt, 220–221.

408 Intelligence report of Andrew Elliot, Oct. 4–7, 1780, in Commager and Morris, *Spirit of 'Seventy-Six*, 752.

409 Mr. Lear's diary quoting Washington's recollection in 1786, cited in Rush, *Washington in Domestic Life*, 28.

410 *Varick*, 189–193; Flexner, 370–372; Walker, 294–295.

411 Crutchfield, *George Washington*, 117.

412 Owen, speech, *Family Magazine* 5:383.

413 Alexander Hamilton to Elizabeth Schuyler, Sept. 25–26, 1780, in Walker, 25:149. In describing Washington's visit to Peggy, Hamilton writes: "Sometimes she pressed her infant to her bosom and lamented its fate." But during other times of the day, it's unclear when baby Edward was with Peggy or with servants. Surely officers and staff must have worried about entrusting the child to a woman in the throes of apparent insanity. But Peggy may have refused to give him up, since she said people were trying to kill him.

414 Flexner, 372.

415 Flexner, 372.

416 Benedict Arnold to George Washington, Sept. 25, 1780, in Brandt, 221–222.

417 Benedict Arnold to Peggy Shippen, Sept. 25, 1780, McHenry Papers, Library of Congress.

418 Hatch, 263.

419 Hatch, 250–251.

420 Marquis de Lafayette to Chevalier de la Luzerne, Sept. 25–26, 1780, in Walker, 25:294–295.

421 Neddy Burd to Jasper Yeates, Oct. 7, 1780, in "Notes and Queries," *Pennsylvania Magazine of History and Biography*, 40:380.

422 Hamilton, *Fate of Major André*, 13.

423 Alexander Hamilton to Elizabeth Schuyler, Sept. 25–26, 1780, in Walker, 25:149.

424 Peggy Shippen to Richard Varick, Sept. 26, 1780, Varick Papers, New-York Historical Society.

Chapter 15

425 Mrs. James Gibson's recollection of Franks's account, in I. N. Arnold, *Life*, 319.

426 Robert Walsh in the *American Quarterly Review* 21 (1837): 105.
427 I. N. Arnold, *Life,* 321.
428 Ellet, *Revolutionary Women,* 197.
429 Ellet, 198.
430 Ibid.
431 Hamilton, *Fate of Major André,* 13.
432 *Varick,* 136.
433 Van Doren, 382; Randall, 570–571.
434 David Franks to Richard Varick, Sept. 28, 1780, in Van Doren, 382.
435 Isenberg, *Fallen Founder: The Life of Aaron Burr,* 27.
436 Isenberg, 66.
437 Burr, *Memoirs of Aaron Burr,* 1:219–220. Burr had deep connections with the Shippen family, having stayed with the family of the elder Dr. William Shippen after being orphaned as a boy.
438 Walker, 25:155.
439 Irvin, 32–33; *Pennsylvania Packet,* Oct. 3, 1780.
440 William Church Houston to William Livingston, Sept. 27, 1780, in *Letters of Delegates,* 15:114–115, quoted in Irvin, 41.
441 "Memorandum of General Arnold's property confiscated and sold in Philadelphia 1779 or 1781," private collection of Hugh Arnold.
442 *Pennsylvania Packet,* Sept. 30, 1780.
443 Neddy Burd to Jasper Yeates, Oct. 7, 1780, in "Notes and Queries," *Pennsylvania Magazine of History and Biography,* 40:380.
444 Ibid., 40:380–381.
445 Edward Shippen to William Moore, Oct. 5, 1780, in Brandt, 313.
446 Neddy Burd to Col. James Burd, Nov. 10, 1780, *Historical Magazine* 8 (1864): 363.
447 *Colonial Records of Pennsylvania,* 12:520.
448 See note 445.

Chapter 16
449 See note 446.
450 George Grieve's footnote in Chastellux, 1:312. Grieve, a colorful character who translated Chastellux's travel diary and added his own commentary, earned a reputation as an agitator during the French Revolution, and some accused him of helping send the official mistress of Louis XV, Madame du Barry, to the guillotine. He spelled his last name Greive in his later years.
451 University of Pennsylvania biographies, "Edward Shippen," www.archives.upenn .edu/people/1700s/shippen_ed.html.
452 Chastellux, 1:147.
453 Randall, 577; Brandt, 239.
454 Randall, 577.

455 Brandt, 230–236; Van Doren, 374–381; Randall, 580–581. Randall notes that one British officer found Arnold a "very unpopular character," and that Admiral George Rodney warned that the jealousy of fellow officers might impair Arnold's effectiveness.

456 Moore, *Diary of the American Revolution,* 2:344.

457 *Royal Gazette,* Oct. 25, 1780, in Brandt, 233.

458 *Royal Gazette,* Oct. 25, 1780, in Van Doren, 379.

459 Benedict Arnold to Benjamin Tallmadge, written October 1780, sent January 1781, in Van Doren, 380.

460 Benedict Arnold to Lord George Germain, October 1780, in *Documents of the American Revolution,* 18:213.

461 Augustus Reebkomp to Lord Herbert, Oct. 26, 1780, *Ninth Report of the Royal Commission on Historical Manuscripts,* pt. 2, 383.

462 Van Doren, 279, 384–388; Randall, 575–577; Brandt, 230.

463 Benedict Arnold to Henry Clinton, Oct. 18, 1780, in Van Doren, 372.

464 http://measuringworth.com/, accessed Aug. 17, 2011.

465 Benjamin Franklin to Marquis de Lafayette, May 14, 1781, in Franklin, *Memoirs,* 1:377.

466 Randall, 575–576.

467 Hatch, 253–255, 258–272; Walsh, 137–139; Flexner, 383–390.

468 Benjamin Tallmadge to Jared Sparks, in Sparks, *Life and Treason of Benedict Arnold,* 257–258.

469 Benjamin Tallmadge to Samuel B. Webb, Sept. 30, 1780, in Webb, *Reminiscences,* 297.

470 Alexander Hamilton to Elizabeth Schuyler, Oct. 2, 1780, in Hamilton, *Writings,* 92.

471 Benedict Arnold to George Washington, Oct. 1, 1780, in *Gentleman's Magazine* 50 (1780): 616.

472 John André to George Washington, Oct. 2, 1780, in *Gentleman's Magazine* 50 (1780): 616.

473 Hendrickson, *Rise and Fall of Alexander Hamilton,* 128.

474 Thacher, 228. Quotations during André's execution vary in a number of histories. We choose Thacher for André's final sentence because the doctor was a witness to the hanging. For many of the other quotes, we rely on Hatch because of the authoritative nature of his book. Hatch states André's final sentence as: "I have nothing more than this—that I would have you gentlemen bear me witness that I die like a brave man."

475 Hatch, 272–275; Walsh, 140–151; Flexner, 391–393; Thacher, 226–230.

476 Flexner, 381; Walsh, 146–147; Randall, 570; Van Doren, 494.

Chapter 17

477 Rebecca Warner Rawle Shoemaker to daughters Anna and Margaret Rawle, Jan. 8, 1780, in Brandt, 248; Rawle, "Laurel Hill," 399. The real Lady Clinton died in 1772 a few days after giving birth to a child.

478 Anna Rawle to Rebecca Shoemaker, Sept. 20, 1780, in Rawle, 400.

479 Anna Rawle to Rebecca Shoemaker, Feb. 8, 1781, in Rawle, 400.

480 Rebecca Shoemaker to daughters Anna and Margaret, Sept. 22, 1781, in Rawle, 400.

481 Becky Franks to sister Abigail Hamilton, Aug. 10, 1781, in "Letter from Miss Becky Franks," *Pennsylvania Magazine of History and Biography* 23 (1899): 307.

482 Randall, 572–573.

483 Robertson, *Twilight of British*, 155.

484 Randall, 572.

485 Brandt, 235; Randall, 573.

486 George Washington to Henry Lee, Oct. 20, 1780, in Brandt, 237.

487 Brandt, 237; Randall, 578–579, 582; Herbert, *God Knows All Your Names*, 7–12.

488 Flexner, 396–397; Brandt, 240–247; Randall, 581–585; Kranish, 164–167.

489 Brandt, 243.

490 Norton, 82. Upper-class women generally avoided strenuous activity for a month after childbirth.

491 Klein, 182.

492 Randall, 586–589; Brandt, 249–250; McCain, *It Happened in Connecticut*, 40–45.

493 Tuchman, 257–259.

494 *Magazine of American History*, 6:156.

495 Anna Rawle to Rebecca Shoemaker, Oct. 25, 1781, in Rawle, 402.

496 Entry for Aug. 1, 1781, in W. Smith, *Historical Memoirs*, 2:428–429.

497 Entry for Nov. 8, 1781, in W. Smith, 2:463.

498 Brandt, 253.

499 Anna Rawle to Rebecca Shoemaker, Dec. 5, 1781, in Walker, 25:163.

500 D. D. Wallace, *Life of Henry Laurens*, 386–388.

501 Rebecca Shoemaker to Anna and Margaret Rawle, Dec. 15, 1781, in Walker, 25:163.

502 Jasanoff, 6.

503 I. N. Arnold, "Arnold at the Court of George III," 678–682; Randall, 592–593; Brandt, 254–255; Lomask, 85.

504 Townsend, *American Indian History*, 76–77.

505 Stirling, *The Stirlings of Cadder*, 94–95. Some histories have confused Sir Walter Stirling with his same-named son and asserted erroneously that Arnold was presented at court by a London banker. We know by a contemporary letter that Arnold was presented by "Sir Walter Stirling." The admiral was a "Sir" at that time, but his son, the banker, was not. The son added "Sir" to his name when he became a baronet in 1800.

506 Mayo, *Jeffery Amherst*, 251; thePeerage.com, s.v. "Elizabeth Cary" (Lady Amherst), http://thepeerage.com/p630.htm#i6292.

507 Clinton's notes on a conversation with William Pitt about Arnold, Nov. 14, 1792, cited in Van Doren, 386.

508 Timbs, *Romance of London*, 3:110–112.

509 William Rawle to family, in Glenn, 2:148, 163–164.

510 Westcott, *Historic Mansions*, 479; "Oatmeal for the Foxhounds: Banastre Tarleton and the British Legion," http://home.golden.net/~marg/bansite/_entry.html. The name Banastre is pronounced "banister." Tarleton led the horsemen who captured Patriot general Charles Lee while he was visiting a woman of loose morals (see chapter 6). Tarleton also was the inspiration for the cruel British colonel William Tavington in the 2000 film *The Patriot*.

511 Benjamin Franklin to R. R. Livingston, March 4, 1782, in *Memoirs of Benjamin Franklin*, 1:416.

512 Verse in *Pennsylvania Packet*, July 17, 1781, in Brandt, 257.

513 Letters in *General Advertiser and Morning Intelligencer*, Feb. 9 and 22, 1782, in Brandt, 255.

514 Gerald Warner, "The New Politics?" *London Telegraph*, May 13, 2010, http://blogs .telegraph.co.uk/news/geraldwarner/100039646/the-new-politics-raising-the-bar-for-no-confidence-votes-to-55-per-cent-is-more-like-a-coup-detat/.

515 Seward, *Monody on Major André*, 1-2. Seward's monody was first published in 1781.

516 Brandt, 256.

517 Van Schaack, *Life of Peter Van Schaack*, 147. The author was Peter's son.

518 George Johnstone to Benedict Arnold, July 21, 1784, in *Magazine of American History*, 10:316.

519 Keith, 65.

520 Joanna Robinson to Ann Robinson, March 9, 1784, Robinson Family Papers, New Brunswick Museum. Joanna was Beverley Robinson's daughter; Ann was Robinson's daughter-in-law.

521 Becky Franks to Williamina Bond, Feb. 19, 1784, in Stern, 204.

522 Jasanoff, 123–124.

523 Joanna Robinson to Ann Robinson, Oct. 29, 1784, in Jasanoff, 124. The word "lusty" did not have the sexual connotation it has today. Joanna Robinson was simply describing Peggy as robust and physically strong.

524 James H. Watmough to his wife, Anna, Jan. 10, 1787, in Watmough, "Letters," 303. Despite the article's title, the correspondence covers years beyond 1785.

Chapter 18

525 Brandt, 259; Randall, 595.

526 Brandt, 259–261; Van Doren, 424; Randall, 597–601.

527 *St. John Royal Gazette*, June 6, 1786, in Brandt, 261.

528 Norton, 6.
529 Peggy Shippen to Judge Edward Shippen, March 6, 1786, in Walker 24:453–454.
530 Randall, 600; Brandt, 263.
531 Peggy Shippen to Edward Arnold, Oct. 16, 1802, private collection of Hugh Arnold.
532 Peggy, Arnold, and their children arrived in St. John in July 1787. Richard's whereabouts while his father fetched the family in England are uncertain, as is the date when Hannah and Henry arrived from New Haven. The children's ages are as of July 15, 1787.
533 Van Doren, 424; Brandt, 264. Brandt makes the excellent point that the "best of husbands" praise happened before the affair was known, and that such descriptions were not repeated afterward in his lifetime.
534 W. M. Wallace, 291. Wallace, a respected and careful historian, states explicitly but without stated source that Arnold "confessed the affair to her and presumably was forgiven." Other Arnold biographers do not go as far. But Peggy's letter to Neddy Burd after Arnold's death suggests that she knew of Arnold's failing for a long time, not through the reading of his will.
535 Peggy Shippen to Betsy Shippen Burd, June 30, 1788, in Walker, 24:455.
536 Ibid.
537 Randall, 603; Brandt, 263; W. M. Wallace, 292–293.
538 Peggy Shippen to Betsy Shippen Burd, Aug. 14, 1788, in Walker, 24:455–456.
539 Lomask, 88; Randall, 602; Flexner, 400–401.
540 Nash, *First City,* 108–110.
541 Lippincott, 32–33.
542 Tinkcom, "The Revolutionary City," 151.
543 Miller and Pencak, *Pennsylvania,* 132.
544 Roche, 219.
545 University of Pennsylvania biographies, Timothy Matlack, www.archives.upenn .edu/people/1700s/matlack_tim.html.
546 Klein, 207.
547 Keith, 59–62, 70.
548 Sabine, *Biographical Sketches of Loyalists,* 1:179.
548 Peggy Shippen to Betsy Shippen Burd, July 5, 1790, in Walker, 24:456–457.
550 Munson Hayt affidavit, May 7, 1790, in Randall, 603. Randall notes that Arnold's former partner, Munson Hayt, also owed Arnold more than twenty-five hundred pounds.
551 Lawrence, *Judges of New Brunswick,* 68–69; *Bangor Historical Magazine* 2 (1886): 190; Randall, 603–604.
552 Benedict Arnold to Jonathan Bliss, Feb. 16, 1792, Benedict Arnold Papers, New Brunswick Museum.
553 Elze, *Lord Byron,* 11, 440.

Chapter 19

554 Peggy Shippen to Judge Edward Shippen, June 26 and July 6, 1792, in Walker, 24:460–463. Some historians have set the date of the duel as July 6, but it is clear from Peggy's July 6 letter that the duel occurred several days earlier. Van Doren gives the date as July 1.

555 *Parliamentary History of England,* 29:1518–1519.

556 Neilson, *Trial by Combat,* 330–331.

557 Baird, *Goodwood,* 158.

558 Cronin, *Paper Pellets,* 203.

559 Fleming, *Duel,* 321–332.

560 I. N. Arnold, *Life,* 378–381.

561 Henry Clinton to Benedict Arnold, May 26, 1787, in Brandt, 268.

562 Peggy Shippen to Henry Clinton, Nov. 13, 1792, in Brandt, 268.

563 http://measuringworth.com/, accessed Aug. 17, 2011.

564 Brandt, 267–269; Van Doren, 386, 425–426.

565 Wheatley, *London, Past and Present,* 3:139.

566 Taylor, 36–37. Some sources have put William Fitch Arnold's birth in 1798 rather than 1794, but that seems impossible for a number of reasons. Peggy's last will and testament notes a bequest from William Fitch to Peggy's son William; William Fitch died in 1795. Also, Benedict Arnold noted in an 1800 letter that his son William had written his first letter without help—hardly something that a two-year-old was likely to do.

567 Peggy Shippen to the Bliss family, Dec. 5, 1795, in Randall, 611.

568 Judge Edward Shippen to Peggy Shippen, June 29, 1794, in Walker, 26:76.

569 Peggy Shippen to Judge Edward Shippen, July 29, 1796, Shippen Papers, Historical Society of Pennsylvania.

570 Talleyrand-Périgord, *Memoirs,* 1:174–175.

571 Randall, 607–609; Brandt, 268–269.

572 Peggy Shippen to Richard Arnold, August 1794, in Walker, 25:464.

573 Fortescue, *History of the British Army,* 4:376.

574 Benedict Arnold to Ward Chipman, Jan. 14, 1795, in Randall, 608.

575 Benedict Arnold to Jonathan Bliss, Sept. 15, 1795, Benedict Arnold Papers, New Brunswick Museum.

576 Peggy Shippen to Judge Edward Shippen, Feb. 5, 1800, in Walker, 25:470.

577 Peggy Shippen to Judge Edward Shippen, May 2, 1796, in Walker, 25:465.

578 Peggy Shippen to Richard Arnold, August 1794, in Walker, 25:464.

579 Brandt, 271.

580 Brandt, 271–272; Randall, 611; Flexner, 402–403.

581 Duke of Portland's order, in I. N. Arnold, *Life,* 389.

582 Peggy Shippen to Richard and Henry Arnold, July 27, 1803, in Walker, 25:488.

583 Benedict Arnold to Jonathan Bliss, March 7, 1798, Benedict Arnold Papers, New Brunswick Museum.

584 Peggy Shippen to Elizabeth Shippen Burd, May 10, 1800, in Walker, 25:470.

585 Benedict Arnold to Jonathan Bliss, Sept. 19, 1800, Benedict Arnold Papers, New Brunswick Museum.
586 Peggy Shippen to Edward Arnold, in E. Shippen, "Two or Three Old Letters," 191.
587 Ann Fitch to Judge Edward Shippen, June 29, 1801, in Walker, 25:472.
588 Walker, 25:472; Taylor, 26, 70.
589 Ann Fitch to Judge Edward Shippen, June 29, 1801, in Walker, 25:472.
590 Peggy Shippen to Neddy Burd, Aug. 15, 1801, in Walker, 25:474.
591 Peggy Shippen to Judge Edward Shippen, July 29, 1796, Shippen Papers, Historical Society of Pennsylvania.

Chapter 20

592 Peggy Shippen to Judge Edward Shippen, autumn 1801, Shippen Papers, Historical Society of Pennsylvania.
593 Peggy Shippen to Judge Edward Shippen, June 2, 1802, in Walker, 25:477.
594 Peggy Shippen to Edward Arnold, Oct. 16, 1802, private collection of Hugh Arnold.
595 Peggy Shippen to Richard and Henry Arnold, Nov. 5, 1802, in Goodfriend, "Widowhood of Margaret Shippen Arnold," 240–241.
596 Peggy Shippen to Judge Edward Shippen, Oct. 5, 1802, in Walker, 25:481.
597 Peggy Shippen to Judge Edward Shippen, autumn 1801, in Walker, 25:474–476.
598 Peggy Shippen to Edward Arnold, Oct. 16, 1802, private collection of Hugh Arnold. Close readers will see the odd coincidence of Arnold partnering with a Mr. Moore—one of Arnold's pseudonyms in the West Point conspiracy. Moore, elected to Parliament in 1803, was a friend of playwright Richard Brinsley Sheridan (*The School for Scandal*). According to the *Dictionary of National Biography*, 38:376, Moore was "the last wearer of a pigtail in London society."
599 Peggy Shippen to Edward Arnold, March 20, 1803, private collection of Hugh Arnold.
600 Peggy Shippen to Judge Edward Shippen, Feb. 5, 1800, in Walker, 25:469.
601 Peggy Shippen to Judge Edward Shippen, June 26, 1792, in Walker, 25:458–461. The italics represent a word underlined by Peggy.
602 Markham, *Financial History*, 1:86–87.
603 Walker, 25:473.
604 Peggy Shippen to Judge Edward Shippen, Jan. 5, 1803, in Walker, 25:483–485.
605 Peggy Shippen to Richard and Henry Arnold, April 13, 1803, in Goodfriend, 246.
606 Peggy Shippen to Richard and Henry Arnold, Aug. 28, 1803, in Goodfriend, 249.
607 Peggy Shippen to Richard and Henry Arnold, March 31, 1803, in Goodfriend, 243–244.
608 Peggy Shippen to Richard and Henry Arnold, Aug. 28, 1803, in Goodfriend, 250.
609 Peggy Shippen to Judge Edward Shippen, Nov. 2, 1803, in Walker, 25:490.
610 Peggy Shippen to Richard Arnold, July 28, 1793, in Walker, 25:463.

611 Peggy Shippen to Richard and Henry Arnold, Nov. 5, 1802, in Goodfriend, 239. The capitalization of "Boy" is Peggy's.

612 Peggy Shippen to Richard and Henry Arnold, Nov. 5, 1802, in Goodfriend, 239.

613 W. M. Wallace, 310–313; Jasanoff, 338–339; Walker, 463, 86; Keith, 64–67; Taylor, 28; Van Doren, 426; *Gentleman's Magazine* 197 (1927): 190–191; Phipps, *Life*, 88.

614 Peggy Shippen to Betsy Shippen Burd, May 10, 1800, in Walker, 25:470.

615 Keith, 64.

616 Edward Shippen Arnold's will, in Jasanoff, 339.

617 Jasanoff, 339. Peggy's granddaughter was named Louisa Harriet Arnold, but her last name was changed to Adams.

618 Jasanoff, 338–339. Ironically, Peggy once wrote to her son Edward to warn him against marrying any woman who was an "adventuress to India." That letter from Peggy Shippen to Edward Arnold, July 16, 1802, is in the private collection of Hugh Arnold.

619 Peggy Shippen to Richard and Henry Arnold, July 27, 1803, in Goodfriend, 246.

620 Peggy Shippen to Betsy Burd Shippen, July 3, 1803, in Walker, 25:486–487.

621 Ibid., 25:487.

622 Ibid.

623 Peggy Shippen to Judge Edward Shippen, in Walker, 25:490.

624 Peggy Shippen to Betsy Shippen Burd, May 14, 1804, Shippen Papers, Historical Society of Pennsylvania.

625 Ibid.

626 Peggy Shippen to Edward Arnold, March 20, 1803, private collection of Hugh Arnold.

627 Taylor, 80–81.

628 Randall, 615; Van Doren, 198; Phipps, 90. According to family lore cited by some historians, Peggy never revealed to Arnold that she kept a lock of André's hair. That is indeed possible, though it seems illogical to accept as fact. If Arnold didn't know, he couldn't have told anyone. It is possible Peggy told friends, but the story comes with no such explanation. Some historians say André's lock of hair was kept in a golden locket; that assertion is logical but not well documented. What evidence do we have for even the basic detail that a lock of hair was kept? Only the writings of Pownoll W. Phipps, whose father's second wife was Peggy's daughter Sophia. Phipps wrote in 1894 that Peggy kept a lock of André's hair, "which we still have." The authors have attempted to track down Phipps's descendants but have not found the lock of hair.

Epilogue
629 Gottlieb, "Theater of Death"; Banner, *The Death Penalty*, 71. Hanging was a common form of execution in eighteenth-century America, but there were exceptions. Catherine Bevan of Pennsylvania was burned at the stake in 1731 for killing her husband.

630 Gillespie, *Executed Women,* 67.

631 Kerber, *Women of the Republic,* 122.

632 "An Intercepted Letter of Dr. Benjamin Church, Loyalist," *Pennsylvania Magazine of History and Biography* 41 (1917): 507–508.

633 Norton, 175–176; De Pauw, *Founding Mothers,* 137–138.

634 Fortescue, 332–333.

Bibliography

Adams, John. *The Works of John Adams*. Edited by Charles Francis Adams. 10 vols. Boston: Little, Brown, 1850–56.

Alden, John R. *A History of the American Revolution*. New York: Knopf, 1969.

Allen, Thomas B. *Tories: Fighting for the King in America's First Civil War*. New York: Harper, 2010.

Anderson, Fred. *Crucible of War: The Seven Years' War and the Fate of Empire in British North America, 1754–1766*. New York: Knopf, 2000.

André, John. "Major André's Story of the 'Mischianza.'" Preface by Sophie Howard. *Century* 47 (1894): 687–692.

———. "Particulars of the Mischianza in America." *Gentleman's Magazine* 48 (August 1778): 353–357.

Arnold Collection. Houghton Library. Harvard University.

Arnold Collection. New Haven Museum.

Arnold Family Papers. Penrose Library. University of Denver.

Arnold, Isaac N. "Arnold at the Court of George III." *Magazine of American History* 3, no. 11 (1879): 676–684.

———. *The Life of Benedict Arnold*. 1880. New York: Arno, 1979.

Baird, Rosemary. *Goodwood: Art and Architecture, Sport and Family*. London: Frances Lincoln, 2007.

Balch, Thomas Willing. "Dr. William Shippen, the Elder." *Pennsylvania Magazine of History and Biography* 1 (1877): 212–332.

———. *The Philadelphia Assemblies*. Philadelphia: Allen, Lane & Scott, 1916.

Banner, Stuart. *The Death Penalty: An American History*. Cambridge, MA: Harvard University Press, 2002.

Bartlett, Josiah. *The Papers of Josiah Bartlett*. Edited by Frank C. Mevers. Hanover, NH: University Press of New England for the New Hampshire Historical Society, 1979.

Benedict Arnold Papers. New Brunswick Museum, St. John, NB.

Bersten, Ian. *Tea: How Tradition Stood in the Way of the Perfect Cup*. Fremantle, WA: Vivid, 2009.

Bingham, Caleb. *The American Preceptor: Being a New Selection of Lessons for Reading and Speaking*. 42nd ed. Boston: Manning & Loring, 1811.

Bishop, Morris. "You are Invited to a Mischianza." *American Heritage* 25, no. 5 (August 1974): 69–75.

Bizarre, for Fireside and Wayside. Edited by Joseph M. Church. Vol. 4 (October 1853–April 1854).

Brandt, Clare. *The Man in the Mirror: A Life of Benedict Arnold.* New York: Random House, 1994.

Bridenbaugh, Carl, and Jessica Bridenbaugh. *Rebels and Gentlemen: Philadelphia in the Age of Franklin.* New York: Reynal & Hitchcock, 1942.

Bronfen, Elisabeth. *The Knotted Subject: Hysteria and its Discontents.* Princeton, NJ: Princeton University Press, 1998.

Brooks, Lynn Matluck. "The Philadelphia Dancing Assembly in the Eighteenth Century." *Dance Research Journal* 21, no. 1 (Spring 1989): 1–6.

Browning, Charles Henry. *Americans of Royal Descent.* 2nd ed. Philadelphia: Porter & Coates, 1891.

Bruce, William Cabell. *Benjamin Franklin, Self-Revealed.* 2 vols. New York: Putnam, 1917.

Burr, Aaron. *Memoirs of Aaron Burr.* Edited by Matthew L. Davis. 2 vols. New York: Harper & Bros., 1836.

Burrows, Edwin G. *Forgotten Patriots: The Untold Story of American Prisoners During the Revolutionary War.* New York: Basic Books, 2008.

Burstein, Andrew, and Nancy Isenberg. *Madison and Jefferson.* New York: Random House, 2010.

Chastellux, François Jean, Marquis de. *Travels in North America in the Years 1780, 1781 and 1782.* Edited by Howard C. Rice. 2 vols. Chapel Hill: University of North Carolina Press for the Institute of Early American History and Culture, 1963.

Chernow, Ron. *Washington: A Life.* New York: Penguin, 2010.

Clinton Papers. William C. Clements Library. University of Michigan.

Cogliano, Francis D. *Revolutionary America, 1763–1815: A Political History.* 2nd ed. New York: Routledge, 2009.

Colonial Records of Pennsylvania. 16 vols. Philadelphia: J. Severns; Harrisburg: T. Fenn, 1851–53.

Commager, Henry Steele, and Richard B. Morris, eds. *The Spirit of 'Seventy-Six.* 1958. New York: Harper & Row, 1967.

Complete Peerage of England, Scotland, Ireland, Great Britain and the United Kingdom, Extant, Extinct, or Dormant. Edited by George Edward Cokayne. 13 vols. in 14. London: St. Catherine Press, 1910–59.

Conway, Moncure Daniel. *The Life of Thomas Paine.* 2 vols. New York: Putnam, 1892.

Cooley, John. *Currency Wars: How Forged Money Is the New Weapon of Mass Destruction.* New York: Skyhorse, 2008.

Correspondence of the American Revolution: Being Letters of Eminent Men to George Washington, From the Time of His Taking Command of the Army to the End of His Presidency. Edited by Jared Sparks. 4 vols. Boston: Little, Brown, 1853.

Cotter, John L., Daniel G. Roberts, and Michael Parrington. *The Buried Past: An Archaeological History of Philadelphia.* Philadelphia: University of Pennsylvania Press, 1992.

Cronin, Richard. *Paper Pellets: British Literary Culture after Waterloo.* Oxford: Oxford University Press, 2010.

Crutchfield, James A. *George Washington: First in War, First in Peace.* New York: Forge, 2005.

Cushman, Paul. *Richard Varick: A Forgotten Founding Father.* Amherst, MA: Modern Memoirs, 2010.

Danson, Edwin. *Drawing the Line: How Mason and Dixon Surveyed the Most Famous Border in America.* New York: Wiley, 2001.

Davis, Andrew. *America's Longest Run: A History of the Walnut Street Theatre.* University Park: Pennsylvania State University Press, 2010.

Deane, Silas, et al. *Deane Papers.* 5 vols. New York: New-York Historical Society, 1887–90.

De Pauw, Linda Grant. *Founding Mothers: Women of America in the Revolutionary Era.* Boston: Houghton Mifflin, 1975.

Desjardin, Thomas A. *Through a Howling Wilderness: Benedict Arnold's March to Quebec, 1775.* New York: St. Martin's, 2006.

Dickinson, John. *Letters from a Farmer in Pennsylvania to the Inhabitants of the British Colonies.* Philadelphia; London: J. Almon, 1774.

Documents of the American Revolution, 1770–1783. Colonial Office series. Edited by K. Gordon Davies. 21 vols. Shannon: Irish University Press, 1972–81.

Dos Passos, John. *The Head and Heart of Thomas Jefferson.* Garden City, NY: Doubleday, 1954.

Durang, Charles. "History of the Philadelphia Stage Between the Years 1749 and 1855." Multipart series. *Philadelphia Sunday Dispatch*, 1854.

Eaton, Arthur Wentworth Hamilton. "Old Boston Families: The De Blois Family." *New England Historical and Genealogical Register* 67 (1913).

Eberlein, Harold Donaldson, and Horace Mather Lippincott. *The Colonial Homes of Philadelphia and Its Neighbourhood.* Philadelphia: J.B. Lippincott, 1912.

Edgeworth, Richard Lovell, and Maria Edgeworth. *Memoirs of Richard Lovell Edgeworth, Esq. Begun by Himself and Concluded by His Daughter, Maria Edgeworth.* 2 vols. 1820. Cambridge: Cambridge University Press, 2011.

Ellet, Elizabeth. *Revolutionary Women in the War for American Independence.* Edited by Lincoln Daimant. Westport, CT: Praeger, 1998.

Elze, Karl Friedrich. *Lord Byron.* London: John Murray, 1872.

Fabian, Ann. *Card Sharps and Bucket Shops: Gambling in Nineteenth-Century America.* New York: Routledge, 1999.

Fiske, John. *The American Revolution.* 2 vols. Boston: Houghton Mifflin, 1891.

Fleming, Thomas. *Duel: Alexander Hamilton, Aaron Burr, and the Future of America.* New York: Basic Books, 1999.

Flexner, James Thomas. *The Traitor and the Spy: Benedict Arnold and John André.* 1953. Boston: Little, Brown, 1975.

Fortescue, Sir John William. *A History of the British Army.* 13 vols. in 14. London: Macmillan, 1899–1930.

Franklin, Benjamin. *Memoirs of Benjamin Franklin*. 2 vols. Philadelphia: McCarty & Davis, 1832–34.

Fraser, Walter J., Jr. *Charleston! Charleston! The History of a Southern City*. Columbia: University of South Carolina Press, 1989.

Freeman, Douglas Southall. *George Washington: A Biography*. 7 vols. New York: Scribner, 1948–57.

Frost, John. *The American Generals: From the Founding of the Republic to the Present Time*. Boston: Horace Wentworth, 1850.

Gabriel, Michael P. *Major General Richard Montgomery: The Making of an American Hero*. Madison, NJ: Fairleigh Dickinson University Press, 2002.

Galloway, Grace Growden. *Diary of Grace Growden Galloway*. New York: Arno, 1971.

A Genealogical and Heraldic Dictionary of the Peerage and Baronetage of the British Empire. 68th ed. London: Henry Colburn, 1906.

Giles Family Papers. New-York Historical Society. Guide at http://dlib.nyu.edu/finding aids/html/nyhs/giles_content.html.

Gillespie, L. Kay. *Executed Women of the 20th and 21st Centuries*. Lanham, MD: University Press of America, 2009.

Glenn, Thomas Allen. *Some Colonial Mansions and Those Who Lived in Them*. 2 vols. Philadelphia: H. T. Coates, 1898–99.

Goodfriend, Joyce D. "The Widowhood of Margaret Shippen Arnold: Letters from England, 1801–1803." *Pennsylvania Magazine of History and Biography* 115, no. 1 (1991): 221–255.

Gottlieb, Gabriele. "Theater of Death: Capital Punishment in Early America, 1750–1800." PhD diss., University of Pittsburgh, 2005. http://etd.library.pitt.edu/ETD/available/etd-12082005-165901/unrestricted/gottlieb.pdf.

Graydon, Alexander. *Memoirs of His Own Time: With Reminiscences of the Men and Events of the Revolution*. Edited by John Stockton Littell. Philadelphia: Lindsay & Blakiston, 1846.

Greene, George Washington. *The Life of Nathanael Greene*. 3 vols. New York: Hurd and Houghton, 1878.

Greene, Jerome A. *The Guns of Independence: The Siege of Yorktown, 1781*. New York: Savas Beatie, 2005.

Hamilton, Alexander. *The Fate of Major André: A Letter from Alexander Hamilton to John Laurens*. New York: C. F. Heartman, 1916.

———. *Writings*. New York: Library of America, 2001.

Hamond Naval Papers. University of Virginia. Microfilm at David Library of the American Revolution, Washington Crossing, PA.

Harland, Marion. *Some Colonial Homesteads and Their Stories*. New York: Putnam, 1897.

Harvey, Oscar Jewell. *A History of Wilkes-Barre, Luzerne County, Pennsylvania*. Wilkes-Barre: Raeder Press, 1909–30.

Harvey, Robert. *"A Few Bloody Noses": The Realities and Mythologies of the American Revolution*. Woodstock, NY: Overlook Press, 2001.

Hatch, Robert McConnell. *Major John André: A Gallant in Spy's Clothing*. Boston: Houghton Mifflin, 1986.

Haulman, Kate. "Object Lessons: A Short History of the High Roll." *Common-Place* 2, no. 1 (October 2001). www.historycooperative.org/journals/cp/vol-02/no-01/lessons.

Hazard's Register of Pennsylvania. Vol. 1 (1828).

Hendrickson, Robert A. *The Rise and Fall of Alexander Hamilton*. New York: Dodd, Mead, 1985.

Herbert, Paul N. *God Knows All Your Names: Stories in American History*. Bloomington, IN: Author House, 2009.

Hibbert, Christopher. *Redcoats and Rebels: The American Revolution Through British Eyes*. New York: Norton, 2002.

Hirschfeld, Fritz. *George Washington and Slavery*. Columbia: University of Missouri Press, 1997.

Hornor, William S. *This Old Monmouth of Ours*. Freehold, NJ: Moreau Brothers, 1932.

Illick, Joseph E. *Colonial Pennsylvania: A History*. New York: Scribner, 1976.

Irvin, Benjamin H. "The Streets of Philadelphia: Crowds, Congress, and the Political Culture of Revolution, 1774–1783." *Pennsylvania Magazine of History and Biography* 129, no. 1 (2005): 7–44.

Irving, Washington. *Life of George Washington*. 5 vols. New York: Putnam, 1857.

Isaacson, Walter. *Benjamin Franklin: An American Life*. New York: Simon & Schuster, 2003.

Isenberg, Nancy. *Fallen Founder: The Life of Aaron Burr*. New York: Viking, 2007.

Jackson, John W. *With the British Army in Philadelphia, 1777–1778*. San Rafael, CA: Presidio Press, 1979.

Jasanoff, Maya. *Liberty's Exiles: American Loyalists in the Revolutionary World*. New York: Knopf, 2011.

Jones, M. *Biographies of Great Men*. London: T. Nelson and Sons, 1866.

Jones, Thomas. *History of New York During the Revolutionary War*. 2 vols. New York: Printed for the New-York Historical Society, 1879.

Jordan, John W. *Colonial and Revolutionary Families of Pennsylvania*. Baltimore: Genealogical, 1978–.

Joyce, John St. George, ed. *Story of Philadelphia*. Philadelphia: Rex, 1919.

Keith, Charles Penrose. *The Provincial Councillors of Pennsylvania, 1733–1776*. 1883. Baltimore: Genealogical, 1997.

Kelley, Joseph J., Jr. *Life and Times in Colonial Philadelphia*. Harrisburg, PA: Stackpole, 1971.

Kemble, Stephen. *Journals of Lieut. Col. Stephen Kemble, 1773–1789*. Boston: Gregg Press, 1972.

Kerber, Linda K. *Women of the Republic*. Chapel Hill: University of North Carolina Press for the Institute of Early American History and Culture, 1980.

Ketchum, Richard M. *The Winter Soldiers: The Battles for Trenton and Princeton*. 1973. New York: Henry Holt, 1999.

Kimsey, Kenneth Roeland. "The Edward Shippen Family: A Search for Stability in Revolutionary Pennsylvania." Ph.D diss., University of Arizona, 1973.

Kingsford, William. *The History of Canada*. 10 vols. Toronto: Rowsell & Hutchison, 1887–98.

Klein, Randolph Shipley. *Portrait of an Early American Family: The Shippens of Pennsylvania Across Five Generations*. Philadelphia: University of Pennsylvania Press, 1975.

Knott, Sarah. *Sensibility and the American Revolution*. Chapel Hill: University of North Carolina Press for the Omohundro Institute of Early American History and Culture, 2009.

Kochan, James. *The United States Army 1783–1811*. Oxford: Osprey Military, 2001.

Koke, Richard J. *Accomplice in Treason: Joshua Hett Smith and the Arnold Conspiracy*. New York: New-York Historical Society, 1973.

Konkle, Burton Alva. *Benjamin Chew*. Philadelphia: University of Pennsylvania Press, 1932.

Kranish, Michael. *Flight from Monticello: Thomas Jefferson at War*. Oxford: Oxford University Press, 2010.

Laurens, Henry. *The Papers of Henry Laurens*. Vol. 14. Edited by David R. Chesnutt, C. James Taylor, and Peggy J. Clark. Columbia: University of South Carolina Press, 1994.

Lawrence, Joseph Wilson. *The Judges of New Brunswick and Their Times*. Edited by Alfred A. Stockton. St. John: 1907.

Leake, John. *Medical Instructions Toward the Prevention and Cure of Chronic Diseases Peculiar to Women*. London: R. Baldwin, 1785.

Leckie, Robert. *George Washington's War: The Saga of the American Revolution*. New York: HarperCollins, 1993.

Lee, Katharine. "Peggy Shippen Arnold, Philadelphia Belle, Military Wife, and American Exile." Master's thesis, University of Tulsa, 2009.

Lefkowitz, Arthur S. *The Long Retreat: The Calamitous Defense of New Jersey, 1776*. New Brunswick, NJ: Rutgers University Press, 1999.

Letters of Delegates to Congress, 1774–1789. Edited by Paul H. Smith. 26 vols. Washington, D.C.: Library of Congress, 1976–2000.

Lewis, Lawrence, Jr. "Edward Shippen, Chief-Justice of Pennsylvania." *Pennsylvania Magazine of History and Biography* 7, no. 1 (1883): 11–34.

Lippincott, Horace Mather. *Early Philadelphia: Its People, Life and Progress*. Philadelphia: J. B. Lippincott, 1917.

Loewenberg, Richard D. "A Letter on Major André in Germany." *American Historical Review* 49 (1943–44): 260.

Lomask, Milton. "Benedict Arnold: The Aftermath of Treason." *American Heritage* 18, no. 6 (1967): 16–17, 84–92.

The Loyal Verses of Joseph Stansbury and Doctor Jonathan Odell. Edited by Winthrop Sargent. Albany, NY: J. Munsell, 1860.

Lyons, Clare A. *Sex Among the Rabble: An Intimate History of Gender and Power in the Age of Revolution, Philadelphia, 1730–1830.* Chapel Hill: University of North Carolina Press for the Omohundro Institute of Early American History and Culture, 2006.

Mackesy, Piers. *The War for America, 1775–1783.* Cambridge, MA: Harvard University Press, 1964.

Markham, Jerry W. *A Financial History of the United States.* 3 vols. Armonk, NY: M. E. Sharpe, 2002.

Martin, James Kirby. *Benedict Arnold, Revolutionary Hero: An American Warrior Reconsidered.* New York: New York University Press, 1997.

Mayo, Lawrence Shaw. *Jeffery Amherst: A Biography.* New York: Longmans, Green, 1916.

McCain, Diana Ross. *It Happened in Connecticut.* Guilford, CT: TwoDot, 2008.

McHenry Papers. Library of Congress.

Meek, Heather. "Of Wandering Wombs and Wrongs of Women: Evolving Conceptions of Hysteria in the Age of Reason." *English Studies in Canada* 35, nos. 2–3 (2009): 105–128.

Miller, Randall M., and William Pencak, eds. *Pennsylvania: A History of the Commonwealth.* University Park: Pennsylvania State University Press; Harrisburg: Pennsylvania Historical and Museum Commission, 2002.

Minutes of the Supreme Executive Council of Pennsylvania, From its Organization to the Termination of the Revolution. Vol. 12. Harrisburg: Theo Fenn, 1853.

Mishoff, Willard O. "Business in Philadelphia during the British Occupation, 1777–1778." *Pennsylvania Magazine of History and Biography* 61, no. 2 (1937): 165–181.

Moore, Frank. *Diary of the American Revolution: From Newspapers and Original Documents.* 2 vols. New York: Scribner, 1859.

Moses, Montrose Jonas. *Representative Plays by American Dramatists.* 3 vols. New York: Dutton, 1918.

Moss, Roger W., and Tom Crane. *Historic Houses of Philadelphia: A Tour of the Region's Museum Homes.* Philadelphia: University of Pennsylvania Press, 1998.

Murdoch, Richard K. "Benedict Arnold and the Owners of the Charming Nancy." *Pennsylvania Magazine of History and Biography* 84, no. 1 (1960): 22–55.

Musto, R. J. "Captive in Jersey." *Patriots of the American Revolution* 4, no. 4 (2011), 10–12.

Nash, Gary B. *First City: Philadelphia and the Forging of Historical Memory.* Philadelphia: University of Pennsylvania Press, 2002.

Neilson, George. *Trial by Combat from Before the Middle Ages to 1819 A.D.* Glasgow: W. Hodge, 1890.

Neimeyer, Charles P. *The Revolutionary War.* Westport, CT: Greenwood, 2007.

Nelson, Paul David. *Francis Rawdon-Hastings, Marquess of Hastings.* Madison, NJ: Fairleigh Dickinson University Press, 2005.

Newman, Richard S. *Freedom's Prophet: Bishop Richard Allen, the AME Church, and the Black Founding Fathers.* New York: New York University Press, 2008.

Ninth Report of the Royal Commission on Historical Manuscripts. Pt. 2, appendix and index. London: Eyre and Spottiswoode, 1884.

Norton, Mary Beth. *Liberty's Daughters: The Revolutionary Experience of American Women, 1750–1800*. 1980. Ithaca, NY: Cornell University Press, 1996.

Notable American Women: 1607-1950. 3 vols. Edward T. James, editor. Cambridge, MA: Belknap Press of Harvard University Press, 1971.

Notes and Queries: A Medium of Inter-Communication for Literary Men, Artists, Antiquaries, Genealogists, Etc. London: George Bell, 1854.

Oaks, Robert F. "Big Wheels in Philadelphia: Du Simitière's List of Carriage Owners." *Pennsylvania Magazine of History and Biography* 95, no. 3 (1971): 351–362.

Owen, Robert Dale. Speech on February 22, 1840, based on interview with the Marquis de Lafayette. *Family Magazine*, 1840.

Paine, Lauran. *Benedict Arnold: Hero and Traitor*. London: Robert Hale, 1965.

Paine, Thomas. *Collected Writings*. New York: Penguin, 1995.

Palmer, Dave R. *George Washington and Benedict Arnold: A Tale of Two Patriots*. Washington, D.C.: Regnery, 2010.

The Parliamentary History of England, From the Earliest Period to the Year 1803. Vol. 29. London: T. C. Hansard, 1817.

Pension Claims AO/13 and AO/12. David Library of the American Revolution, Washington Crossing, PA.

Phipps, Pownoll William. *The Life of Colonel Pownoll Phipps*. London: Richard Bentley and Son, 1894.

Puls, Mark. *Henry Knox: Visionary General of the American Revolution*. New York: Palgrave Macmillan, 2008.

Purvis, Thomas L. *Colonial America to 1763*. New York: Facts on File, 1999.

Randall, Willard Sterne. *Benedict Arnold: Patriot and Traitor*. New York: Morrow, 1990.

Raphael, Ray. *A People's History of the American Revolution*. New York: Perennial, 2002.

Rappleye, Charles. *Robert Morris: Financier of the American Revolution*. New York: Simon & Schuster, 2010.

Rauser, Amelia F. "Hair, Authenticity, and the Self-Made Macaroni." *Eighteenth-Century Studies* 38, no. 1 (Fall 2004): 101–117.

Rawle, William Brooke, "Laurel Hill and Some Colonial Dames Who Once Lived There." *Pennsylvania Magazine of History and Biography* 35, no. 4 (1911): 385–414.

Reading, John. *John Reading's Diary*. Edited by David R. Reading. Alexandria, VA: Mount Amwell Project, 2010.

Reed, Joseph. *Life and Correspondence of Joseph Reed*. 2 vols. Edited by William B. Reed. Philadelphia: Lindsay & Blakiston, 1847.

Reed Papers. New-York Historical Society.

Reich, Jerome R. *British Friends of the American Revolution*. Armonk, NY: M.E. Sharpe, 1998. Richardson, Robert Charlwood. *West Point*. New York; London: Putnam, 1917.

Risse, Guenter B. "Hysteria at the Edinburgh Infirmary: The Construction and Treatment of a Disease, 1770–1800," *Medical History* 32, no. 1 (1988): 1–22.

The Riverside Shakespeare. Edited by G. Blakemore Evans. Boston: Houghton Mifflin, 1974.

Roberts, Kenneth. *March to Quebec: Journal of the Members of Arnold's Expedition.* New York: Doubleday, Doran, 1938.

Robertson, James. *The Twilight of British Rule in Revolutionary America: The New York Letter Book of General James Robertson, 1780–1783.* Edited by Milton M. Klein and Ronald W. Howard. Cooperstown: New York State Historical Association, 1983.

Robinson Family Papers. New Brunswick Museum, St. John, NB.

Roche, John F. *Joseph Reed: A Moderate in the American Revolution.* New York: Columbia University Press, 1957.

Rooks, Judith Pence. *Midwifery and Childbirth in America.* Philadelphia: Temple University Press, 1997.

Rose, Alexander. *Washington's Spies: The Story of America's First Spy Ring.* New York: Bantam, 2006.

The Royal Military Calendar, or Army Service and Commission Book. 3rd ed. 5 vols. London: A. J. Valpy, 1820.

Royster, Charles. "'The Nature of Treason': Revolutionary Virtue and American Reactions to Benedict Arnold." *William and Mary Quarterly* 36, no. 2 (1979): 163–193.

Rush, Richard. *Washington in Domestic Life.* Philadelphia: J. B. Lippincott, 1857.

Sabine, Lorenzo. *Biographical Sketches of Loyalists of the American Revolution.* 2 vols. Boston: Little, Brown, 1864.

Sale, Edith Tunis. *Old Time Belles and Cavaliers.* Philadelphia: J. B. Lippincott, 1912.

Sargent, Winthrop. *The Life and Career of Major John André.* New ed. New York: William Abbatt, 1902.

Scharf, J. Thomas, and Thompson Westcott. *History of Philadelphia, 1609–1884.* 3 vols. Philadelphia: L. H. Everts, 1884.

Schroeder, John Frederick, and Benson John Lossing, *Life and Times of Washington.* 4 vols. Albany, NY: M. M. Belcher, 1903.

Seilhamer, George Oberkirsh. *History of the American Theatre.* 3 vols. Philadelphia: Globe, 1888–91.

Seward, Anna. *Monody on Major André: and Elegy on Captain Cook.* London: Longman Hurst, Rees, Orme, and Brown, et al., 1812.

Shippen, Edward. "Two or Three Old Letters." *Pennsylvania Magazine of History and Biography* 23, no. 2 (1899): 184–195. Shippen Family Papers. American Philosophical Society, Philadelphia.

Shippen Papers. Historical Society of Pennsylvania, Philadelphia.

Shippen Papers. Library of Congress microfilm.

Shippen-Burd Papers. William C. Clements Library, University of Michigan.

Shreve, L. G. *Tench Tilghman: The Life and Times of Washington's Aide-de-Camp.* Centreville, MD: Tidewater, 1982.

Skillion, Anne, ed. *New York Public Library Literature Companion.* New York: Free Press, 2001.

Smith, Joshua Hett. *An Authentic Narrative of the Causes Which Led to the Death of Major André.* London: Mathews & Leigh, 1808.

Smith, William. *Historical Memoirs of William Smith, 1778–1783*. Edited by W.H.W. Sabine. 2 vols. New York: Arno, 1969–71.

Snyder, June Avery, and Martin P. Snyder. *The Story of the Naomi Wood Collection and Woodford Mansion*. Wayne, PA: Haverford House, 1981.

Sparks, Jared. *The Life and Treason of Benedict Arnold*. Boston: Hilliard, Gray, 1835.

Stern, Mark Abbott. *David Franks: Colonial Merchant*. University Park: Pennsylvania State University Press, 2010.

Stirling, Thomas Willing. *The Stirlings of Cadder*. St. Andrews, Scotland: W.C. Henderson & Son, University Press, 1933.

Talleyrand-Périgord, Charles Maurice de. *Memoirs of the Prince de Talleyrand*. 5 vols. New York: Putnam, 1891.

Taylor, J. G. *Some New Light on the Later Life and Last Resting Place of Benedict Arnold and of His Wife Margaret Shippen*. London: George White, 1931.

Thacher, James. *Eyewitness to the American Revolution*. Stamford, CT: Longmeadow, 1994.

Thomas, Cynthia Lee. "Margaret Shippen Arnold: The Life of an Eighteenth-Century Upper-Class Woman." Master's thesis, University of Houston, 1982.

Timbs, John. *Romance of London: Strange Stories, Scenes and Remarkable Persons of the Great Town*. 3 vols. London: Richard Bentley, 1865.

Tinkcom, Harry M. "The Revolutionary City, 1765–1783." In *Philadelphia: A 300-Year History*, edited by Russell F. Weigley, 109–154. New York: Norton, 1982.

Tomlinson Collection. New York Public Library/New York Mercantile Library.

Townsend, Camilla, ed. *American Indian History: A Documentary Reader*. Malden, MA: Wiley-Blackwell, 2009.

Tuchman, Barbara W. *The First Salute: A View of the American Revolution*. New York: Knopf, 1988.

Van Doren, Carl. *Secret History of the American Revolution*. New York: Viking, 1941.

Van Schaack, Henry C. *The Life of Peter Van Schaack, LL.D.* New York: John F. Trow, 1842.

The Varick Court of Inquiry. Edited by Albert Bushnell Hart. Boston: Bibliophile Society, 1907. www.archive.org/stream/varickcourtofinq00vari#page/n11/mode/2up.

Varick Papers. New-York Historical Society.

Walker, Lewis Burd. "Life of Margaret Shippen, Wife of Benedict Arnold." *Pennsylvania Magazine of History and Biography* 24-26 (1900–1902).

Wallace, David Duncan. *The Life of Henry Laurens*. New York: Putnam, 1915.

Wallace, Willard M. *Traitorous Hero: The Life and Fortunes of Benedict Arnold*. New York: Harper & Brothers, 1954.

Walpole, Horace. *Letters of Horace Walpole, Fourth Earl of Orford*. Edited by Peter Cunningham. Vol. 7. London: Richard Bentley and Son, 1891.

Walsh, John Evangelist. *The Execution of Major André*. New York: Palgrave, 2001.

Washington, George. *The Writings of George Washington*. Edited by John C. Fitzpatrick. 39 vols. Washington, D.C.: US Government Printing Office, 1931–44.

———. *The Writings of George Washington*. Edited by Worthington Chauncey Ford. 14 vols. New York: Putnam, 1889–93.

———. *The Writings of George Washington*. Edited by Jared Sparks. 12 vols. Boston: Ferdinand Andrews; Russell, Odiorne and Metcalf; Hilliard, Gray, 1833–39.

Watmough, James H. "Letters of James H. Watmough to His Wife, 1785." *Pennsylvania Magazine of History and Biography* 29, no. 1 (1905): 31–43.

Watson, John F. *Annals of Philadelphia and Pennsylvania in the Olden Time*. 3 vols. Philadelphia, Edwin S. Stuart, 1884.

Weaver, William Woys. *A Quaker Woman's Cookbook: The Domestic Cookery of Elizabeth Ellicott Lea*. Rev. ed. Mechanicsburg, PA: Stackpole, 2004.

Webb, James Watson. *Reminiscences of Gen'l Samuel B. Webb, of the Revolutionary Army*. New York: Globe, 1882.

Weir, William. *Fatal Victories: From the Crusades to Bunker Hill to the Vietnam War: History's Most Tragic Military Triumphs and the High Cost of Victory*. 1993. New York: Pegasus, 2006.

Westcott, Thompson. *Historic Mansions and Buildings of Philadelphia*. Philadelphia: Porter & Coates, 1877.

Wheatley, Henry B. *London, Past and Present: Its History, Associations, and Traditions*. 3 vols. London: John Murray, 1891.

Wilson, Barry K. *Benedict Arnold: A Traitor in Our Midst*. Montreal: McGill–Queen's University Press, 2001.

Worner, William Frederic. "A Benjamin Franklin Letter." *Papers Read Before the Lancaster County Historical Society* 25 (1921).

Young, John Russell, Howard Malcolm Jenkins, and George Overcash Seilhamer. *Memorial History of the City of Philadelphia from Its First Settlement to the Year 1895*. 2 vols. New York: New-York History Company, 1895–98.

Index

About the Authors

Mark Jacob, deputy metro editor at the *Chicago Tribune,* was part of the team that won the 2001 Pulitzer Prize for explanatory journalism. He is co-author of the newspaper's "10 Things You Might Not Know" feature. He has co-written four other books. Jacob's articles have been published in *Library Quarterly, Chicago* magazine, and *Chicago History* magazine. His short fiction has appeared in the literary magazines *Other Voices, Pikestaff Forum, Samsara,* and *Minnesota Review.* He has served as an adjunct professor at Northwestern University's Medill Graduate School of Journalism.

Stephen H. Case is managing director and general counsel of Emerald Development Managers LP, which provides equity capital for project-finance transactions. From 2009 to 2011, he also was chairman of the board of Motors Liquidation Company, the non-government-owned remnant of General Motors Corporation. Case served for fourteen years on the boards of trustees of Columbia University and New York Presbyterian Hospital. He has served as secretary of the board of trustees of Glimmerglass Opera Company near Cooperstown, New York, and is a trustee of the American Revolution Center in Philadelphia. From 1975 to 2004 he was a partner in the law firm of Davis Polk & Wardwell. Case has been an adjunct professor at Georgetown University Law Center in Washington, D.C. To satisfy his personal curiosity, Case has made himself an expert in the Peggy Shippen story, reading all available histories that examine her story and tracking down Peggy's letters at various repositories of historical manuscript.